CW00347655

A TIMES BARTHOLOMEW GUIDE
LONDON

Published by Times Books and
John Bartholomew and Son Ltd

Authors
Alan Blackwood and Hedley Jane

This edition published in Great Britain by
John Bartholomew & Son Ltd and Times Books Ltd,
16 Golden Square, London W1R 4BN

© Hachette Guides Bleus, 1987.
Maps © TCI, Milan 1987, © Hachette Guides
Bleus, Paris, 1987.

Manufactured in France by Aubin, Poitiers

British Library Cataloguing in Publication Data

Blackwood, Alan; Jane, Hedley.
    London. — (A Times Bartholomew guide)
    1. London (England) — Description — 1981– —
    — Guide-books
I. Title
914.21'04858   DA679
ISBN 0-7230-0288-6

CONTENTS

Photo credits: British Museum, p.176; British Tourist Authority, pp.22, 30/31, 43, 47, 79, 93, 104, 136, 152, 172, 212, 228, 232; Angelo Hornak, pp. 70, 84, 89, 116/7, 128, 148, 217, 224; Museum of London, pp.74/5; National Gallery, p.189; Tate Gallery, p.192; Tim Woodcock, pp.96, 120, 144, 160, 216.

HOW TO USE YOUR GUIDE

The *Guide to London* describes all the main features of the city and its suburbs, setting the various buildings, monuments, squares and parks in their historical context. Together with the practical information it will enable you to make the most of your visit, to experience the capital's history and pageantry, and explore its lesser known corners.

Maps are provided in the opening pages – general maps of Inner and Outer London, with more detailed maps for the central areas. These are followed by basic information on the city, including transport services, shopping, entertainment, pubs, calendar of events, sport, and a selected list of hotels and restaurants by area.

The major sights of London are divided into **nine itineraries.** Included within each one is a route map and each of the main sites or areas (shown as headings) is followed by a map number with grid references, which relate to the maps on pp.8–21. (To find a building, a place or an artist, refer to the index on pp.238–40.) Each itinerary is followed by Places to Stop, which lists pubs, hotels, restaurants and cafés where you can have tea, a drink or a snack; and a selection of the more interesting shops. The section on **London's River** covers sites of interest along the Thames, from Teddington Lock upstream to the Thames Barrier at Woolwich, and includes a list of pubs to visit.

The **main museums** and galleries are covered in detail in the next section, with 'not to be missed' items featured in bold type.

Many of London's historic sites are further away from the centre and these are covered in the **Outer London** section, as well as the capital's many riverside areas or picturesque 'villages' such as Chiswick, Kew, Richmond and Hampstead. Separate sections are devoted to **Hampton Court, Greenwich** and **Blackheath.** Lastly, although not part of London but only an hour or so away, there is a section on **Windsor** and **Eton,** well worth a day trip.

Note

As London street names are often duplicated in different areas, you need to check the postal district (or name of suburb) given in addresses, e.g. WC1, SW6. This will also give you a rough idea of where the area is, i.e. West Central, South West.

TRAVEL IN LONDON

Underground stations (⊖) and British Rail stations (⇌) are shown throughout the *Guide*. Bus routes are also given when a particular place cannot be reached by train or Underground. (See also Getting About, p.34.)

FEATURES OF SPECIAL INTEREST

★   interesting
★★   remarkable
★★★   exceptional

SYMBOLS AND ABREVIATIONS USED IN GUIDE

☎   Telephone
Tx.   Telex
⊖   London Transport Underground station
⇌   British Rail station
🅿   Parking

Special symbols for Hotels and Restaurants are listed on p.51

▬ MAPS, ITINERARIES AND PLANS

Maps

Itineraries

Plans

©Copyright London Regional Transport

Travel to London's main sites by Underground:

Buckingham Palace ⊖ Victoria (District, Circle and Victoria)
Westminster Abbey and Houses of Parliament ⊖ Westminster
    (District and Circle)
Tate Gallery ⊖ Pimlico (Victoria)
National Theatre and South Bank Arts Centre ⊖ Waterloo
    (Bakerloo and Northern)
British Museum ⊖ Tottenham Court Road (Central and Northern),
    Russell Square (Piccadilly)
National Gallery and Trafalgar Square ⊖ Charing Cross (Northern,
    Bakerloo and Jubilee)
Piccadilly Circus ⊖ Piccadilly (Piccadilly and Bakerloo)
Covent Garden ⊖ Covent Garden (Piccadilly)

Barbican Arts Centre and London Museum ⊖ Barbican (Metropolitan and Circle), Moorgate (Metropolitan, Circle and Northern)
St Paul's Cathedral ⊖ St Paul's (Central)
The City ⊖ Bank (Central and Northern)
Tower of London ⊖ Tower Hill (District and Circle)
Madame Tussaud's ⊖ Baker Street (Metropolitan, Circle, Bakerloo and Jubilee)
Zoo ⊖ Regent's Park (Bakerloo), Camden Town (Northern)
Harrods and **Knightsbridge** ⊖ Knightsbridge (Piccadilly)
South Kensington Museums and **Albert Hall** ⊖ South Kensington (Piccadilly, District and Circle)
Kew Gardens ⊖ Kew Gardens (District)

Itineraries

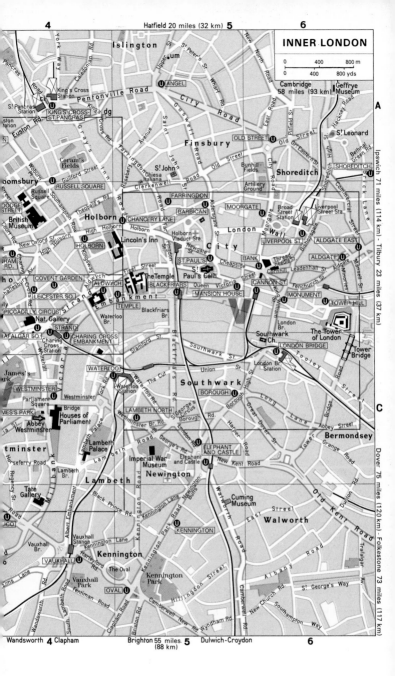

INNER · LONDON

Hatfield 20 miles (32 km)

Cambridge 58 miles (93 km)

Ipswich 71 miles (114 km) - Tilbury 23 miles (37 km)

Dover 75 miles (120 km) - Folkestone 73 miles (117 km)

Wandsworth   Clapham   Brighton 55 miles (88 km)   Dulwich-Croydon

Principal Museums

British Museum   B4
National Gallery   B4
Tate Gallery   D4
Victoria and Albert Museum   C2
Natural History Museum   C2
Science Museum   C2
Museum of London   B5

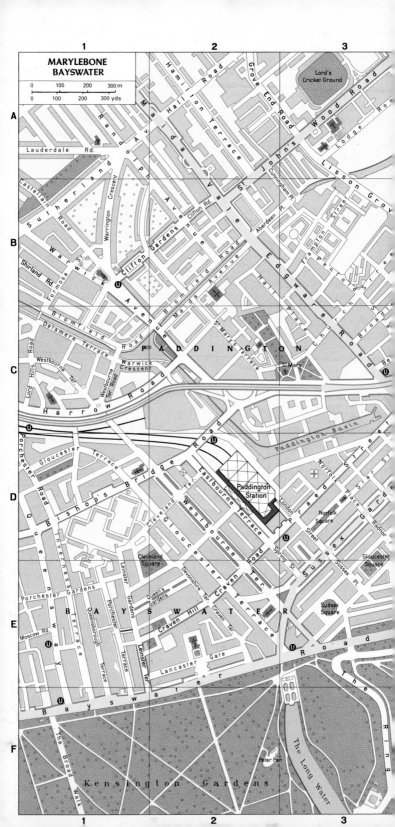

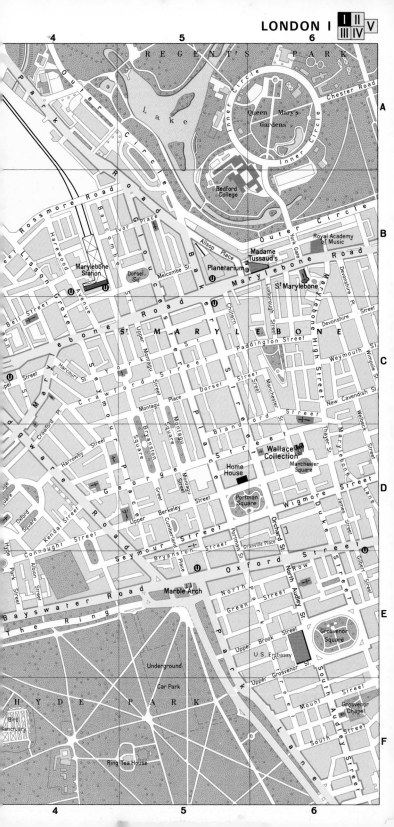

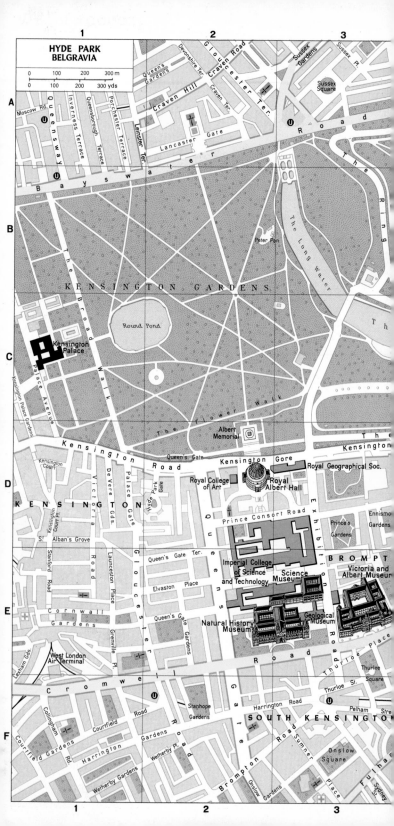

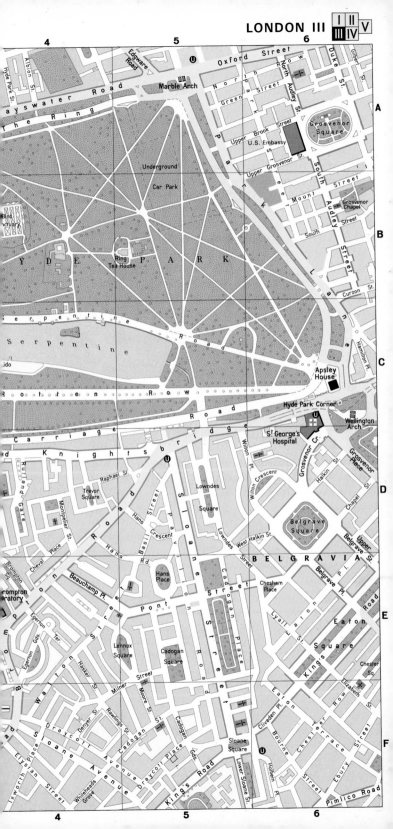

4   5   6

Edgware Road

Oxford Street

North Row

Duke St.

Green Street

North Audley St.

Albion St.

Hyde Park St.

Marble Arch

U

Bayswater Road

The Ring

A

Grosvenor Square

Upper Brook Street

U.S. Embassy

Upper Grosvenor St.

Underground
Car Park

South Audley Street

Mount Street

Grosvenor Chapel

B

Bird
Sanctuary

HYDE PARK

Ring
Tea House

South Street

Park Lane

Curzon St.

Hamilton Pl.

Serpentine Road

Serpentine

Lido

C

Apsley House

Rotten Row

Carriage Road

Hyde Park Corner

U

Wellington Arch

Grosvenor Pl.

S.t George's Hospital

Grosvenor Cr.

Knightsbridge

U

Wilton Pl.

Wilton Crescent

Grosvenor Place

Rutland Gate

Raphael St.

Trevor Square

Hans Road

Brompton Road

Montpelier St.

Basil Street

Sloane Street

Lowndes Square

Lowndes Square

West Halkin St.

Wilton Crescent

Halkin St.

Chapel St.

Belgrave Square

Upper Belgrave St.

D

Hans Crescent

Cheval Place

Hans Place

Pont Street

Cadogan Place

BELGRAVIA

Belgrave Pl.

Chesham Place

Belgrave Sq.

Lyall St.

Eaton Place

Brompton
Oratory

Beauchamp Pl.

Egerton Gds.

Egerton Ter.

Walton Street

Sloane Street

Lennox Square

Cadogan Square

Cadogan Street

Eaton Square

E

Milner Street

Hasker St.

Moore St.

Draycott Place

Draycott Gds.

Denyer St.

Rawlings St.

Cadogan Gds.

King's Road

Chester Sq.

Elizabeth St.

Cliveden Pl.

Eaton Terrace

Chester Row

Draycott Avenue

Sloane Square

U

Bourne Street

Holbein

Ebury Street

F

Ixworth Street

Elystan Street

Sloane Avenue

Whiteheads Grove

Kings Road

Lower Sloane St.

Pimlico Road

4   5   6

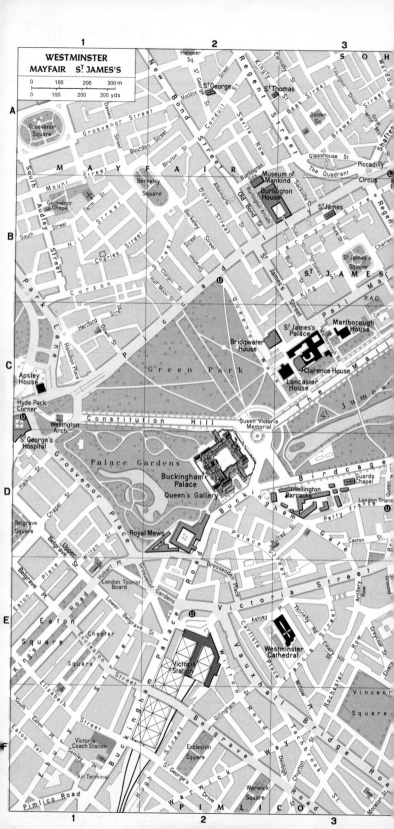

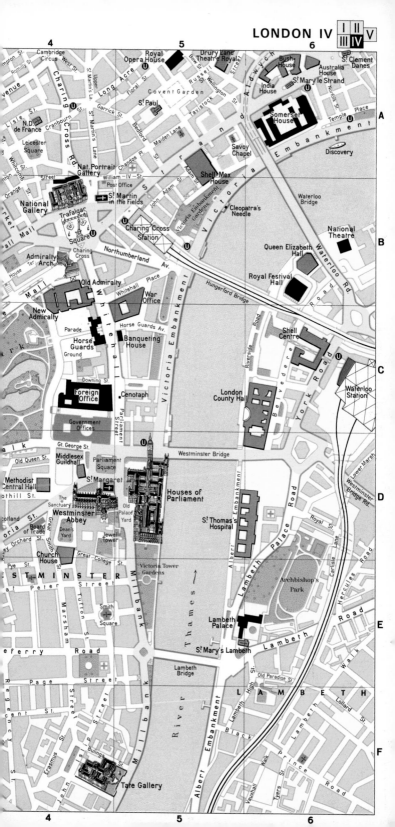

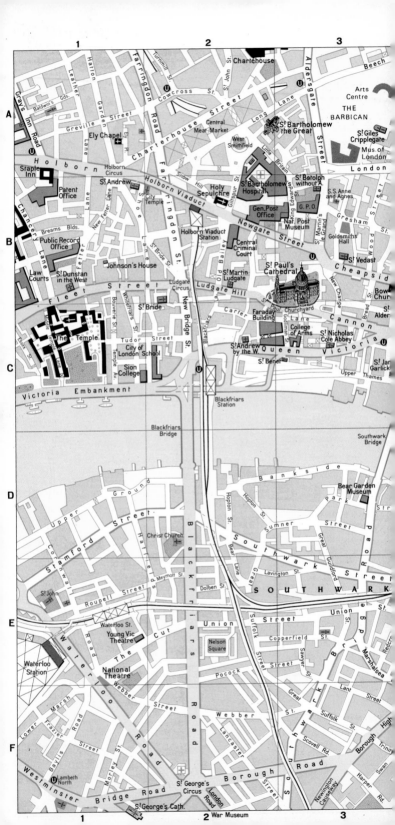

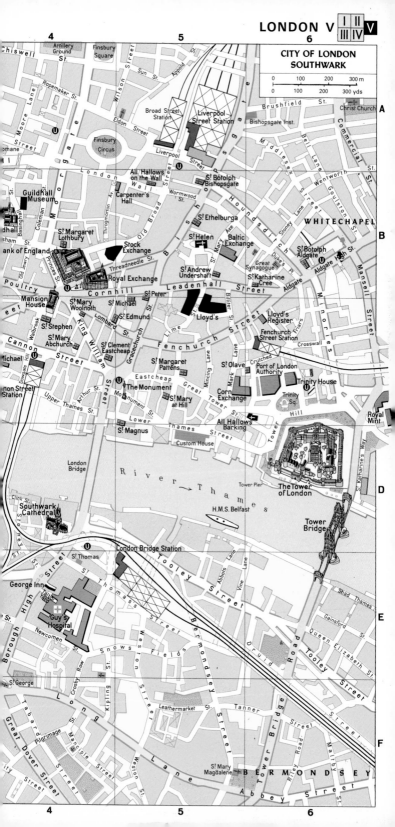

© SERVIZIO CARTOGRAFICO DEL TOURING CLUB ITALIANO, MILANO-1985

Main localities referred to in text:

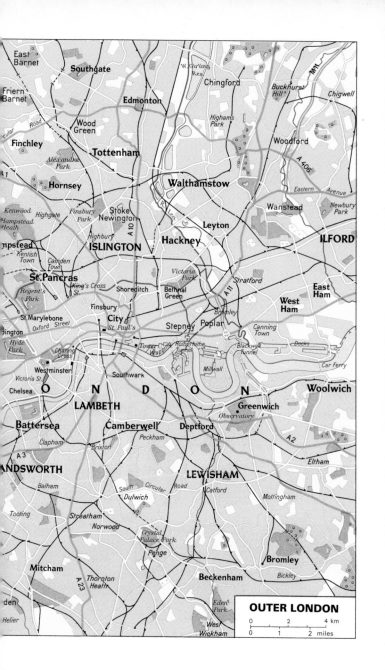

OUTER LONDON

0   2   4 km

0   1   2 miles

INTRODUCTION

London differs from most other great European cities in at least two important respects. As the capital of an island kingdom, London has not seriously been threatened with foreign land attack since the Norman Conquest of 1066. Consequently, it was spreading freely over the countryside, linking up with neighbouring towns and villages, while cities like Paris, Vienna and Florence were still contained behind fortified walls. This largely unimpeded growth accounts for London's relatively open and sprawling pattern (except for the most central parts), and for so many fine buildings and other places of interest spread over such a wide area. It also explains why the Londoner's own pride in his city operates at so many levels. He is, of course, proud of London as a whole, but he will claim equal allegiance to London south of the river, London east of the City, or London north of Regent's Park. His strongest loyalty, however, is reserved for his own special bit of London: Hammersmith, Hampstead, Camden Town, Stepney, Camberwell – wherever he lives is his 'village' or 'manor', with its own history, personality, atmosphere. This multi-faceted 'London Pride' is something special for the visitor to seek out and to savour – among the people, in the bustling streets and local markets, and in the thousands of friendly pubs.

London is also the capital of a nation that has thrived on what the historians called 'gradualism' – a process of slow but continuous political and social change. London has witnessed civil war and the execution of a king, been largely destroyed by fire, and devastated again by war, but it has avoided the often violent upheavals that have ruptured the life of many other cities. This is what keeps its traditions so strong, and lends a special lustre to its pageantry.

This sense of the present nourished by the past exists at a deeper level. City thoroughfares, now in the shadow of gleaming office blocks, still commemorate in name events and circumstances already old when Richard Whittington was Lord Mayor. The titles of once illustrious estates are enshrined in the names of more famous streets and squares. London's magnificent parks are living memorials, in name and extent, to royal hunting reserves, pleasure gardens,

St Martin-in-the-Fields from Trafalgar Square

parade grounds and the gardens of noble houses. Law courts and hospitals remain on the sites of medieval tribunals and monasteries. The nation's seat of government has not moved for close on a thousand years. London also has some of the oldest-established shops in the world. Discovering these countless links with the past makes every visit to Britain's capital an adventure and a delight.

London is sustained by its past, but not burdened by it. It is no longer the grimy industrial capital of an empire, although it remains an international centre of finance and trade. Otherwise, the whole tenor of its life has changed enormously in less than fifty years. Until recently Londoners never thought of their city as a mecca for the arts. But that is what it has become. As well as collections of art treasures – among the world's finest – London has new concert halls, theatres and art galleries, offering the visitor a year-round abundance of music, opera, drama and every other kind of entertainment, second to none in quality and variety. It also boasts some of the world's finest hotels and restaurants. In keeping with this new image, it has cleaned its great public buildings, extended and spruced up its famous Underground, dispelled the smoke and the smog, and made Old Father Thames a cleaner river than it has been for centuries. The words of the poet William Dunbar, written nearly 500 years ago, again ring true:

Above all ryvers thy Ryver hath renowne,
  Whose beryall stremys, pleasaunt and preclare,
Under thy lusty wallys renneth down,
  Where many a swan doth swymme with wyngis fair;
  Where many a barge doth saile and row with are;
Where many a ship doth rest with top-royalle.
  O, towne of townes! patrone and not compare,
London, thou art the flour of Cities all.

COMING TO LONDON

This section contains all the necessary information for reaching London by sea or by air, with details of customs and immigration formalities, currency and climate, as well as addresses of British Tourist Authority offices overseas.

ARRIVING BY AIR

London has two main airports, Heathrow and Gatwick, while some flights (mainly charters) arrive at Stansted or Luton. All are well served by London's transport systems.

Heathrow:

One of the world's busiest airports, situated 15 miles west of London, Heathrow has four terminals. British Airways and KLM international flights arrive at Terminal 4, other intercontinental flights at Terminal 3, European flights at Terminal 2 and domestic flights at Terminal 1. The journey to central London can be made by Underground, bus or taxi.

London Underground (Piccadilly Line) trains serve the airport 20 hours a day. There are two stations – one for terminals 1, 2 and 3 and the other for terminal 4. The trains go directly into London's centre in about 40 minutes, but they have no luggage-handling facilities. Only take the Underground if you can walk with your luggage.

Two **Airbus** routes serve Heathrow. They have facilities for luggage and go by direct routes to some of London's main hotels and then to railway terminals: Route A1 via Cromwell Road to Victoria (60 mins), A2 via Notting Hill Gate to Euston (60 mins). There are also **Flightline** coaches (Route 767) to Victoria Coach Station (50 mins). (Ask at the Underground Information Centre or phone London Regional Transport enquiries on 222 1234 for information about buses or Underground).

Black **taxis** are always available at Heathrow; the average fare from Heathrow to London's centre is £15, but you will be taken door to door, and the driver will help you with your luggage.

Gatwick:

The airport is some 30 miles south of London and is served by train and bus. **British Rail** operates a service to London's Victoria Station (30 mins). Trains run every 15 minutes during the day, and hourly from midnight to 6am. **Flightline** coaches (Route 777) go to Victoria Coach Station (80 mins).

ARRIVING BY SEA

There are several ports in the south and east of England which offer easy access to London. All those listed offer car ferry services:

Plymouth (ferries from St Malo, Roscoff and Santander): 220 miles by road (A3-M5-M4); trains (4 hrs) to Paddington.
Portsmouth (ferries from Cherbourg and Le Havre): 65 miles by road (A3); trains (2 hrs) to Waterloo.
Newhaven (ferries from Dieppe): 70 miles by road (A26-B2116-A23-M23); trains (1½ hrs) to Victoria.
Folkestone (ferries from Ostend, Boulogne): 72 miles by road (M20-A20); trains (1½ hrs) to Charing Cross.
Dover (ferries from Boulogne, Dunkirk, Calais, Zeebrugge, Ostend): 75 miles by road (A2-M2-A2); trains (1½ hrs) to Charing Cross or Victoria.
Ramsgate (ferries from Calais): 70 miles by road (A299-M2-A2); trains (3 hrs) to Victoria.
Harwich (ferries from Scandinavia, Hamburg and Hook of Holland): 70 miles by road (A604-A12); trains (1½ hrs) to Liverpool Street.
Continental train services have direct connections to either Victoria (from French destinations) or Liverpool Street (from destinations in northern Europe). Continental coach services terminate at Victoria Coach Station. For coach and rail travellers there are bus and Underground connections at all London stations as well as taxi-cab ranks. For travellers arriving by car, there are **AA** (Automobile Association) information offices at all ports.

▬▬ ENQUIRIES

Offices of the British Tourist Authority throughout the world will offer friendly and helpful advice on your visit to London, including details of package tours and special opportunities for visitors. Offices are located at the following addresses:

Australia: 171 Clarence Street, Sydney N.S.W. 2000. ☎(02) 29-8627
Belgium: Rue de la Montagne 52, Bergstraat B2, 1000 Brussels. ☎(02) 511.43.90
Brazil: Avenida Ipiranga 318A, 12° Andar, conj. 1201, Edificio Vila Normanda, 01046 São Paulo. ☎011 257−1834
Canada: 94 Cumberland Street, Suite 600, Toronto, Ontario M5R 3N3. ☎(416) 925 6326
Denmark: Møntergade 3, DK 1110 Copenhagen. ☎(01) 12 07 93
France: 6 Place Vendôme, 75001 Paris. ☎(01) 42 96 47 60
Germany: Neue Mainzer Str. 22, 6000 Frankfurt am Main 1. ☎(069) 2380750
Hong Kong: Suite 903, 1 Hysan Avenue, Hong Kong. ☎(5) 764 366
Ireland: Clerys, O'Connell Street, Dublin 1. ☎(01) 614 188
Italy: Via S. Eufemia 5, 00187 Rome. ☎(06) 78.4998 or 678.5548
Japan: Tokyo Club Building, 3-2-6 Kasumigaseki, Chiyoda-ku, Tokyo 100. ☎(03) 581 3603
Mexico: Edificio Alber, Paseo de la Reforma 332-5 Piso, 06600 Mexico DF. ☎(05) 533 6375
Netherlands: Leidseplein 5, 1017 PR Amsterdam. ☎(020) 23.46.67
New Zealand: 8th Floor, Norwich Insurance House, Cnr. Queen and Durham Streets, Auckland 1. ☎(09) 31 446
Norway: Mariboes gt. 11, 0183 Oslo 1. ☎(02) 41 18 49
Singapore: 14 Collyer Quay 05-03, Singapore Rubber House, Singapore 0104. ☎224 2966/7
South Africa: 7th Floor, JBS Building, 107 Commissioner Street, 2001 Johannesburg. PO Box 6256, Johannesburg 2000. ☎(011) 29 67 70
Spain: Torre de Madrid 6/4, Plaza de España, Madrid 28008. ☎(01) 241 13 96
Sweden: For visitors: Malmskillnadsgatan 42, 1st floor. For mail: Box 7293, S-103 90 Stockholm. ☎(08) 21 24 44
Switzerland: Limmatquai 78, 8001 Zurich. ☎(01) 47 42 77/97
USA: 40 West 57th Street, New York, NY10019. ☎(212) 581 4700

Tx: 237798; 612 South Flower Street, Los Angeles, CA 90017. ☎(213) 623-8196; John Hancock Centre (Suite 3320), 875 North Michigan Avenue, Chicago, IL 60611. ☎(312) 787 0490; Plaza of the Americas, North Tower, Suite 750, Dallas, Texas 75201. ☎(214) 720 4040

FORMALITIES

Non-British subjects require a valid passport for entry into the United Kingdom, and certain nationalities also require a visa. Check in good time with the British Embassy or High Commission in your home country. Normal customs restrictions apply on entering Britain, and there is strict enforcement of the ban on importing any live animal without its having a 6 month quarantine period, because of the danger of rabies. There is no limit to the amount of currency (sterling) that you can bring in or take out of Britain. The amount of duty-free goods that you can import will vary according to your nationality – ask at the airline desk or on board ship. No inoculations are normally required to enter Britain.

CURRENCY

The monetary unit of the United Kingdom is the pound (£). It is divided into one hundred pence. Notes are circulated with the value of £5, £10, £20, and £50. The coins of the realm are 1p, 2p, 5p, 10p, 20p, 50p, £1 and £2. A few £1 notes are still in circulation and will be accepted. The banks of Northern Ireland and Scotland produce their own notes, which can be seen in London from time to time, these also are legal tender.

THE CLIMATE

The English weather is famous for its unpredictability, and from day to day it is uncertain whether Londoners will be warmed by a breeze from the Gulf Stream or buffeted by a cold wind from Siberia. Frequently the weather changes in the course of a day, but there are seldom extremes of heat or cold, and London's notorious 'pea-souper' fogs are a thing of the past. Rain is not often very heavy, but can occur at almost any time, so it is wise to have some protection. Temperatures are highest in July and August, but there are frequent summer showers. London is generally pleasant and mild from April through to October.

Temperatures (average)

	Jan	Feb	Mar	Apr	May	Jun	Jul	Aug	Sep	Oct	Nov	Dec
°F	40	40	44	49	55	61	64	64	59	52	46	42
°C	4	4	7	9	13	16	18	18	15	11	8	6

Rainfall (average)

	Jan	Feb	Mar	Apr	May	Jun	Jul	Aug	Sep	Oct	Nov	Dec
ins	2.1	1.6	1.5	1.5	1.8	1.8	2.2	2.3	1.9	2.2	2.5	1.9
mm	54	40	37	37	46	45	57	59	49	57	64	48

VISITING LONDON

L ondon is no longer the world's largest city, but Greater
  London does cover an area of over 600 sq miles (1,500
km²). Nevertheless, the majority of places of interest to visitors
are close to the centre, and an excellent system of public
transport makes it easy to find one's way about. 'Ask a police-
man' is still sound advice if you are lost or need help, since the
police – and traffic wardens – are normally well-informed.

▬▬ INFORMATION

The visitor to London need never be at a loss for information on events,
sights, transport etc., and the wealth of publications gives an embarrassment of choice. The centres below have been chosen for their
reliability, broad coverage and up-to-date information.

Information Centres

The following offices can give information to tourists concerning
sightseeing, tours, tickets to West End cinemas and theatres and, in
some cases, can book accommodation. Staff are often multilingual.

London Tourist Board and Convention Bureau, 26 Grosvenor Gardens, London SW1W OUD ☎730 3488 (written and telephone enqui-
ries only). **LTB Tourist Information Centres** are located at **Victoria
Station** forecourt, SW1 (*open daily 9am–8.30pm, 10pm Jul–Aug;
bookshop closes at 8pm; book for guided tours before 7.30pm*),
Selfridges Department Store (ground floor), Oxford Street, W1
(*open Mon–Fri 9am–6pm, Thu to 7.30pm*), **Harrods Department
Store** (fourth floor), Brompton Road, SW1 (*open Mon–Fri 9am–5pm,
Wed 9.30am–7pm, Sat 9am–6pm*), the **Tower of London,** West Gate,
EC3, (*open Apr–Sep, daily 10am–6pm*) and **Heathrow Central Underground Station** (*open daily 9am–6pm*). The **City of London Information Centre,** St Paul's Churchyard, EC4, ☎606 3030 (*open daily
9.30am–5pm*) offers information on the City business district and a
guide to local events.

   London Transport travel information centres are located at certain Underground stations: **Heathrow** (both stations), **Piccadilly Circus, Oxford Circus, Victoria, St James's Park, Charing Cross,
Euston,** and **King's Cross/St Pancras.** These information centres are
open every day from morning until evening, although the hours vary
slightly. ☎222 1234 (24 hours) for London Transport travel information.
The **British Travel Centre,** 12 Lower Regent Street, W1, houses the
British Tourist Authority information centre, American Express Travel
Service, and a British Rail ticket office. It also handles bookings for
trips, theatres, and concerts, and has a bookshop. (*Open Mon–Sat
9am–6.30pm, Sun 10am–4pm; personal callers only*).

Publications

The most detailed sources of information for the visitor are the weeklies *Time Out, City Limits,* and *What's On in London,* which come out on Wednesdays and are sold at most newsagents and newsstands; these publications provide full information on theatres, shows, cinemas, concerts, exhibitions, festivals, TV, radio, children's activities etc., along with practical information, compiled for Londoners as much as for the visitor. Information is also availabe from Britain's main daily newspapers, which all have London editions: *The Times, Independent, Guardian, Daily Telegraph, Daily Mail, Today, Sun, Daily Express, Daily Mirror, Daily News* and *Star.* These newspapers are published in the morning and give British news as a whole, world news in less detail, and news of current events, including theatre and cinema programmes. There are also London's evening papers, the *London Standard* and the *Evening News,* sold from lunchtime until late at night. All these newspapers are available from newsagents or street vendors and are priced from 10 to 30 pence. Sunday newspapers are larger, with more news and more arts information; most include a colour supplement, and their prices are somewhat higher: *The Observer, Sunday Times, Sunday Telegraph, Mail on Sunday, Today, News of the World, Sunday Express, Sunday Mirror* and *Sunday People.* Many London newsagents carry a wide selection of foreign newspapers, and a European edition of the *International Herald Tribune* is published Mon–Sat.

Telephone Information

Time Line (the exact time) ☎123; *Sportsline* (sports news) ☎246 8020; *Daily Express Cricketline* (giving news during major matches) ☎154; *Dataline* (a general information service) ☎200 0200; *Weather Forecast* ☎246 8091; *Children's London* (information on events for the young) ☎246 8007; *Leisureline* (a daily selection of main events in and around London) ☎246 8041 (English); ☎246 8043 (French); ☎246 8045 (German).

▬ TOURING LONDON

London is particularly enjoyable when seen from a comfortable seat, and touring buses and boats are very popular – especially as there is often a knowledgeable guide who will tell you about the places you visit. The city's 500 or so Blue Badge guides (trained by the LTB) can also be booked for tours by car, and walking tours. There are a number of bus rides around London, the most famous being London Transport's red bus tour. Boat tours of the Thames are particularly fascinating, and if an aerial view of the city is required there are even helicopter tours. Details of London tours are obtainable from travel agents or Tourist Information Centres.

London by Bus

Book for escorted coach tours of London sights at any **London Transport** travel information centre (see opposite), or ☎222 1234 (24 hours) for London Transport travel information. Tickets can also be booked at the Wilton Road Coach Station, SW1, and the **British Travel Centre** (see opposite). **Cityrama** (☎720 6663) offers tours with a taped commentary in eight languages. With the independent **Culture Bus** (☎629 4999) you can get on and off as you please at any of the 20 bus stops for particular sights. Luxury coach tours, complete with stewardess, are available through **Harrods** (☎581 3603). Tour companies using Blue Badge guides are **Evans Evans Tours** (☎930 2377) and **Frames Rickards** (☎837 3111).

Houses of Parliament from across the Thames

Excursions on the Thames

Upstream: Boats leave from Westminster Pier, opposite Big Ben, and travel upstream to Kew every 30 mins, 10.30am–3.30pm. Trips upstream to Hampton Court leave at 10am, 10.30am, 11.30am and noon (☎930 4721). Downstream: Boats leave Westminster Pier to the Tower of London (20-min journey) every 20 mins, 10.30am–4pm; and to Greenwich (45-min journey) every 20 mins 10.30am–4pm. Three-hour round trip cruises to the Thames Flood Barrier leave from Westminster Pier at 10am and 1.30pm; one-hour cruises every 30 mins, 11.30am–5pm.

On the Regents Canal

Zoo Waterbus travels between Little Venice and Camden Lock, ☎ 482 2550 ⊖ Warwick Avenue, Camden Town. **Jason's Trip** cruise along the canal ☎286 3428 ⊖ Camden Town. Recorded **River-boat Information Service** ☎730 4812.

Aerial Views of London

UK Air Taxis, Westland Heliport, Lombard Road, SW11, ☎228 9114 ⇌ Clapham Junction. **Tempus Aviation,** Grove House, 628 London Road, Colnbrook, Buckinghamshire ☎02812 4750.

EMBASSIES, CONSULATES AND HIGH COMMISSIONS

Australia, Australia House, Strand, WC2
Austria, 18 Belgrave Mews West, SW1
Bangladesh, 28 Queen's Gate, SW7
Belgium, 103 Eaton Square, SW1
Bulgaria, 186 Queen's Gate Gardens, SW7
Canada, 1 Grosvenor Square, W1
China, 31 Portland Place, W1
Czechoslovakia, 25 Kensington Palace Gardens, W8
Denmark, 55 Sloane Street, SW1
Egypt, (Arab Republic), 19 Kensington Palace Gardens, W8
Finland, 38 Chesham Place, SW1
France, 58 Knightsbridge, SW1
Germany: Democratic Republic, 34 Belgrave Square, SW1; Federal Republic, 23 Belgrave Square, SW1
Greece, 1a Holland Park, W11
Hungary, 35 Eaton Place, SW1
Iceland, 1 Eaton Terrace, SW1
India, India House, Aldwych, WC2
Ireland (Republic), 17 Grosvenor Place, SW1
Israel, 2 Palace Green, Kensington Palace Gardens, W8
Italy, 14 Three Kings Yard, Davies Street, W1
Luxembourg, 27 Wilton Crescent, SW1
Netherlands, 38 Hyde Park Gate, SW7
New Zealand, New Zealand House, Haymarket, SW1
Norway, 25 Belgrave Square, SW1
Poland, 47 Portland Place, W1
Portugal, 11 Belgrave Square, SW1
Romania, 4 Palace Green, W8
Saudi Arabia, 22 Holland Park, W11
South Africa, South Africa House, Trafalgar Square, WC2
Spain, 24 Belgrave Square, SW1
Sweden, 11 Montagu Place, W1
Switzerland, 16 Montagu Place, W1
United States, 1 Grosvenor Square, W1
U.S.S.R., 13 Kensington Palace Gardens, W8
Yugoslavia, 5 Lexham Gardens, W8

SERVICES

Money

If you want to change money or travellers' cheques, a bank will charge the smallest commissions and offer the best rates. Outside banking hours there are bureaux de change, whose rates are still not unreasonable. When changing money, you will normally be required to show some form of identity, preferably your passport. The principal clearing banks (**National Westminster, Midland, Barclays, Lloyds**) have foreign departments that cash travellers' cheques during banking hours: Mon–Fri 9.30am–3.30pm. Certain branches are open 9.30am–noon or 2.30pm on Saturdays. The following bureaux de change are open 24 hours a day, 7 days a week and display their charges clearly: **Chequepoint,** 548 Oxford Street, W1, ☎723 2646; **Erskine,** 15 Shaftesbury Avenue, W1, ☎734 1400; **Lenlyn,** Victoria Station, SW1, ☎828 8367. Heathrow and Gatwick Airports both have 24-hour banks and **American Express,** 6 Haymarket, SW1, ☎930 4411 (*open Mon–Fri 9am–5pm, Sat 9am–noon*) and **Thomas Cook,** 45 Berkeley Street, W1, ☎499 4000 (*open Mon–Fri 9am–5.30pm, Sat 9am–noon*) both have money changing facilities.

Telephones

Public phones in London and elsewhere in Britain are usually in red (or yellow) kiosks. They may also be in chrome kiosks with green, blue, or yellow bands. There are different types, but all display clear instructions for use. The older (dial) telephones operate thus: lift receiver, dial number, and on hearing the call answered, insert your coin (minimum 10p). Newer (push button) types require the money to be put in before you make your call. The most recent design accepts a 'phonecard' only – these are green cards, available at post offices and newsagents, which contain a fixed number of units which are used up as you make your calls. If you do not have a phonecard, the relevant kiosks list the nearest place where you can buy one. If in difficulty call the operator (100). For directory enquiries (information) call 142 for London numbers, 192 for numbers outside London, giving the town; name and address that you require.

Emergencies

Emergency calls (which are free on any phone) are sent through to a central exchange and then directed to the police, ambulance or fire brigade. (In areas near the sea, the coast guard can also be contacted.) The number for emergencies is ☎999.

Other emergency services: **Capital Helpline,** ☎388 7575, open Mon–Fri 9.30am–5.30pm will direct callers to organizations that can help with their problem. **The Samaritans,** St Stephens, 39 Walbrook Road, EC4, ☎283 3400, open 24 hours to the depressed and suicidal. **Teledata** ☎200 0200, 24-hour service with details of all emergency services.

Chemists (pharmacies):

Warman Freed, 45 Golders Green Road, NW11, ☎455 4351 ⊖ Golders Green (*open 9.30am–midnight*).
H.D. Bliss, 5 Marble Arch, W1, ☎723 6116 ⊖ Marble Arch (*open 9am–midnight*); 50 Willesden Lane, NW6, ☎624 8000 ⊖ Kilburn (*open 9am–2am*).

Dental Emergency Care ☎677 6363, 584 1008 (*24 hours*).

Hospitals in London offering emergency services are:
University College, Gower Street, W1, ☎387 9300 ⊖ Warren Street
St Bartholomew's, West Smithfield, EC1, ☎600 9000 ⊖ St Paul's
Charing Cross, Fulham Palace Road, W6, ☎748 2040 ⊖ Hammersmith
Westminster, Dean Ryle Street, Horseferry Road, SW1, ☎828 9811 ⊖ Westminster or Victoria
St Stephen's, 369 Fulham Palace Road, SW10, ☎352 8161 ⊖ Fulham Broadway or South Kensington, then bus No. 14
St Thomas's, Lambeth Palace Road, SE1, ☎928 9292 ⊖ Westminster or Waterloo
Royal Free, Pond Street, NW3, ☎794 0500 ⊖ Belsize Park or Hampstead

Post Offices

Central Post Office, Trafalgar Square, 24 William IV Street, WC2, ☎930 9580. (*Open Mon–Sat 8am–8pm, Sun and bank hols 10am–5pm.*) Apart from this one, there are post offices all over London (*opening hours normally 9am–5.30pm weekdays, 9am–noon Sat*) offering a great number of services, including the sale of stamps, express mail services, postal orders etc. **Datapost** guarantees to deliver letters and packages safely to any address normally within a day. Sub-post offices, often in newsagents' shops, cannot offer the full range of postal services but do provide most requirements.

Lost Property

If something is mislaid or stolen, your first move is to inform the police so as to validate any subsequent insurance claims. Then, depending where the loss occurred, contact one of the following if appropriate. **Airports:** Gatwick ☎0293 31299 (*daily 8.30am–4pm*), Heathrow ☎745 7727/8 (*daily 9am–4pm*). **Ports:** Sealink ☎387 1234. **Bus** and **Underground:** 200 Baker Street, NW1, ☎486 2496 (*Mon–Fri 9.30am– 2pm*). **Taxi:** 15 Penton Street, N1, ☎278 1744 (*Mon–Fri 9am–4pm*). **British Rail:** There are Lost Property Offices at all main London stations.

If you lose your passport go first to the nearest police station and then your consulate. If you lose a credit card, phone the emergency number given to you, to avoid being charged if someone else uses your card.

▬▬ *GETTING ABOUT*

All the itineraries described in the guide are best followed on foot. London is a wonderful city for walking, with many parks and spacious squares, as well as quaint old corners which conjure up the city's richly patterned history. To get to each of the districts, there is a wide choice of transportation, and the top of a London bus gives a wonderful perspective on the bustling streets. However, the traffic in central London is always dense, and the fastest way to get around is certainly the Underground.

Underground and Bus

London Transport controls both buses and Underground trains. ☎222 1234 for their 24-hour travel information service (English only).

London is served by an extensive underground railway system (the 'tube'). Trains run at regular intervals, and there are stations at every main-line terminus and near all the popular tourist attractions. The trains are quick and comfortable. A map of the Underground system is shown on pp.6–7. Check which line you want to travel on (they are clearly colour-coded) and in which direction (platforms are indicated as northbound, southbound, eastbound or westbound). Several of the lines have more than one branch, so check the destination shown on the indicator on the platform. The first trains run from 6 or 6.30am (later on Sundays), and the last at approximately midnight.

The bus service in London is also good, although strangers may find it more difficult to get around this way, and buses are, of course, subject to delays in the traffic. There are two types of red buses: one-person operated, where you pay your fare to the driver, and two-person buses, with a conductor collecting fares. Buses cover a greater area of London than the Underground, and there are many different routes serving all parts of the city. Bus routes are given in the *Guide* when a particular place cannot be reached by train or Underground. The all-night bus services are useful after British Rail and the Underground close down.

London Transport fares are reduced for children under 14, and for 14- and 15-year olds with a Child Rate Photocard (available from post offices in the London area). Under 5s travel free. Free maps of Underground and bus services and a large number of ever-changing leaflets describing various fares and special passes are available from Underground and bus stations.

Tourist Passes

The **London Explorer** pass is available from London Transport or LTB

Tourist Information Centres, or any Underground station. It allows unlimited travel on all London's red buses (except special sightseeing tours) and almost all the Underground (including Heathrow by Airbus or tube) for 1, 3, 4 or 7 days (special prices for those under 16). This is ideal for longer excursions into London's hinterland. The **Capitalcard** offers unlimited off-peak travel (i.e. Mon–Fri after 9.30am) for the day, throughout London, by train, Underground or bus. Available from British Rail and Underground stations. Note also the one-day off-peak **Travelcard,** which allows unlimited travel on the Underground and buses after 9.30am weekdays and all day at weekends. Passes issued for a week, month, or longer can be used at all times of the day.

British Rail

British Travel Centre (personal callers only): 12 Lower Regent Street, W1. (*Open Mon–Sat 9am–6.30pm, Sun 10am–4pm*). **InterCity general enquiries:** ☎834 2345. A central stacking system ensures that all phone calls are answered in strict rotation, so be patient and wait for a reply. British Rail runs an extensive commuter network in and around London, with frequent interchanges with the Underground system. Several places not served by the Underground are accessible by British Rail, including Greenwich, Hampton Court and Windsor. Longer journeys throughout Britain can be made on the InterCity network, and there are many special prices for off-peak travel. London's main-line terminals are: Charing Cross ☎928 5100; Euston ☎387 7070; Holborn Viaduct ☎928 5100; King's Cross ☎278 2477; Liverpool Street ☎283 7171; London Bridge ☎928 5100; Marylebone ☎387 7070; Paddington ☎262 6767; Victoria ☎928 5100; Waterloo ☎928 5100. Timetables giving details of journeys all over the country are available from many British Rail stations (including all those listed above).

Taxis

London's **black cabs** are rated the best in the world. Any cab with its yellow 'For Hire' sign lit up should stop if you flag it down, and provided your journey is within six miles and within the London borders, the cab must take you where you want to go. Taxis are harder to find on the street in outer districts. Either phone **Radio Taxis** ☎272 0272, 272 3030, 235 5000 (24 hours) or a local **minicab** (check in *Yellow Pages*). Minicabs are unlicensed and have no meters, so check the fare to your destination before starting the journey. In general, they offer a good service at a fair price – much the same as a taxi for short journeys, less for longer ones.

Driving in London

Do not use your car in London unless it is absolutely necessary; traffic is extremely dense, with numerous traffic jams. Parking places must nearly always be paid for, either on parking meters or in one of the **National Car Parks** throughout the city ☎499 7050. The **North** and **South Circular ringroads,** although often congested, are accessible from the centre and link up to all major motorways around London. The **M25 motorway,** although further out, may often be the fastest way of driving from one side of the capital to the other. Many suburban Underground and British Rail stations close to main routes into London have large car parks, and this is often the quickest and easiest way to come into town.

Car-Hire

Avis: 68 North Row, W1, ☎629 7811; Gatwick Airport ☎0293 29721; Heathrow Airport ☎897 9321. **Budget:** Central reservations ☎441 5882; British Rail King's Cross ☎833 0972; Victoria NCP car park, Semley Place, SW1, ☎730 5233. **Godfrey Davis Rail Drive**: King's Cross Station ☎278 5228; Paddington Station ☎262 5655; Heathrow Airport ☎897 0811. **Hertz:** Victoria Coach Station ☎730 8323. To hire a car you must be at least 21, and have held a licence valid in the UK for a year. It is also useful to have a credit card, otherwise rental firms will require a sizeable deposit.

Cycling

One of the most enjoyable and independent methods of travelling around London is by bicycle, and there are now many cycle routes. If you can avoid the main traffic routes and keep your eyes open, you will find cycling a leisurely and comfortable way to see the sights. **The London Cycling Campaign** ☎928 7220 has been set up to provide cyclists with advice and information, and bicycles are availabe for hire from the following firms: **Bell Street Bikes** 73 Bell Street, NW1, ☎724 0456; **Bicycle Revival,** 17-19 Elizabeth Street, SW1, ☎730 6716; **Dial-a-bike,** 18 Gillingham Street, SW1, ☎828 4040. It is also possible to hire a motorcycle from **Scootabout Limited,** 59 Albert Embankment, SE1, ☎582 0055, but a valid licence is needed.

▬ ENTERTAINMENT

London is the theatre capital of the world. The National Theatre has three stages (Olivier, Lyttelton and Cottesloe), and productions featuring the company are often to be seen at other London theatres as well, while the Royal Shakespeare Company, based in Stratford-upon-Avon, has its London home at the Barbican Centre, using both the Barbican Theatre and The Pit for different productions. These apart, there are more than forty other theatres in London's West End, offering a wide range of performances from musicals to contemporary drama. Agatha Christie's **The Mousetrap** has been running since 1954. There are several repertory companies, mainly in the suburbs, and 'fringe' theatres throughout London. Most of the first-run cinemas are in the West End.

London is also famous for its music, with two resident opera companies, four symphony orchestras and countless instrumental and chamber music groups. There is also a lively jazz and rock music scene.

Theatre

Tickets can be booked at the theatres themselves (many now have a credit card telephone booking system for confirmed reservations) or through a theatre ticket agency. The agency will charge a commission, but may be able to obtain tickets for shows that are advertised as 'sold out'. Most major hotels also have booking offices in the foyer. Half-price tickets can be obtained on the day of a performance from the **Society of West End Theatre Half-Price Ticket Booth,** west side of Leicester Square, WC2 (*open 2.30–6.30pm*) and at some theatres.

Ticket agencies include:
Fringe Box Office, Duke of York's Theatre, St Martin's Lane, WC2, ☎379 6002
Keith Prowse, 44 Shaftesbury Avenue, W1, ☎437 8976, bookings ☎741 9999
Premier Box Office, 188 Shaftesbury Avenue, W1, ☎240 2245/7
Ticket Master, 78 St Martin's Lane, WC2, ☎404 5768

Details of current productions can be found in *Time Out, City Limits, What's on and Where to Go* and in the principal daily newspapers, but the following list shows the location of the main venues and their specialities, with phone numbers for booking and credit-card (CC) booking. Some fringe theatres are clubs requiring memberhip, but this can normally be obtained when purchasing tickets.

West End

Opera, ballet and dance
Coliseum (English National Opera), St Martin's Lane, WC2, ☎836 3161, 240 5258 (CC) ⊖ Leicester Square, Charing Cross
Covent Garden (Royal Opera House), Bow Street, WC2, ☎240 1066 (CC), 240 1911 (information) ⊖ Covent Garden
The Place (London Contemporary Dance Theatre), 17 Duke's Road, WC1, ☎387 0031 ⊖ Euston
Sadler's Wells (New Sadler's Wells Opera and touring companies), Rosebery Avenue, EC1, ☎278 8916/5916 ⊖ Angel

Mainly musicals
Adelphi, Strand, WC2, ☎836 7611, 836 7358 (CC) ⊖ Charing Cross
Apollo, Shaftesbury Avenue, W1, ☎437 2663, 434 3598 (CC) ⊖ Piccadilly Circus
Apollo Victoria, 17 Wilton Road, SW1, ☎828 8665, 630 6262 (CC) ⊖ Victoria
Dominion, Tottenham Court Road, W1, ☎580 8845 ⊖ Tottenham Court Road
Drury Lane (Theatre Royal), Catherine Street, WC2, ☎836 8108, 240 9066/7 (CC) ⊖ Covent Garden
Her Majesty's, Haymarket, SW1, ☎839 2244, 930 6606, 930 4025, (CC) ⊖ Piccadilly Circus
London Palladium, 8 Argyll Street, W1, ☎437 7373 ⊖ Oxford Circus
New London, Drury Lane, WC2, ☎405 0072, 404 4079 (CC) ⊖ Holborn
Palace, Shaftesbury Avenue, W1, ☎434 0909 (CC) ⊖ Leicester Square
Prince Edward, Old Compton Street, W1, ☎734 8951, 836 3464 (CC) ⊖ Leicester Square
Prince of Wales, Coventry Street, W1, ☎930 8681, 930 0844 (CC) ⊖ Piccadilly Circus
Victoria Palace, Victoria Street, SW1, ☎834 1317, 828 4735 (CC) ⊖ Victoria

Drama, comedy or musicals
Albery, St Martin's Lane, WC2, ☎836 3878, 379 6565 (CC) ⊖ Leicester Square
Aldwych, Aldwych, WC2, ☎836 6404 ⊖ Holborn, Covent Garden, Temple
Criterion, Piccadilly Circus, W1, ☎930 3216 ⊖ Piccadilly Circus
Duchess, Catherine Street, WC2, ☎836 8243, 379 6433 (CC) ⊖ Covent Garden
Duke of York's, St Martin's Lane, WC2, ☎836 5122, 836 9837 (CC) ⊖ Leicester Square
Garrick, Charing Cross Road, WC2, ☎379 6107 (CC) ⊖ Leicester Square
Globe, Shaftesbury Avenue, W1, ☎437 1592, 240 7200 (CC) ⊖ Piccadilly Circus
Haymarket (Theatre Royal), Haymarket, SW1, ☎930 9832 (CC) ⊖ Piccadilly Circus
Lyric, Shaftesbury Avenue, W1, ☎437 3686, 434 1050 (CC) ⊖ Piccadilly Circus
Phoenix, Charing Cross Road, WC2, ☎836 2294, 240 9661 (CC) ⊖ Tottenham Court Road, Leicester Square
Piccadilly, Denman Street, W1, ☎437 4506, 379 6565 (CC) ⊖ Piccadilly Circus
Queen's, Shaftesbury Avenue, W1, ☎734 1166, 240 7200 (CC) ⊖ Piccadilly Circus

Savoy, Strand, WC2, ☎836 8888, 379 6219 (CC)   ⊖ Charing Cross
Shaftesbury, Shaftesbury Avenue, W1, ☎379 5399, 741 9999 (CC)
⊖ Tottenham Court Road
Strand, Aldwych, WC2, ☎836 2660, 836 5190 (CC)   ⊖ Holborn,
Covent Garden, Temple
Vaudeville, Strand, WC2, ☎836 9987 (CC)   ⊖ Charing Cross
Westminster, Palace Street, SW1, ☎834 0283   ⊖ Victoria
Whitehall, Whitehall, SW1, ☎930 7765, 379 6565 (CC)   ⊖ Charing
Cross

Smaller, more intimate theatres
Ambassadors, West Street, WC2, ☎836 6111, 836 1171 (CC)
⊖ Leicester Square
Comedy, Panton Street, SW1, ☎930 2578, 240 7200 (CC)
⊖ Piccadilly Circus
Fortune, Russell Street, WC2, ☎836 2238 (CC)   ⊖ Covent Garden
Mayfair, Stratton Street, W1, ☎629 3036 (CC)   ⊖ Green Park
St Martin's, (current home of *The Mousetrap*), West Street, WC2,
☎836 1443 (CC)   ⊖ Leicester Square
Wyndham's, Charing Cross Road, WC2, ☎836 3028, 379 6565 (CC)
⊖ Leicester Square

Miscellaneous theatres
Arts Theatre, 6–7 Great Newport Street, WC2, ☎836 2132 ⊖ Leicester
Square
Café Theatre, Bear and Staff pub, 37 Charing Cross Road, WC2,
☎240 0794   ⊖ Leicester Square
Donmar Warehouse, 42 Earlham Street, WC2, ☎240 8230, 379 6565
(CC)   ⊖ Leicester Square
Drill Hall, 16 Chenies Street, WC1, ☎637 8270   ⊖ Goodge Street
ICA (Institute of Contemporary Arts), The Mall, SW1, ☎930 3647
⊖ Charing Cross
Shaw, 100 Euston Road, NW1, ☎388 1394   ⊖ Euston
Vanbrugh (Royal Academy of Dramatic Art), Malet Street, WC1,
☎636 7076   ⊖ Goodge Street

Open air
Regent's Park Open-Air Theatre (Jun–Aug), Inner Circle, Regent's
Park, NW1, ☎486 2431   ⊖ Baker Street

City and South Bank
National Companies
Barbican Theatre and **The Pit** (Royal Shakespeare Company), Barbican
Centre, EC2, ☎628 8795, 638 8891 (CC)   ⊖ Barbican, Moorgate
Olivier, Lyttelton and **Cottesloe,** (National Theatre Company), South
Bank, SE1, ☎928 2252 (CC)   ⊖ Waterloo

Drama and fringe
Mermaid, Puddle Dock, EC4, ☎236 5568 (CC)   ⊖ Blackfriars
Old Vic, The Cut, SE1, ☎928 7616, 261 1821 (CC)   ⊖ Waterloo
Oval House, 54 Kennington Oval, SE11, ☎582 7680   ⊖ Oval
Young Vic and **Studio,** 66 The Cut, SE1, ☎928 6363   ⊖ Waterloo

East and South-east London
Albany Empire (fringe), Douglas Way, Deptford, SE14, ☎691 3333
⊖ ⇌ New Cross
Ashcroft (drama), Fairfield Hall, Park Lane, Croydon, ☎688 9291
⇌ East Croydon
Greenwich Theatre (drama), Crooms Hill, SE10, ☎858 7755 ⇌ Green-
wich
Half Moon (fringe), 213 Mile End Road, E1, ☎790 4000   ⊖ Stepney
Green

Theatre Royal, Stratford East (new plays and musicals), Gerry Raffles Square, E15, ☎534 0310 ⊖ Stratford
Warehouse (fringe), 62 Dingwall Road, Croydon, ☎680 4060 ⇌ East Croydon

North and North-west London

Almeida (fringe), Almeida Street, N1, ☎359 4404 ⊖ Angel, Highbury & Islington
Cockpit (theatre workshop and fringe productions), Gateforth Street, NW8, ☎402 5081 ⊖ Marylebone, Edgware Road
Corner (pub theatre), Hen and Chicken, Highbury Corner, N5, ☎226 3724 ⊖ Highbury & Islington
Hampstead (new plays), Swiss Cottage Centre, Avenue Road, NW3, ☎722 9301 ⊖ Swiss Cottage
King's Head (original pub theatre), 115 Upper Street, N1, ☎226 1916 ⊖ Angel, Highbury & Islington
Little Angel (marionettes), 14 Dagmar Passage, Cross Street, N1, ☎226 1787 ⊖ Angel
Old Red Lion (fringe), St John Street, EC1, ☎837 7816 ⊖ Angel
Tricycle (fringe), 269 Kilburn High Road, NW6, ☎328 8626 ⊖ Kilburn ⇌ Brondesbury
Village (fringe), The Production Village, 100 Cricklewood Lane, NW2, ☎452 3922⊖ Golders Green, Willesden Green then bus nos. 245, 260.

West and South-west London

Battersea Arts Centre (fringe), Old Town Hall, Lavender Hill, SW11, ☎223 8413 ⇌ Clapham Junction
Bush (pub theatre), Shepherd's Bush Green, W12, ☎743 3388 ⊖ Shepherd's Bush, Goldhawk Road
Canal Café (fringe), Bridge House, Delamere Terrace, Little Venice, W2, ☎289 6054 ⊖ Warwick Avenue
Gate (pub theatre), Prince Albert, 11 Pembridge Road, W11, ☎229 0706 ⊖ Notting Hill Gate
Kensington Park Theatre (fringe), 139 Ladbroke Grove, W10, ☎736 9793 ⊖ Ladbroke Grove
Latchmere (fringe), 503 Battersea Park Road, SW11, ☎228 2620 ⇌ Clapham Junction
Lyric and **Studio** (drama), King Street, W6, ☎741 2311 ⊖ Hammersmith
Man in the Moon (fringe), 392 King's Road, SW3, ☎351 2876 ⊖ Sloane Square then bus.
Orange Tree (fringe), 45 Kew Road, ☎940 3633 ⊖ ⇌ Richmond
Polka (children's theatre), 240 Wimbledon Broadway, SW19, ☎543 4888 ⊖ ⇌ Wimbledon
Questors (fringe), Mattock Lane, W13, ☎567 5184 ⊖ Ealing Broadway
Richmond (drama), The Green, ☎940 0088 ⊖ ⇌ Richmond
Riverside Studios (arts centre), Crisp Road, W6, ☎748 3354 ⊖ Hammersmith
Royal Court and **Theatre Upstairs** (English Stage Company), Sloane Square, SW1, ☎730 1745, 730 1857 (CC), 730 2554 (Theatre Upstairs) ⊖ Sloane Square
Tabard (pub theatre), 2 Bath Road, W4, ☎995 6035 ⊖ Turnham Green
Watermans Arts Centre (fringe), 40 High Street, Brentford ☎400 3400 ⇌ Kew Bridge
Wimbledon (drama), The Broadway, SW19, ☎540 0362 ⊖ ⇌ Wimbledon

Cinema

The National Film Theatre (South Bank, ☎928 3232) has extremely interesting programming, but it is necessary to become a member and for most performances to book well in advance. Full cinema listings are found in *Time Out, City Limits* and *What's on and Where to Go*. There are various offers for reduced rates, and matinees are usually cheaper. Children under 16 can generally enter for half the standard price. Films are given various certificates, depending on their suitability for children. 'U': Universal, anyone can watch. 'PG': Parental Guidance, there may be strong language in these films, and cinemas often refuse entry to unaccompanied children after 6pm. '15': no one under the age of fifteen may see them. '18': no one under the age of eighteen may see them.

Music

Full details of London's rock music scene can be found in music magazines such as *New Musical Express, City Limits, Time Out* etc. Some of the most popular venues are listed below:

Bull & Gate, 389 Kentish Town Road, NW5, ☎485 5358 ⊖ Kentish Town

Dingwalls, Camden Lock, NW1, ☎267 4967 ⊖ Camden Town, Chalk Farm

Hammersmith Palais, 242 Shepherd's Bush Road, W6, ☎748 2812 ⊖ Hammersmith

Hog's Grunt, Production Village, 100 Cricklewood Lane, NW2, ☎450 8969 ⊖ Golders Green, Willesden Green

Marquee, 90 Wardour Street, W1, ☎437 6603 ⊖ Piccadilly Circus

Odeon, Hammersmith Broadway, W6, ☎748 4081 ⊖ Hammersmith

Red Lion pub, 318 High Street, Brentford, ☎560 6181 ⊖ South Ealing, Gunnersbury

Wembley Arena, Empire Way, Wembley, ☎902 1234 ⊖ Wembley Park

The best-known jazz clubs are:

Bull's Head, 373 Lonsdale Road, SW13, ☎876 5241 ⇌ Barnes Bridge ⊖ Hammersmith then bus No. 9.

Ronnie Scott's, 47 Frith Street, W1, ☎439 0747 ⊖ Leicester Square

100 Club, 100 Oxford Street, W1, ☎636 0933 ⊖ Tottenham Court Road

Classical concerts are given at:

Barbican Hall, Barbican Centre, EC2, ☎628 8795, 638 8891 (CC) ⊖ Barbican, Moorgate

Royal Albert Hall, Kensington Gore, SW7, ☎589 8212, 589 9465 (CC) ⊖ South Kensington

St John's, Smith Square, SW1, ☎222 1061 ⊖ Westminster

The **South Bank Arts Centre,** SE1, includes three concert halls: the **Royal Festival Hall, Queen Elizabeth Hall,** and the **Purcell Room,** ☎928 3191, 928 8800 (CC) ⊖ Embankment, Waterloo ⇌ Waterloo

Wigmore Hall, 36 Wigmore Street, W1, ☎935 2141 ⊖ Bond Street

Open-air concerts are given in summer by the lake at **Crystal Palace Park,** SE26, (⇌ Crystal Palace), in **Holland Park,** Kensington, W8, (⊖ Holland Park), and by the lake at **Kenwood,** Hampstead, N6, (⊖ Archway, Golders Green then bus No. 210).

▬ SHOPPING

Shopping in London offers endless possibilities, from the fashionable jewellers and art galleries of Bond Street to colourful markets where nearly everything is a bargain. Most shops are open Monday to

Saturday from 9 or 9.30am till 5.30pm, with many in the West End and Kensington High Street staying open till 7.30 or 8pm on Thursdays. Knightsbridge and the King's Road have late-night shopping on Wednesday. You will find some shops open on Sundays, especially in tourist areas such as Covent Garden.

In the West End, Oxford Street (from Marble Arch to Tottenham Court Road) is the most popular, and busiest, shopping area, with several department stores (**Selfridges, Debenhams, John Lewis, D.H. Evans**), branches of most of the leading chain stores (**C & A, Marks & Spencer, Mothercare, Littlewoods, British Home Stores, Boots**) and the **HMV** and **Virgin** record megastores. Nearby Regent Street (from Oxford Circus to Piccadilly) is slightly more upmarket (**Liberty, Dickins & Jones, Jaeger, Aquascutum, Austin Reed, Lillywhites**) and boasts the biggest toy shop in the world, **Hamleys**. Bond Street has **Fenwick** department store and exclusive designer boutiques (**Gianni Versace, Guy Laroche, Daniel Hechter, Yamamoto, Kenzo, Roland Klein, Karl Lagerfeld, Loewe, Ralph Lauren**) and shoe shops (**Gucci, Kurt Geiger, Rayne, Russell & Bromley**). South Molton Street, which runs parallel with the north of Bond Street, is an attractive pedestrian area with pavement cafés and more high fashion (**Browns, Joseph Bis, Butler & Wilson,** jewellery, **Katharine Hamnett, Hobbs,** shoes).

Covent Garden is rapidly becoming one of London's most fashionable shopping districts, with numerous smart clothes and shoe shops: **Hobbs** and **Whistles** for women's shoes and clothing, **S. Fisher** for trendy, quality menswear, and the **Body Shop,** a branch of the worldwide herbal cosmetic and perfume chain. Beside the Piazza, the **Apple Market** is Covent Garden's other half, a long string of stalls, many changing each day of the week, selling mainly crafts, but specializing in antiques on Mondays. If you are looking for a particular article, listed below are some of London's specialist shops.

Fashion Addresses

Hardy Amies, 14 Savile Row, W1, ☎734 2436
Christian Dior, 9 Conduit Street, W1, ☎499 6255
Norman Hartnell, 26 Bruton Street, W1 ☎629 0992
Lachasse, 4 Farm Street, W1, ☎499 2906
(Appointments are needed for the above four.)
Aquascutum, 100 Regent Street, W1, ☎743 6090
Austin Reed, 103 Regent Street, W1, ☎734 6789
Blades (men), 8 Burlington Gardens, W1, ☎734 8911
Browns, 23–27 South Molton Street, W1, ☎499 5630
Bugatti, 59 Kensington Church Street, W8, ☎937 2624
Burberrys, 18 Haymarket, SW1, ☎930 3343
S. Fisher, 22–23 and 32 Burlington Arcade, W1, ☎493 4180
Moss Bros, Bedford Street, WC2, ☎240 4567
Janet Reger (lingerie), 2 Beauchamp Place, SW3, ☎584 9368
Yves St Laurent, 84 Brompton Road, SW3, ☎584 4993
The Scotch House, 2 Brompton Road, SW1, ☎581 2151
Scottish Merchant, 16 New Row, WC2, ☎836 2207
Simpson, 203 Piccadilly, W1, ☎734 2002
Wardrobe, 17 Crawford Street, W1, ☎935 4086
Westaway and Westaway, 65 Great Russell Street, WC1, ☎405 4479

Shoes

Bally (women), 30 Old Bond Street, W1, ☎493 2250
Chelsea Cobbler, 54 King's Road, SW3, ☎584 2602
Church and Co (men), 58–59 Burlington Arcade, W1, ☎493 8307

Maxwell's (men), 11 Savile Row, W1, ☎734 9714
Russell & Bromley, 24 New Bond Street, W1, ☎629 6903
Sacha, 351 New Oxford Street, W1, ☎499 7272
Zapata, 49–51 Old Church Street, SW3, ☎352 8622

Classics

Ava (women), 73 Walton Street, SW3, ☎581 3973
James Drew (women), 3 Burlington Arcade, W1, ☎493 0714
H. Huntsman and Sons (men), 11 Savile Row, W1, ☎734 7441
Nutters of Savile Row (men), 35a Savile Row, W1, ☎437 6850
Panache (women), 24 Beauchamp Place, SW3, ☎584 9807

Books

Compendium, 234 Camden High Street, NW1, ☎485 8944
Dillons, 82 Gower Street, WC1, ☎636 1577
Foyles, 119 Charing Cross Road, WC1, ☎437 5660
Hatchards, 187 Piccadilly, W1, ☎437 3924
Waterstones, 88 Regent Street, W1, ☎734 0713; 121 Charing Cross Road, WC2, ☎434 4291; 99 Old Brompton Road, SW7, ☎581 8522 and 195 Kensington High Street, W8, ☎937 8432

Antiques

Barrett Street Antique Supermarket, W1, ☎493 5833
Chelsea Antique Market, 245–253 King's Road, SW3, ☎352 9695
Gray's Antique Market, 58 Davies Street, W1, ☎629 7034
Pelham Galleries, 163 and 165 Fulham Road, SW3, ☎589 2686

Jewellery and Silver

Bentley, 65 New Bond Street, W1, ☎629 0651
Bond Street Silver Galleries, 111 New Bond Street, W1, ☎493 6180
Collingwood, 171 New Bond Street, W1, ☎734 2656
Garrard, 112 Regent Street, W1, ☎734 7020 jewellers to the Queen
London Silver Vaults, Chancery Lane, WC2, ☎242 3844, for antique and modern silver
S.J. Phillips, 139 New Bond Street, W1, ☎629 6261

▬ MARKETS

London has an enormous variety of markets, catering to different tastes and pockets. They can be found all over the capital, selling items of all kinds – fruit or antique silver, fish or clothing. There are too many street markets in London to mention them all but those below are famous, and a visitor may be able to pick up a bargain or two.

Berwick Street, W1 (*Mon–Sat*) for fruit and vegetables ⊖ Piccadilly Circus
Camden Lock, NW1 (*Sat–Sun*) for crafts, antiques, bric-à-brac, second-hand and new clothing ⊖ Camden Town, Chalk Farm
Camden Passage, NW1 (*Wed 6.30am–4pm, Thu, Sat 8am–4pm*) shops and stalls selling a wide range of antiques, books, prints and bric-à-brac ⊖ Angel
Columbia Road, Shoreditch, E2 (*Sun am*) for flowers and plants ⊖ Bethnal Green
Electric Avenue, Brixton, SW9 (*Mon–Tue, Wed am, Thu–Sat*) for second-hand clothing and Afro-Caribbean foods ⊖ Brixton
Greenwich Antiques Market, Greenwich High Road, SE10 (*Sat–Sun*) for antiques ⇌ Greenwich
Leather Lane, EC1 (*Mon–Fri*) for fruit and vegetables, plants, clothing ⊖ Chancery Lane
Petticoat Lane, Middlesex Street, E1 (*Sun am*) for general goods ⊖ Liverpool Street

Petticoat Lane market

Portobello Road, W11 *(Mon–Sat)* for fruit, vegetables, and general goods; *(Fri–Sat)* bric-à-brac and flea market; *(Sat)* antiques ⊖ Notting Hill Gate, Ladbroke Grove
Shepherd's Bush, Goldhawk Road, W12 *(Mon–Wed, Thu am, Fri–Sat)* for general goods ⊖ Shepherd's Bush, Goldhawk Road
Wembley, Wembley Stadium Car Park *(Sun am)* for clothing, jewellery, food, bric-à-brac ⊖ Wembley Park

London's wholesale markets are almost institutions in themselves, well worth a visit for the lively atmosphere, the range of fresh poultry, game, flowers and fish on display and the continual bartering. Since they are primarily there to serve retailers, hoteliers and restaurateurs who want fresh produce, the markets begin very early (4am onwards) and are all closed by midday:

Billingsgate, North Quay, West India Dock Road (*Tue–Sat*), London's principal fish market ☏ Mile End then bus No. 106

New Covent Garden, Nine Elms, SW8 (*Mon–Sat 4am–9am*), London's principal fruit and vegetable market, with flowers on Sat ☏ Vauxhall

Smithfield, EC1 (*Mon–Fri*) for meat, poultry and game ☏ Farringdon

Spitalfields, E1 (*Mon–Sat 4.30am–9am*) for fruit, vegetables and flowers ☏ Liverpool Street

▬▬ AUCTIONS

London has retained its position as the world's centre for art auctions, partly because of the lenient laws on the export of works of art. Even if you do not intend to make a purchase, go along to one of London's auction houses to see how things work and enjoy the atmosphere.

Bonhams, Montpelier Galleries, Montpelier Street, SW7, ☎584 9161 ☏ Knightsbridge

Christie's Fine Art, 8 King Street, SW1, ☎839 9060 ☏ Piccadilly Circus

Christie's (South Kensington), 85 Old Brompton Road, SW7, ☎581 2231, art and antiques, ☏ South Kensington

Phillips, 7 Blenheim Street, W1, ☎629 6602 ☏ Bond Street

Sotheby's, 34–35 New Bond Street, W1, ☎493 8080 and 19 Motcomb Street, SW1, ☎235 4311 ☏ Bond Street

▬▬ ART GALLERIES

London has a flourishing art market, particularly in old masters and in Victorian art, while there are also a number of excellent contemporary galleries. Most of the principal galleries are in the Bond Street area. For a full listing of current exhibitions, see the art press or *Time Out* etc.

Agnew, 43 Old Bond Street, W1, ☎629 6176, Old Masters ☏ Green Park

Christie's Contemporary Art, 8 Dover Street, W1, ☎499 6701 ☏ Green Park

Fischer Fine Art, 30 King Street, St James's, SW1, ☎839 3942, 20th-century European artists and British realists ☏ Piccadilly

Marlborough Fine Art, 6 Albemarle Street, W1, ☎629 5161, 19th–20th-century art ☏ Green Park

Anthony d'Offay, 9 and 23 Dering Street, W1, ☎629 1578, British and international contemporary art ☏ Bond Street

Waddington, 2, 4, 31 and 34 Cork Street, W1, ☎439 1866, contemporary painting and sculpture ☏ Piccadilly Circus

▬▬ SPORT

Apart from the huge variety of spectator sports in London, there are many opportunities to participate in your chosen activity. Most boroughs have well-equipped sports centres and swimming pools, while excellent golf courses are to be found in the suburbs. Some of the most important societies and organizations that can help you find a place to play your particular sport in London are listed below.

The Greater London and South Eastern Region Sports Council, (P.O Box 480), Crystal Palace National Sports Centre, Leadrington Road, SE19, ☎778 8600, provides general information concerning all sports.

Sports Council Information Centre, 16 Upper Woburn Place, WC1, ☎388 1277.

Sportsline, ☎222 8000, offers information on every sport imaginable and will give you the name of the nearest centre for any sport.

Sports Centres

Crystal Palace National Sports Centre, SE19, ☎778 0131 ≉ Crystal Palace

Ealing Northern, Greenford Road, ☎422 4428 ⊖ Greenford

Elephant and Castle Recreation Centre, 22 Elephant and Castle, SE1 ☎582 5505 ⊖ Elephant and Castle

Eltham, Messeter Place, Eltham High Street, SE9, ☎850 9217 ≉ Eltham Park

Eternit Wharf, Stevenage Road, SW6, ☎381 5266 ⊖ Hammersmith

Hendon, Algernon Road, NW4, ☎202 6027 ≉ Hendon

Jubilee, Queen's Park Estate, Caird Street, W10, ☎960 5511 ⊖ Queen's Park

Kensington, Walmer Road, W11, ☎727 9923 ⊖ Latimer Road

Merton YMCA, 200 The Broadway, SW19, ☎540 7255 ⊖ Wimbledon

Michael Sobell Sports Centre, Hornsey Road, N7, ☎607 1632 ⊖ Holloway Road

Mornington Sports and Leisure Centre, 142–150 Arlington Road, NW1, ⊖ Mornington Crescent

Queen Mother Sports Centre, 223 Vauxhall Bridge Road, SW1, ☎834 4726 ⊖ Victoria, Pimlico

Swiss Cottage, Winchester Road, NW3, ☎278 4444 ⊖ Swiss Cottage

Swimming Pools

Most of the above sports centres have swimming pools. There are other indoor and outdoor pools in London, including:

The Oasis, (indoor and outdoor) 32 Endell Street, WC2, ☎836 9555 ⊖ Tottenham Court Road

Porchester Baths, (indoor) Porchester Road, W2, ☎798 3688 ⊖ Royal Oak

Serpentine Lido, (outdoor) Hyde Park, SW7, ☎724 3104 ⊖ Lancaster Gate, Knightsbridge

Seymour Baths, (indoor) Seymour Place, W1, ☎723 8019 ⊖ Edgware Road

Golf

Many membership courses will extend guest facilities to members of comparable clubs overseas.

Royal Mid-Surrey, Old Deer Park, Twickenham Road, Richmond ☎940 1894. 18-hole parkland course open Mon–Fri. Players must be members of recognized clubs and hold a handicap certificate ⊖ ≉ Richmond

South Herts, Links Drive, N20, ☎445 2035. 18-hole parkland course, open Mon–Fri. Players must be members of recognized clubs. ⊖ Totteridge & Whetstone

Municipal courses where it is not necessary to be a member:

Brent Valley Golf Course, Church Road, W7, ☎567 1287. 18-hole course in Brent River Park. ⊖ ≉ Hanwell

Home Park, Hampton Court, ☎997 6645 ≉ Hampton Court, Hampton Wick

Richmond Park, Roehampton Gate, SW15, ☎876 3205. Two 18-hole parkland courses with advanced booking necessary at weekends. ≉ Barnes

Royal Epping Forest, Forest Approach, Station Road, E4, ☎529 1039. 18-hole. ≉ Chingford

Twickenham, Staines Road, ☎979 6946. 9-hole course. ≉ Fulwell

Riding

Bathurst Riding Stables, 63 Bathurst Mews, ☎723 2813 ⊖ Lancaster Gate

Lilo Blum, 32 Grosvenor Crescent Mews, SW1, ☎235 6846, includes rides in Hyde Park. ⊖ Hyde Park Corner

Roehampton Gate Riding and Livery Stables, Priory Lane, SW15, adjacent to Richmond Park, ☎876 7089 ≹ Barnes

Skating

Michael Sobell Sports Centre, Hornsey Road, N7, ☎607 1632 ⊖ Holloway Road

Queens Ice Skating Club, 17 Queensway, W2, ☎229 0172 ⊖ Bayswater, Queensway

Richmond Ice Rink, Clevedon Road, East Twickenham, ☎892 3646 ⊖ ≹ Richmond

Streatham Ice Rink, 386 Streatham High Road, SW16, ☎769 7861 ≹ Streatham

▬ PARKS

London has more parks and open spaces than any other major city in the world. There are more than 80 parks within 7 miles of Piccadilly, while Greater London includes nearly 400 parks larger than 20 acres (8ha), totalling some 45,000 acres (18,200ha). Even in central London several are situated only minutes away from main shopping centres and business areas, providing peaceful havens and a refuge from the bustle of city streets and traffic.

The ten Royal Parks are justly famous, and part of our national heritage. Originally royal hunting grounds, pleasure gardens and deer parks, they are now delightful leisure spots for the enjoyment of everyone. Details of these parks and their historic buildings can be found in the itineraries.

London's parks and open spaces vary enormously in size and character, ranging from small formal flower gardens to the vast grasslands of Richmond Park and Hampstead Heath, and the natural woodlands of Epping Forest. There are trim lawns and secluded walks, sunken gardens, rivers and lakes, and many splendid stately homes, galleries and museums to visit. They also offer a wide range of leisure and sporting facilities, including tennis courts, golf courses, bowling greens, lakes and ponds for swimming, boating and fishing, and areas for riding horses or flying kites. They have also been the site of many exhibitions, concerts, fairs, festivals and firework displays. Most parks have special areas for young children, and adventure playgrounds provide hours of fun for the older ones.

The city's open spaces are carefully protected and many are able to support a wide variety of wildlife. Apart from the ducks, squirrels and rabbits living minutes away from busy streets, many a rarer species can be spotted. The lake and island in St James's Park are a designated bird sanctuary, where specially introduced species include exotic ducks, geese and pelicans. Wild animals include numerous herds of deer ranging over Richmond Park, as they have for 350 years. London Zoo, at the north end of Regent's Park, is a must for family visits. (*See p.158*.)

Most parks offer some kind of refreshments. Whether you have a cooling drink, a snack from a kiosk, or a gourmet meal in a comfortable restaurant, there is a good chance you will also enjoy a pleasant view.

Open from dawn till dusk, London's parks are an integral part of city life, providing areas for the enjoyment and recreation of Londoners and visitors alike.

Dickens Inn, St Katharine's Dock

PUBS

The pub (public house) is first and foremost a place to enjoy a drink among congenial company, although pubs are also among the best places for good inexpensive food, and many offer entertainment of various kinds, but their greatest attraction to the visitor is perhaps the opportunity they give to savour the atmosphere of local London in all its variety.

Among the 7,000 pubs in the capital there are still taverns hundreds of years old tucked away in numerous lanes, particularly in the City of London, and one galleried coaching inn, the George in Southwark, survives from Shakespeare's day. From the last century there are a few superb Victorian 'gin-palaces' resplendent with carved mahogany, brass fittings and engraved mirrors. Other pubs have gardens or terraces, and those beside the river Thames (*see p. 175*) or the Regent's Canal are particularly attractive. Pubs are also very much part of the entertainment scene in London, many having regular sessions with jazz, folk or rock groups (see *City Limits* and *Time Out* for details). Several pubs also hold regular theatrical performances, often of high quality, which will later transfer to the West End. Others are the venue for numerous experimental and fringe theatre groups. Some pubs are quiet and intimate, others brash and noisy; some are wedded to their local community, others cater particularly for visitors; each one reflects a different aspect of London life.

The opening times of pubs are limited by law, and most London pubs open from 11 or 11.30am to 3pm and again from 5 or 5.30pm to 11pm. These times do vary slightly in different parts of London, and many pubs in the City, which cater for the business community, close as early as 8 or 9pm in the evening and stay closed on Saturdays and Sundays. A few pubs close to the main wholesale markets (Smithfield,

Southwark etc.) are licensed to open very early in the morning, although drinking is restricted to market users. Children under the age of 14 are not permitted to enter pubs, and may not buy or drink alcohol until they are 18. However, younger children are usually allowed on terraces or in gardens and in restaurants if these are separate from the bars.

Beer is the main drink sold in pubs, and there are hundreds of different types. The principal choice is between lager – similar to American and European beers – and bitter, draught English ale, or bottled light ale. Most pubs also offer a stronger best bitter. Beer is sold in half-pints or pints (20% more than a US pint). Many pubs are owned by breweries, and there are still two traditional breweries in London – Young's of Wandsworth and Fuller's of Chiswick – that brew particularly good 'real' ales. Pubs also sell spirits (the standard measure is 1⅔ fl.oz.) and a very limited choice of wine by the glass as well as some non-alcoholic drinks. Pub food can vary from snacks at the bar to a full-scale restaurant meal, but many pubs offer a limited range of excellent hot dishes, especially at lunchtime on weekdays.

A selection of pubs and wine-bars (which are subject to the same laws on opening hours) appears at the end of the itineraries. When a pub is owned by a brewery, this is shown in brackets after the name.

▬ PLACES OF WORSHIP

All around London services are held for most of the major religions; the visitor is likely to be able to worship whatever his or her faith.

Listed below are only a few of the many places which hold services daily:

St Paul's Cathedral, Ludgate Hill, EC4 (*services: Sun 8, 10.30, 11.30am, 3.15pm; Mon–Thu 7.30, 10am, 12.30, 5pm; Fri 7.30, 10am, 5pm; Sat 8, 10am, 12.30pm. During winter the 5pm service is replaced by one at 4pm*) ⊖ St Paul's. **Westminster Abbey,** Broad Sanctuary, SW1 (*services: Sun 8, 10.30, 11.40am, 3, 6.30pm; Mon–Fri: 7.30, 8am, 12.30, 5pm; Sat 8am, 3pm*) ⊖ Westminster, St James's Park. **Queen's Chapel,** Marlborough Road, W1 (*Services: Sun 8.30, 11.15am, Easter Day–end July*) ⊖ Green Park. **Westminster Cathedral** (RC) Ashley Place, SW1 (*High Mass: Sun 10.30am*) ⊖ Victoria. **Central Synagogue,** Great Portland Street, W1 (*services daily 8am; Sat 9.30am*) ⊖ Great Portland Street. **West London Synagogue,** Upper Berkeley Street, W1 (*services Fri 6pm; Sat 11am*) ⊖ Marble Arch.

Amongst the churches in London famous for their music of outstanding quality are:

All Saints, Margaret Street, W1. ⊖ Oxford Circus
Brompton Oratory (RC), Brompton Road, SW7. ⊖ South Kensington
Chapel Royal of St John, White Tower, Tower of London, EC3. ⊖ Tower Hill
Church of the Immaculate Conception (RC), Farm Street, W1. ⊖ Green Park, Bond Street
St James's, Piccadilly, SW1. ⊖ Piccadilly Circus
St Martin-in-the-Fields, Trafalgar Square, WC2. ⊖ Trafalgar Square
St Paul's Cathedral, see above
St Paul's, Wilton Place, SW1. ⊖ Knightsbridge
Temple Church, Inner Temple Lane, EC4. ⊖ Temple
Westminster Abbey, see above
Westminster Cathedral (RC), see above

FACILITIES FOR CHILDREN

Places of special interest to children include:
Natural History Museum (*see p.204*). **Science Museum** (*see p.206*).
Guinness World of Records Exhibition, The Trocadero, Piccadilly
Circus – a chance to see some of the most fascinating world records
'close up'. **London Dungeon** (*see p.137*) – a very effective and
frightening display of some of London's more unpleasant history.
Don't take very young children. **Planetarium** (*see p.156*) – star and
laser displays are projected onto its dome ceiling. **Pollock's Toy
Museum** (*see p.146*) – a collection of old and rare toys, which are
beautiful and fascinating. **London Transport Museum,** Covent Garden (*see p.150*) – an exciting presentation of some of LT's old
equipment. Children are given the opportunity to try out some of the
machines – pressing buttons and pulling levers.

All around London in borough parks are so-called 'adventure
playgrounds' offering supervised play facilities, which are unique to
each one. Such delights as high cat-walks and long swings will
entertain your child indefinitely.

If you want an evening or a day without the worry of children,
London has a number of babysitting agencies, which will arrange to
fetch and look after them:

Babysitters/Childminders, 67A Marylebone High Street, W1, ☎935
9763/2049
Babysitters Unlimited, 271–273 King Street, W6, ☎741 5566
Universal Aunts, 250 King's Road, SW3, ☎351 5676

'Mother and baby' facilities are available at Harrods (Knightsbridge),
John Lewis (Oxford Street), and Selfridges (Oxford Street).

FACILITIES FOR THE DISABLED

Artsline, ☎388 2227: Information service concerning access for the
disabled to the major entertainments and arts centres in London.
Greater London Association of the Disabled, ☎274 0107: General
queries concerning accommodation, access etc.
LTB Tourist Information Centre, ☎730 3488, Victoria Station forecourt, SW1, offers *London for the Disabled Visitor* – a booklet concerning all aspects of being in London if you are disabled.
Holiday Care Service, ☎0293-774 535: Free information service for
all disabled, mentally handicapped and elderly people.

LONDON EVENTS

January: International Boat Show; West London Antiques Fair; Holiday on Ice, Wembley Arena; Brent Festival of Music and Dance;
Benson and Hedges Masters Snooker Tournament.

February: International Food and Drink Exhibition; Crufts Dogs Show;
Stratford and East London Music Festival; Stampex – International
Stamp Exhibition.

March: Chelsea Antiques Fair; London International Opera Festival;
British Designer Show; London Photography Fair; Devizes to West-
minster International Canoe Race; Oxford v Cambridge University Boat
Race – Putney to Mortlake; International Festival of Country Music;
Daily Mail Ideal Home Exhibition; Camden Festival.

April: London Book Fair; London Beer Drinker Festival; Champions All
International Gymnastics; Craft Fair; London Marathon; Littlewoods
Cup Football Final; FA Vase Final; Easter Parade, Battersea Park

May: Rugby League Challenge Cup Final; Historic Commercial Vehicle Run, Battersea Park to Brighton; Royal Windsor Horse Trials; FA Cup Final; Chelsea Flower Show; International Contemporary Art Fair; Fine Art and Antiques Fair, Olympia; Greenwich Festival.

June: Horse Guards Parade 'Beating the Retreat'; Stella Artois Tennis Championships; Grosvenor House Antiques Fair; Trooping the Colour; All England Club Lawn Tennis Championships, Wimbledon; Metropolitan Police Horse Show; London to Brighton Bicycle Ride; Putney Show, Putney Lower Common; Summer Exhibition – Royal Academy of Arts.

July: Festival of the City of London; Berkeley Square Charity Ball; Royal Tournament, Earls Court; Richmond Festival; Henry Wood Promenade Concerts (Proms); Finchley Carnival; Chelsea Village Fair; Swan Upping – River Thames; Doggetts Coat and Badge Race, Tower Bridge to Chelsea.

August: West London Antiques Fair; Greater London Horse Show, Clapham Common; Greenwich Clipper Weeks; Notting Hill Carnival.

September: Chelsea Antiques Fair; Battle of Britain Service; Sunday Times Fun Run, Hyde Park; Punch and Judy Festival, Covent Garden Piazza.

October: National Brass Band Championships; Horse of the Year Show; Chelsea Crafts Fair; Trafalgar Day Parade by Sea Cadets; International Bike Show.

November: London to Brighton Veteran Car Run; Kensington Antiques Fair; Caravan and Camping Holiday Show; Lord Mayor's Show; London Craft Fair; Daily Mail International Ski Show; Benson and Hedges Tennis Championships; World Travel Market; State Opening of Parliament.

December: International Showjumping Championships, Olympia; Christmas lights and trees, Oxford Street and Regent Street.

▬ HOTELS AND RESTAURANTS

The following selective listing of hotels and restaurants is divided according to the main areas described in the Guide. London hotels are frequently booked up during the tourist season or at the time of special events, and early booking is always advisable. The Tourist Information Centres at Victoria Station and Heathrow Central Station (see p.28) both have a hotel booking service.

Hotel ratings:

▲	Simple but comfortable
▲▲	Very comfortable
▲▲▲	First class
▲▲▲▲	Luxury

Prices

Hotels: average price for a room for two, with bathroom, breakfast, service and VAT. **Restaurants:** average price for an evening meal for one, including coffee, service (if applicable) and VAT, but excluding wine.

Hotels:		Restaurants:	
£	under £50	£	under £15
££	£50–100	££	£15–20
£££	£100–150	£££	£20–25
££££	£150–200	££££	£25–30
£££££	over £200	£££££	over £30

Credit cards accepted:

A.   Access/Mastercard/Eurocard
Ae. American Express
Dc. Diners Club
V.   Visa/Barclaycard

Symbols:

🅿   Parking
&   Access for disabled
❀   Garden
🏊   Swimming pool

Central London

Westminster, St James's and Mayfair
(Map IV; itineraries 1 and 2)

Hotels

▲▲▲▲ *Athenaeum* (Rank), 116 Piccadilly, W1, ☎499 3464. Tx. 261589. 112 rm. **££££** A. Ae. Dc. V. De-luxe hotel overlooking Green Park, with outstanding service. Restaurant: **£££.**

▲▲▲▲ *Brown's* (Trust House Forte), Albemarle St, W1, ☎493 6020. Tx. 28686. 125 rm. **££££** A. Ae. Dc. V. Distinguished hotel situated in the heart of Mayfair. Restaurant: *L'Aperitif.* **£££**.

▲▲▲▲ *Cavendish* (Trust House Forte), Jermyn St, SW1, ☎930 2111. Tx. 263187. 253 rm. 🅿 **£££** A. Ae. Dc. V. Restaurant: **£££**.

▲▲▲▲ *Chesterfield,* 35 Charles St, W1, ☎491 2622. Tx. 269394. 114 rm. **£££** A. Ae. Dc. V. Restaurant: **££**.

▲▲▲▲ *Claridge's* (Savoy), Brook St, W1, ☎629 8860. Tx. 21872. 205 rm. **££££** A. Ae. Dc. V. Restaurant: **££££**.

▲▲▲▲ *Connaught* (Savoy), Carlos Place, W1, ☎499 7070. 90 rm. **££££** A. World-famous London institution renowned for its traditional service and superb restaurant. Restaurant: **££££**.

▲▲▲▲ *Dorchester,* Park Lane, W1, ☎629 8888. Tx. 887704. 275 rm. 🅿 **£££££** A. Ae. Dc. V. One of London's great hotels with a famous chef, Anton Mosiman. Restaurant: *Terrace.* **££££** *Cl. Sun.*

▲▲▲▲ *Dukes* (Prestige), 35 St James's Place, SW1, ☎491 4840. Tx. 28283. 51 rm. **££££** A. Ae. Dc. V. Privately owned hotel in the heart of St James's. Restaurant: Chicory parcels filled with brill on light red wine sauce. **£££££**.

▲▲▲▲ *Goring,* 15 Beeston Place, SW1, ☎834 8211. Tx. 919166. 100 rm. 🅿 **£££** A. Ae. Dc. V. The first hotel in the world to be equipped with central heating and a private bath for each bedroom. Restaurant: **££**.

▲▲▲▲ *Inn on the Park* (Prestige), Hamilton Place, W1, ☎499 0888. Tx. 22771. 228 rm. 🅿 **££££** A. Ae. Dc. V. Restaurant: *Four Seasons.* **££££**.

▲▲▲▲ *Intercontinental,* 1 Hamilton Place, W1, ☎409 3131. Tx. 25853. 490 rm. 🅿 & **££££** A. Ae. Dc. V. Restaurant: *Le Soufflé.* & Savoury and sweet soufflés, veal mignon, sweetbreads. **£££** *Cl. Sat lunch.*

▲▲▲▲ *London Hilton,* 22 Park Lane, W1, ☎493 8000. Tx. 24873. 445 rm. 🅿 & **££££** A. Ae. Dc. V. Restaurant: *British Harvest.* & **£££**.

▲▲▲▲ *May Fair* (Inter-Continental), Stratton St, W1, ☎629 777. Tx. 262526. 292 rm. & **££££** A. Ae. Dc. V. Luxury hotel with its own theatre. Restaurant: *Le Chateaubriand.* & **£££** *Cl. Sat lunch.*

▲▲▲▲ *New Piccadilly* (Gleneagles), Piccadilly, W1, ☎734 8000. Tx. 25795. 290 rm. 🏊 **££££** A. Ae. Dc. V. Restaurant: **£££**.

▲▲▲▲ *Ritz* (Cunard), Piccadilly, W1, ☎493 8181. Tx. 267200. 139 rm. **££££** A. Ae. Dc. V. Elegant hotel on Piccadilly, overlooking

Green Park. Restaurant: Skewered Oban scampi in fish mousse on saffron sauce. **£££££**.

▲▲▲▲ *Westbury* (Trust House Forte), New Bond St, W1, ☎629 7755. Tx. 24378. 242 rm. **£££** A. Ae. Dc. V. Restaurant: **££££**.

▲▲▲ *Royal Westminster* (Thistle), Buckingham Palace Rd, SW1, ☎834 1821. Tx. 916821. 134 rm. **£££** A. Ae. Dc. V. Restaurant: **£**.

▲▲▲ *St Ermin's* (Stakis), Caxton St, SW1, ☎222 7888. Tx. 917731. 296 rm. **P** **££** A. Ae. Dc. V. Restaurant: *Carvery*. **£**.

▲▲▲ *St James Court,* Buckingham Gate, SW1, ☎834 6655. Tx. 919557. 40 rm. **P** ✔ **££££** A. Ae. Dc. V. Restaurant: Fillet of salmon with aubergines. **££££**.

▲▲▲ *Washington* (Sarova), Curzon St, W1, ☎499 7030. Tx. 24540. 164 rm. **£££** A. Ae. Dc. V. Restaurant: **£££**.

▲▲ *Rubens* (Sarova), 39 Buckingham Palace Rd, SW1, ☎834 6600. Tx. 916577. 172 rm. **£££** A. Ae. Dc. V. Restaurant: **£**.

Restaurants

Le Gavroche, 43 Upper Brook St, W1, ☎730 2820 *Cl. Sat, Sun, Bank hols*. Caneton Gavroche, soufflé suisse. **£££££** A. Ae. Dc. V.

Guinea Grill, 26 Bruton Place, W1, ☎499 1210 *Cl. Sat lunch, Sun*. Steaks. **£££££** Ae. Ae. Dc. V.

Miyama, 38 Clarges St, W1, ☎499 2443 *Cl. Sat lunch, Sun, Easter, 25 Dec–1 Jan, Bank hols*. Japanese. Teppan-yaki. **£££££** A. Ae. Dc. V.

Scotts, 20 Mount St, W1, ☎629 5248 **P** *Cl. Sun lunch, Christmas, Easter, Bank hols*. Fish. Suprême de Turbotin Teymour. **£££££** A. Ae. Dc. V.

Suntory, 72 St James's St, SW1, ☎409 0201 *Cl. Sun, Bank hols*. Japanese. Teppan-yaki, Shabu-shabu. **£££££** A. Ae. Dc. V.

Champagne Exchange, 17c Curzon St, W1, ☎493 4490 *Cl. Sat, Sun lunch*. Caviar, smoked fish, shellfish. **££££** A. Ae. Dc. V.

Greenhouse, 27a Hay's Mews, W1, ☎499 3331 *Cl. Sat lunch, Sun, 25 Dec–1 Jan, Bank hols*. Anglo-French. Roast rack of lamb. **££££** A. Ae. Dc. V.

Ninety Park Lane, 90 Park Lane, W1, ☎409 1290 **P** & *Cl. Sat lunch, Sun, Bank hols*. **££££** A. Ae. Dc. V. Hotel restaurant.

One Two Three, 27 Davies St, W1, ☎409 0750 *Cl. Sat, Sun, Christmas, New Year*. Japanese. **££££** A. Ae. Dc. V.

Mr Kai of Mayfair, 65 South Audley St, W1, ☎493 8988 & *Cl. 25–26 Dec, Bank hols*. Peking duck. **£££** A. Ae. Dc. V.

Le Caprice, Arlington House, Arlington St, SW1, ☎629 2239 *Cl. Sat lunch, 24 Dec–2 Jan*. Noisettes d'agneau bergère. **££** A. Ae. Dc. V.

Golden Carp, 8a Mount St, W1, ☎499 3385 *Cl. Sat lunch, Sun, Bank hols*. **££** A. Ae. Dc. V.

Green's, 36 Duke St, SW1, ☎930 4566 *Cl. Sat, Sun*. Fish cakes, English puddings. **££** A. Ae. Dc. V.

Langan's Brasserie, Stratton St, W1, ☎491 8822 *Cl. Sat lunch, Sun, Christmas, Easter, Bank hols*. Grilled sea bass with herb butter sauce. **££** A. Ae. Dc. V.

Al Hamra, 31 Shepherd Market, W1, ☎493 1954 & *Cl. 25 Dec–1 Jan*. Lebanese. Kibbeh, vamia. **£** A. Ae. Dc. V.

Gaylord, 16 Albemarle St, W1, ☎629 9802 *Cl. 25–26 Dec*. Kashmiri dishes. **£** A. Ae. Dc. V.

Hard Rock Café, 150 Old Park Lane, W1, ☎629 0382 Hamburgers, chips and salad, smoked pork. **£**.

Ho-Ho, 29 Maddox St, W1, ☎493 1228 *Cl. Sun*. Chinese. Steamed scallops. **£** A. Ae. Dc. V.

Justin de Blank, 54 Duke St, W1, ☎629 3174 *Cl. Sat eve, Sun, Bank hols.* Anglo-French. Lamb and aubergine casserole. **£.**
The Magic Moment, 233 Regent St, W1, ☎499 6176. Clam chowder, chargrilled prime rib. **£** A. Ae. Dc. V.
Marquis, 121a Mount St, W1, ☎499 1256 *Cl. Sun, Bank hols.* International. Game in season. **£** A. Ae. Dc. V.
Tandoori of Mayfair, 37a Curzon St, W1, ☎629 0600 ⊛ ⅍ *Cl. 25–26 Dec.* Fish tikka, Sali boti. **£** A. Ae. Dc. V.

Westminster:
Tate Gallery, Millbank, SW1, ☎834 6754 ⅍ *Cl. Sun, 24–26 Dec, 1 Jan.* British. **££.**
Bumbles, 16 Buckingham Palace Rd, SW1, ☎828 2903 ⅍ *Cl. Sat lunch, Sun, Bank hols.* British. Scotch rump steak. **£** A. Ae. Dc. V.
Kundan, 3 Horseferry Rd, SW1, ☎834 3434 ◘ *Cl. Sun, Bank Hols.* Indian. **£** A. Ae. Dc. V.
Methuselah's, 29 Victoria St, SW1, ☎222 0424 ⅍ *Cl. Sat, Sun, Bank hols.* Wine bar. **£** A. Dc. V.

Embankment and the City
(Maps IV, V; itineraries 3 and 4)

Hotels

▲▲▲▲ ***Howard*** (Barclays), Temple Place, WC2, ☎836 3555. Tx. 268047. 141 rm. ◘ ⅍ **£££££** A. Ae. Dc. V. Spacious and comfortable hotel overlooking the Thames. Restaurant: ***Quai d'Or.*** ⅍ Fillets of sole 'Isle de France'. **££££**.
▲▲▲▲ ***Savoy,*** Strand, WC2, ☎836 4343. Tx. 24234. 200 rm. ◘ **£££££** A. Ae. Dc. V. A justly famous London institution with outstanding restaurants overlooking the river. Restaurant: ***River.*** **£££**.
▲▲▲▲ ***Tower*** (Thistle), St Katharine's Way, E1, ☎481 2575. Tx. 885934. 826 rm. ◘ **£££** A. Ae. Dc. V. Restaurant: **£££.**
▲▲▲▲ ***Waldorf*** (Trust House Forte), Aldwych, WC2, ☎836 2400. Tx. 24574. 312 rm. **£££** A. Ae. Dc. V. Restaurant: **££.**
▲▲▲ ***Charing Cross,*** Strand, WC2, ☎839 7282. Tx. 261101. 219 rm. ◘ ⅍ **££** A. Ae. Dc. V. Newly modernized hotel which retains its original sumptuous Victorian interior. Restaurant: ***Betjeman.*** ⅍ **£.** *Cl. Christmas.*
▲▲▲ ***Great Eastern*** (Compass), Liverpool St, EC2, ☎283 4363. Tx. 886812. 163 rm. ◘ **££** A. Ae. Dc. V. Restaurant: ***City Gates.*** Carvery. **£** *Cl. 24 Dec–2 Jan.*
▲▲▲ ***Royal Horseguards*** (Thistle), Whitehall Court, SW1, ☎839 3400. Tx. 917096. 284 rm. **££** A. Ae. Dc. V. Restaurant: **££.**
▲▲▲ ***Strand Palace*** (Trust House Forte), Strand, WC2, ☎836 8080. Tx. 24208. 775 rm. **££** A. Ae. Dc. V. Restaurant: **££.**

Restaurants

The Strand and Aldwych:
Rules, 35 Maiden Lane, WC2, ☎836 5314 ⅍ *Cl. Sun, 24 Dec– 1 Jan, Bank hols.* British. **££** A. Ae. Dc. V.
Shuttleworth's, 1 Aldwych, WC2, ☎836 3346 *Cl. Sat lunch, Sun, Bank hols.* Game, Scotch steaks. **£** A. Ae. Dc. V.
Simpsons, 100 The Strand, WC2, ☎836 9112 *Cl. Sun, Bank hols, Christmas, Easter.* British. Roast sirloin of beef. **£** A. Ae. Dc. V.

The City:
Corney & Barrow, 118 Moorgate, EC2, ☎628 2898 *Cl. Sat, Sun, Christmas, New Year, Easter, Bank hols.* Anglo-French. **£££££** A. Ae. Dc. V.

Baron of Beef, Gutter Lane, EC2, ☎606 6961 *Cl. Sat, Sun.*
British. Sirloin of beef, summer pudding. **£££** A. Ae. Dc. V.
Le Poulbot, 45 Cheapside, EC2, ☎236 4379 *Lunch only. Cl. Sat,
Sun, Christmas, New Year, Bank hols.* French. **£££** A. Ae. Dc. V.
Wheeler's, 33 Foster Lane, EC2, ☎606 0896 *Lunch only. Cl. Sat,
Sun.* Fish and seafood. **£££** A. Ae. Dc. V.
Ginnan, 5 Cathedral Place, EC4, ☎236 4120 ఉ *Cl. Sat eve,
Sun, Bank hols.* Japanese. **££** A. Ae. Dc. V.
Oscar's Brasserie, Temple Chambers, Temple Avenue, EC4,
☎353 6272 *Cl. Sat, Sun, last 3 wks Aug, last wk Dec, Bank hols.*
Turbot marinière, fillet of lamb. **££** A. Ae. Dc. V.
Hana Guruma, 49 Bow Lane, EC2, ☎236 6451 ఉ *Cl. Sat, Sun,
Christmas, New Year.* Yakitori bar. **£** A. Ae. Dc. V.
The Nosherie, 12 Greville St, EC1, ☎242 1591 *Lunch only. Cl.
Sat, Sun.* Jewish. Salt beef, cheese blintzes. **£.**

East End
(Map V, Inner London; itinerary 5)

Restaurants

Bethnal Green:
Cherry Orchard, 241 Globe Rd, E2, ☎980 6678 ఴ ఉ *Cl. 1 wk
Aug, 10 days Christmas.* Vegetarian moussaka. **£.**

Poplar:
New Friends, 53 West India Dock Rd, E14, ☎987 1139 *Cl.
Christmas.* Chinese. Suckling pig. **£** A. Ae. Dc. V.

Hackney:
Seashell, 424 Kingsland Rd, E8, ☎254 6152 🄿 *Cl. Sun, Mon,
10 days Christmas.* Poached salmon, halibut, Dover sole. **£.**

South Bank
(Map IV; itinerary 6)

Restaurants

Mabileau, 61 The Cut, SE1, ☎928 8645 *Cl. Sat lunch, Sun,
Christmas, New Year.* French. **££** A. Ae. Dc. V.
RSJ, 13a Coin St, SE1, ☎928 4554 *Cl. Sat lunch, Sun, 25–26 Dec,
Bank hols.* French. Fresh salmon with saffron cream sauce. **££**
A. Ae. V.
South of the Border, Joan St, SE1, ☎928 6374 🄿 ఴ ఉ Inter-
national. **£** A. Ae. Dc. V.

Soho
(Map II; itinerary 7)

Hotel

▲▲▲ **Royal Trafalgar** (Thistle), Whitcomb St, WC2, ☎930 4477.
Tx. 298564. 108 rm. **££** A. Ae. Dc. V. Restaurant: **Hamilton's
Brasserie. £.**

Restaurants

Han Kuk Hoe Kwan, 2 Lowndes Court, W1, ☎437 3313 ఉ *Cl.
Sun, 3 days Christmas, New Year.* Korean. Bulgoggi – thin sliced
beef. **££££** A. Ae. Dc. V.
Au Jardin des Gourmets, 5 Greek St, W1, ☎437 1816 ఉ *Cl.
Sat lunch, Sun eve, Christmas, Easter.* Fricassé de poissons au
saffron. **£££** A. Ae. Dc. V.
L'Escargot, 48 Greek St, W1, ☎437 2679 ఉ *Cl. Sat lunch, Sun,
Christmas, New Year, Bank hols.* **£££** A. Ae. Dc. V.

Gay Hussar, 2 Greek St, W1, ☎437 0973 *Cl. Sun, Bank hols.* East European. **£££.**

Wheeler's, 19 Old Compton St, W1, ☎437 2706 Fish and seafood. **£££** A. Ae. Dc. V.

Beotys, 79 St Martin's Lane, WC2, ☎836 8768 ♿ *Cl. Sun, Bank hols.* Greek. **££** A. Ae. Dc. V.

Café Pelican, 45 St Martin's Lane, WC2, ☎379 0309 🍷 ♿ *Cl. 25–26 Dec.* French. Toulouse sausages, brasserie dishes. **££** A. Ae. Dc. V.

Chesa (Swiss Centre), 10 Wardour St, W1, ☎734 1291 🅿 *Cl. 25–26 Dec.* Swiss. Fondue, air-cured meats, bratwurst. **££** A. Ae. Dc. V.

Chez Solange, 35 Cranbourn St, WC2, ☎836 0542 ♿ *Cl. Sun, Bank hols.* **££** A. Ae. Dc. V.

Estoril da Luigi e Roberto, 3 Denman St, W1, ☎437 8700 Venison. **££** A. Ae. Dc. V.

Frith's, 14 Frith St, W1, ☎439 3370 ♿ *Cl. Sat & Sun lunch, Bank hols.* Anglo-French. Salmon trout with laver bread and orange sauce. **££** A. Ae. Dc. V.

Saigon, 45 Frith St, W1, ☎437 7109 *Cl. Sun, Bank hols.* Southeast Asian. Vietnamese barbecued beef. **££** Ae. Ae. Dc. V.

La Bastide, 50 Greek St, W1, ☎734 3300 *Cl. Sat lunch, Sun, Bank hols.* Salmon with sorrel sauce. **£** A. Ae. Dc. V.

Brewer Street Buttery, 56 Brewer St, W1, ☎437 7695 *Lunch only. Cl. Sat, Sun, Bank hols.* Polish. Pieroshki, bigos. **£.**

Cork & Bottle Wine Bar, 44 Cranbourn St, WC2, ☎734 7807 *Cl. 25–26 Dec, 1 Jan.* Raised creamy ham and cheese pie. **£** A. Dc. V.

Country Life, 123 Regent St, W1, ☎434 2922 *Lunch only. Cl. Sat, Sun, Bank hols.* Vegetarian. **£.**

Cranks, 8 Marshall St, W1, ☎437 9431 *Cl. Sun, Bank hols.* Vegetarian. **£** A. Ae. Dc. V.

Desaru, 60 Old Compton St, W1, ☎734 4379 *Cl. 25–26 Dec, 1 Jan.* Indonesian/Malaysian. **£** A. Ae. Dc. V.

Gallery Rendezvous, 53 Beak St, W1, ☎734 0445 ♿ *Cl. 25 Dec, 1 Jan.* Chinese. Barbecued Peking duck. **£** A. Ae. Dc. V.

Grahame's Seafare, 38 Poland St, W1, ☎437 3788 ♿ *Cl. last wk Dec, 1st wk Jan.* Halibut with egg and lemon sauce Jewish style. **£** V.

Lee Ho Fook, 15 Gerrard St, W1, ☎734 9578 *Cl. Christmas, New Year.* Duck. **£** A. Ae. Dc. V.

Melati, 21 Great Windmill St, W1, ☎437 2745 ♿ *Cl. 25 Dec.* Malaysian. Satay, Singapore laksa. **£** A. Ae. Dc. V.

New World, 1 Gerrard Place, W1, ☎734 0677 ♿ *Cl. 25 Dec.* Chinese. Lobster with chilli and black bean sauce. **£** A. Ae. Dc. V.

Nuthouse, 26 Kingly St, W1, ☎437 9471 *Cl. Sun.* Vegetarian. **£.**

Old Budapest, 6 Greek St, W1, ☎437 2006 *Cl. Christmas, Easter, Sun, Bank hols.* East European. Smoked goose, red cabbage. **£** A. Ae. V.

Pizza Express, 29 Wardour St, W1, ☎437 7215 Pizza veneziana. **£** A.

Poon's, 4 Leicester St, WC2, ☎437 1528 🅿 *Cl. Sun, Christmas.* Deep-fried squid with garlic, Cantonese dishes. **£.**

Red Fort, 77 Dean St, W1, ☎437 2525 ♿ *Cl. 25–26 Dec, 1 Jan.* Indian. Tandoori quails. **£** A. Ae. Dc. V.

Rugantino, 26 Romilly St, W1, ☎437 5302 ♿ *Cl. Sat lunch, Sun.* Italian. Sea bass in pernod and fennel-seed sauce. **£** A. Ae. Dc. V.

Sheekey's, 29 St Martin's Court, WC2, ☎240 2565 ♿ *Cl. Sat*

lunch, Sun, Christmas, Easter, Bank hols. Fish, oysters. **£** A. Ae. Dc. V.
Soho Brasserie, 23 Old Compton St, W1, ☎439 3758 *Cl. Sun.* French. Magret of duck in sherry vinegar sauce. **£** A. Ae. Dc.
Wong Kei, 41 Wardour St, W1, ☎437 3271 ⅊ *Cl. 25 Dec.* Soya chicken. **£.**

Bloomsbury and Holborn
(Map II; itinerary 7)

Hotels

▲▲▲▲*Regent Crest,* Carburton St, W1, ☎388 2300. Tx. 22453. 322 rm. ⦿ **££** A. Ae. Dc. V. Restaurant: **££.**
▲▲▲*Bedford Corner* (Aquarius), Bayley St, WC1, ☎580 7766. Tx. 296464. 88 rm. **££** A. Ae. Dc. V. Restaurant: ⅊ **££** *Cl. 24 Dec–1 Jan.*
▲▲▲*Berners,* 10 Berners St, W1, ☎636 1629. Tx. 25759. 234 rm. **£££** A. Ae. Dc. V. Restaurant: **££.**
▲▲▲*Kennedy* (Mount Charlotte), 43 Cardington St, NW1, ☎387 4400. Tx. 28250. 320 rm. ⦿ **££** A. Ae. Dc. V. Restaurant: **£.**
▲▲▲*New Ambassadors,* 12 Upper Woburn Place, WC1, ☎387 1456. Tx. 267074. 101 rm. **£** A. Ae. Dc. V. Restaurant: **£.**
▲▲▲*Royal Scot* (Mount Charlotte), 100 King's Cross Rd, WC1, ☎278 2434. Tx. 27657. 349 rm. ⦿ **££** A. Ae. Dc. V. Restaurant: **Bugatti's.** ⅊ **£.**
▲▲▲*Russell* (Trust House Forte), Russell Square, WC1, ☎837 6470. Tx. 24615. 318 rm. **££** A. Ae. Dc. V. Restaurant: **££.**
▲▲ *Bonnington,* 92 Southampton Row, WC1, ☎242 2828. Tx. 261591. 242 rm. **££** A. Ae. Dc. V. Restaurant: **£.**
▲▲ *Great Northern* (Compass), King's Cross, N1, ☎837 5454. Tx. 299041. 87 rm. ⦿ **££** A. Ae. Dc. V. Restaurant: Prime roast beef, traditional steak and kidney pie. **£** *Cl. 25 Dec, 1 Jan.*
▲▲ *Royal National* (Imperial London), Bedford Way, WC1, ☎637 2488. Tx. 21822. 1028 rm. ⦿ ⅊ **££** A. Ae. Dc. V. Restaurant: ⅊ **£.**
▲ *Academy,* 17 Gower St, WC1, ☎636 7612. Tx. 24364. 20 rm. **£** A. V.

Restaurants

L'Etoile, 30 Charlotte St, W1, ☎636 7189 *Cl. Sat, Sun, Aug, Bank hols.* French. **£££££** A. Ae. Dc. V.
Rue St Jacques, 5 Charlotte St, W1, ☎637 0222 ⅊ *Cl. Sat lunch, Sun, Easter, Bank hols, 24 Dec–5 Jan.* **£££££** A. Ae. Dc. V.
White Tower, 1 Percy St, W1, ☎636 8750 *Cl. Sat, Sun, 3 wks Aug, 1 wk Christmas, Bank hols.* Greek dishes, roast duckling. **£££** A. Ae. Dc. V.
Porte de la Cité, 65 Theobalds Rd, WC1, ☎242 1154 *Lunch only. Cl. Sat, Sun, Christmas, Easter, Bank hols.* Suprême de poulet. **££** A. Ae. Dc. V.
Cranks, Tottenham St, W1, ☎631 3912 *Cl. 8pm, Sun, Bank hols.* Health food breakfast, quiche, flans, pizza, salads. **£.**
Elephants & Butterflies, 67 Charlotte St, W1, ☎580 1732 *Cl. Sat lunch, Sun, Bank hols.* Vegetarian. Organic ingredients. **£** A. Ae. Dc. V.
Gaylord (India), 79 Mortimer St, W1, ☎580 3615 ⦿ ⅊ Tandoori dishes. **£** A. Ae. Dc. V.
Gonbei, 151 King's Cross Rd, WC1, ☎278 0619 *Cl. Sun, 25 Dec–1 Jan.* Japanese. Sushi. **£.**

The Greenhouse, 16 Chenies St, WC1, ☎637 8038 *Cl. Sun, 24 Dec–1 Jan.* Wholefood and vegetarian dishes. **£.**
Hare Krishna Curry House, Hanway St, W1, ☎636 5262 ♿ *Cl. Sun.* Hindu vegetarian dishes. **£** A. Ae. Dc. V.
Mandeer, 21 Hanway Place, W1, ☎323 0660 *Cl. Sun, Bank hols, Christmas.* Indian vegetarian dishes. **£** A. Ae. Dc. V.

Covent Garden
(Map II; itinerary 7)

Restaurants

Boulestin, 1a Henrietta St, WC2, ☎836 7061 *Cl. Sat lunch, Sun, last 3 wks Aug, 1 wk Christmas, Bank hols.* French. Pigeon with wild mushrooms. **£££££** A. Ae. Dc. V.
Inigo Jones, 14 Garrick St, WC2, ☎836 6456 ♿ *Cl. Sat lunch, Sun, Bank hols.* French. **£££££** A. Ae. Dc. V.
Peppermint Park, Upper St Martin's Lane, WC2, ☎836 5234 Guacamole, hamburgers, blinis. **££££** Ae. Dc. V.
Neal Street, 26 Neal St, WC2, ☎836 8368 *Cl. Sat, Sun, 25 Dec–2 Jan.* International. Truffles in season, wine-mushroom soup. **£££** A. Ae. Dc. V.
L'Opera, 32 Great Queen St, WC2, ☎405 9020 *Cl. Sat lunch, Sun, Bank hols.* French. **£££** A. Ae. Dc. V.
Grimes, 6 Garrick St, WC2, ☎836 7008 *Cl. Sat lunch, Sun.* Fish, Colchester oysters. **££** A. Ae. Dc. V.
Poons of Covent Garden, 41 King St, WC2, ☎240 1743 *Cl. Sun, 24–27 Dec.* Lap yuck soom, Kam Ling duck. **££** Ae. Dc. V.
Cranks, Unit 11, Covent Garden Market, WC2, ☎379 6508 *Cl. 8pm, Bank hols, Sun.* Vegetarian. Waldorf salad. **£.**
Food for Thought, 31 Neal St, WC2, ☎836 0239 *Cl. Sat, Sun, last wk Dec and 1st wk Jan, Bank hols.* Vegetarian. Fresh tagliatelle verde. **£.**
Plummers, 33 King St, WC2, ☎240 2534 *Cl. Sat lunch, Sun.* British. Clam chowder, salmon pie. **£** A. Ae. Dc. V.
Taste of India, 25 Catherine St, WC2, ☎836 6591 ♿ Tandoori king prawns. **£** A. Ae. Dc. V.
Tourment d'Amour, 19 New Row, WC2, ☎240 5348 *Cl. Sat lunch, Sun, 2 wks Christmas, Bank hols.* **£** A. Ae. Dc. V.

The West End
(Maps I, II; itinerary 8)

Hotels

▲▲▲▲ ***Churchill,*** Portman Square, W1, ☎486 5800. Tx. 264831. 489 rm. 🅿 **££££** A. Ae. Dc. V. Restaurant: ***No. 10.*** **£££.**
▲▲▲▲ ***Cumberland*** (Trust House Forte), Marble Arch, W1, ☎262 1234. Tx. 22215. 905 rm. ♿ **££** A. Ae. Dc. V. Restaurant: ***Wyvern.*** ♿ **££.** *Cl. 26 Dec, 1 Jan.*
▲▲▲▲ ***Holiday Inn Marble Arch,*** 134 George St, W1, ☎723 1277. Tx. 27983. 241 rm. 🅿 ♿ ✂ **£££** A. Ae. Dc. V. Restaurant: ***La Bibliothèque.*** ♿ Steak 'Lucien', scampi maître d'hôtel. **££££.** *Cl. lunch, Sun, Bank hols.*
▲▲▲▲ ***White House*** (Rank), Regent's Park, NW1, ☎387 1200. Tx. 24111. 580 rm. ♿ **£££** A. Ae. Dc. V. Restaurant: **£££.** *Cl. Sat lunch, Sun, Bank hols.*
▲▲▲ ***Bryanston Court,*** 60 Great Cumberland Place, W1, ☎262 3141. Tx. 262076. 56 rm. **££** A. Ae. Dc. V. Restaurant: **£.**
▲▲▲ ***Clifton Ford,*** Welbeck St, W1, ☎486 6600. Tx. 22569. 220 rm. 🅿 **££** A. Ae. Dc. V. Restaurant: Roast rib of beef. **££.**

▲▲▲ *Concorde,* 50 Great Cumberland Place, W1, ☎402 6169. Tx. 262076. 28 rm. **££** Restaurant: **£** *Cl. Sat, Sun*.

▲▲▲ *Harewood* (Inter), Harewood Row, NW1, ☎262 2707. Tx. 297225. 93 rm. 🅿 ⑃ **££** A. Ae. Dc. V. Restaurant: *Street Cars.* **£.**

▲▲▲ *Londoner* (Sarova), Welbeck St, W1, ☎935 4442. Tx. 894630. 142 rm. **££** A. Ae. Dc. V. Restaurant: **£** *Cl. Sat & Sun lunch.*

▲▲▲ *Montcalm,* Great Cumberland Place, W1, ☎402 4288. Tx. 28710. 116 rm. **££££** A. Ae. Dc. V. Small de-luxe hotel in a tree-lined Georgian crescent close to Marble Arch. Restaurant: *La Varenne.* Veal kidneys with wild mushrooms. **££.**

▲▲▲ *St George's* (Trust House Forte), Langham Place, W1, ☎580 0111. Tx. 27274. 85 rm. **£££** A. Ae. Dc. V. Restaurant: **££.**

▲▲▲ *Stratford Court* (Edwardian), 350 Oxford St, W1, ☎629 7474. Tx. 22270. 138 rm. **££** A. Ae. Dc. V. Restaurant: Roast meats. **£.**

▲ *Portman Court,* 30 Seymour St, W1, ☎402 5401. 30 rm. ⑃ **£** A. Ae. Dc. V. Small hotel in the former home of Edward Lear.

Restaurants

Odin's, 27 Devonshire St, W1, ☎935 7296 *Cl. Sat lunch, Sun, Christmas, New Year.* Anglo-French. **££££** Ae.

Defune, 61 Blandford St, W1, ☎935 8311 *Cl. Sun, 10 days Christmas, Bank hols.* Japanese. Sushi, sashimi. **£££** Ae. Dc.

Del Monico's, 114 Crawford St, W1, ☎935 5736 *Cl. Sun, 25–26 Dec, 1 Jan.* Italian. **££** A. Ae. Dc. V.

Green Leaves, 77 York St, W1, ☎262 8164 *Cl. Sat lunch, Sun.* Peking and Szechuan cuisine. Spicy spare ribs. **££** A. Ae. Dc. V.

La Loggia, 68 Edgware Rd, W2, ☎723 0554 *Cl. Sun, Bank hols.* **££** A. Ae. Dc. V.

Langan's Bistro, 26 Devonshire St, W1, ☎935 4531 ⑃ *Cl. Sat lunch, Sun, Christmas, Bank hols.* French. **££** Ae.

Biagi's, 39 Upper Berkeley St, W1, ☎723 0394 *Cl. Bank hols.* Italian. **£** A. Ae. Dc. V.

Caravan Serai, 50 Paddington St, W1, ☎935 1208 🅿 ⑃ *Cl. Sun lunch.* Middle Eastern. Ashak. **£** A. Ae. Dc. V.

Genevieve, 13 Thayer St, W1, ☎935 5023 ⑃ *Cl. Sat, Sun, Bank hols.* French. Guinea fowl in pastry with ginger sauce. **£** A. Ae. Dc. V.

Le Muscadet, 25 Paddington St, W1, ☎935 2883 *Cl. Sat lunch, Sun, 3 wks Aug, 2 wks Christmas, Bank hols.* **£** A. V.

Raw Deal, York St, W1, ☎262 4841 *Cl. Sun, Bank hols.* Vegan dishes. **£.**

Topkapi, 25 Marylebone High St, W1, ☎486 1872 ⑃ *Cl. 25–26 Dec.* Middle Eastern. Lamb kebab. **£** A. Ae. Dc. V.

Viceroy of India, 3 Glentworth St, NW1, ☎486 3401 *Cl. 25 Dec.* Bataire masala (quail). **£** A. Ae. Dc. V.

Kensington
(Map III, Inner London; itinerary 9)

Hotels

▲▲▲▲ *Blakes,* 33 Roland Gardens, SW7, ☎370 6701. Tx. 8813500. 50 rm. **££££** A. Ae. Dc. V. Stylish small hotel of great character. Restaurant: Roast rack of lamb with rosemary. **£££££.** *Cl. 25–26 Dec.*

▲▲▲▲ *Gloucester* (Rank), 4 Harrington Gardens, SW7, ☎373 6030. Tx. 917505. 531 rm. 🅿 **£££** A. Ae. Dc. V. Restaurant: **££.**

▲▲▲▲ *Hilton International Kensington,* 179 Holland Park Avenue, W11, ☎603 3355. Tx. 919763. 606 rm. ⚏ **£££** A. Ae. Dc. V. Restaurant: *Market.* **££.**

▲▲▲▲ *London Tara* (Best Western), Scarsdale Place, Wrights Lane, W8, ☎937 7211. Tx. 918834. 830 rm. ⚏ ⅃ **££** A. Ae. Dc. V. Restaurant: *Poachers.* ⅃**££££.**

▲▲▲▲ *Royal Garden* (Rank), Kensington High St, W8, ☎937 8000. Tx. 263151. 395 rm. ⚏ **£££** A. Ae. Dc. V. Restaurant: *Royal Roof.* **£££** *Cl. Sat lunch, Sun, Bank hols, 3 wks Aug.*

▲▲▲ *Baileys,* 140 Gloucester Rd, SW7, ☎373 6000. Tx. 264221. 158 rm. **££** A. Ae. Dc. V. Restaurant: *Bombay Brasserie.* **££££.**

▲▲▲ *Barkston,* Barkston Gardens, SW5, ☎373 7851. Tx. 8953154. 77 rm. **££** A. Ae. Dc. V. Restaurant: ⅃ **£.**

▲▲▲ *Eden Plaza,* 68 Queen's Gate, SW7, ☎370 6111. Tx. 916228. 65 rm. **££** A. Ae. Dc. V. Restaurant: **£.**

▲▲▲ *John Howard,* 4 Queen's Gate, SW7, ☎581 3011. Tx. 8813397. 40 rm. ⅃ **££** A. Ae. Dc. V. Luxurious hotel in an historic building close to Kensington Gardens. Restaurant: ⅃ Mousse de langouste aux perles de la Caspienne. **£££.**

▲▲▲ *Kensington Palace* (Thistle), De Vere Gardens, W8, ☎937 8121. Tx. 262422. 298 rm. **££** A. Ae. Dc. V. Restaurant: **£** *Cl. Sun.*

▲▲▲ *Regency* (Sarova), 100 Queen's Gate, SW7, ☎370 4595. Tx. 267594. 188 rm. **££** A. Ae. Dc. V. Traditional hotel with modern amenities. Restaurant: **£.**

▲▲▲ *Rembrandt* (Sarova), Thurloe Place, SW7, ☎589 8100. Tx. 295828. 200 rm. ⅌ **££** A. Ae. Dc. V. Restaurant: **££.**

▲▲▲ *Vanderbilt* (Edwardian), 76 Cromwell Rd, SW7, ☎589 2424. Tx. 919867. 230 rm. **££** A. Ae. Dc. V. Restaurant: **£.**

▲▲ *Hogarth* (Inter), Hogarth Rd, SW5, ☎370 6831. Tx. 8591994. 88 rm. ⚏ **££** A. Ae. Dc. V. Restaurant: **£.**

▲▲ *Leicester Court,* 41 Queen's Gate Gardens, SW7, ☎584 0512. Tx. 268821. 7 rm. **££** A. Ae. Dc. V. Restaurant: **£.**

▲▲ *Number Sixteen,* Sumner Place, SW7, ☎589 5232. Tx. 266638. 32 rm. ⚿ **££** A. Ae. Dc. V. Hotel with a spectacular garden and an international reputation.

▲▲ *Prince,* 6 Sumner Place, SW7, ☎589 6488. 20 rm. **£** A. V.

Restaurants

Clarke's, 124 Kensington Church St, W8, ☎221 9225 *Cl. 1 wk Easter, 3 wks Aug, 10 days Christmas.* Anglo-French. Char grills. **££** A. V.

Le Crocodile, 38c/d Kensington Church St, W8, ☎938 2501 ⅃ *Cl. Sat lunch, Sun.* Boudin de fruits de mer au riz sauvage. **££** ACAM Dc. V.

Malabar, 27 Uxbridge St, W8, ☎727 8800 *Cl. last wk Aug.* Indian. Devilled kaleja (chicken livers). **££** A. V.

Mandarin, 197c Kensington High St, W8, ☎937 1551 *Cl. 24–26 Dec.* Peking duck, crispy beef. **££** A. Ae. Dc. V.

Michel, 343 Kensington High St, W8, ☎603 3613 French. **££** A. Ae. Dc. V.

The Ark, 122 Palace Gardens Terrace, W8, ☎229 4024 ⅃ *Cl. Sun lunch.* Rack of lamb, steak and kidney pie. **£** A. Ae. V.

Bahn Thai, 35a Marloes Rd, W8, ☎937 9960 *Cl. 2 wks Aug, 2 wks Christmas.* South-east Asian. **£** A. Ae. Dc.

Holland Street, 33c Holland St, W8, ☎937 3224 *Cl. Sat lunch, Sun eve, Aug, Bank hols.* Chicken breast stuffed with spinach and Stilton. **£** A. V.

La Paesana, 30 Uxbridge St, W8, ☎229 4332 *Cl. Sun, Bank hols.* Italian. **£** A. Ae. Dc. V.

Phoenicia, 11 Abingdon Rd, W8, ☎937 0120 *Cl. 25–26 Dec.* Lebanese. Tabouleh. **£** A. Ae. Dc. V.

Topo d'Oro, 389 Uxbridge St, W8, ☎727 5813 **P** *Cl. 25–26 Dec.* **£** A. Ae. Dc. V.

Earl's Court:

Read's, 152 Old Brompton Rd, SW5, ☎373 2445 **⊛** *Cl. Christmas, Bank hols.* Anglo-French. **£££££** A. Ae. Dc. V.

La Croisette, 168 Ifield Rd, SW10, ☎373 3694 *Cl. Mon, Tue lunch.* Fish. Sea bass. **£££** A. Dc.

L'Oliver, 116 Finborough Rd, SW10, ☎370 4199 *Cl. Sun.* French. A. Ae. Dc. V.

Tiger Lee, 251 Old Brompton Rd, SW5, ☎370 3176 ⅰ *Cl. lunch, 25 Dec.* Lobster, crispy duck. **££** Ae. Dc. V.

L'Aquitaine, 158 Old Brompton Rd, SW5, ☎373 9918 ⅰ *Cl. Sun.* Confit de canard à la creme de flageolets. **£** A. Ae. Dc. V.

Crystal Palace, 10 Hogarth Place, SW5, ☎373 0754 *Cl. Bank hols.* Peking and Szechuan cuisine. **£** A. Ae. Dc. V.

Pontevecchio, 254 Old Brompton Rd, SW5, ☎373 9082 ⅰ *Cl. Bank hols.* Italian. **£** A. Ae. Dc. V.

Holland Park:

Leith's, 92 Kensington Park Rd, W11, ☎229 4481 *Cl. 4 days, Christmas, Bank hols.* International. Brill fillet stuffed with crab mousseline, lobster sauce. **££££** A. Ae. Dc. V.

Julie's, 135 Portland Rd, W11, ☎727 8331 **⊛** *Cl. 4 days Christmas and Easter, Aug Bank hol Mon.* Cotswold duck with peaches, port and cherries. **£££** A. Ae. Dc. V.

La Pomme d'Amour, 128 Holland Park Avenue, W11, ☎229 8532 **⊛** ⅰ *Cl. Sat lunch, Sun, Bank hols.* Caneton au poivre vert et ananas. **£££** A. Ae. Dc. V.

Chez Moi, 1 Addison Avenue, W11, ☎603 8267 *Cl. lunch, Sun, 2 wks Aug, Christmas.* Rack of lamb. **££** A. Ae. Dc. V.

Lilly's, 6 Clarendon Rd, W11, ☎727 9359 *Cl. 1 wk Christmas.* Suprême of halibut with mango and banana. **££** A. Ae. Dc. V.

L'Artiste Assoiffé, 122 Kensington Park Rd, W11, ☎727 4714 **P** *Cl. Sun.* Crab mango. **£** A. Ae. Dc. V.

Knightsbridge, Belgravia and South Kensington
(Map III; itinerary 9)

Hotels

▲▲▲▲ **Berkeley** (Savoy), Wilton Place, W1, ☎235 6000. Tx. 919252. 160 rm. **P** ✔ **££££** A. Ae. V. Hotel famed for style, service and superb cuisine. Restaurant: **Le Perroquet.** **££££** *Cl. Sat.*

▲▲▲▲ **Hyatt Carlton Tower,** 2 Cadogan Place, SW1, ☎235 5411. Tx. 21944. 228 rm. **P** **£££££** A. Ae. Dc. V. Modern hotel close to Sloane Street. Restaurant: **Chelsea Room.** **£££££.** *Cl. 3 days Christmas.*

▲▲▲▲ **Hyde Park** (Trust House Forte), Knightsbridge, SW1, ☎235 2000. Tx. 262057. 179 rm. ⅰ **££££** A. Ae. Dc. V. Restaurant: **Park Room.** ⅰ Roast rib of beef. **££.**

▲▲▲▲ **Sheraton Park Tower,** 101 Knightsbridge, SW1, ☎235 8050. Tx. 917222. 295 rm. **P** **££££** A. Ae. Dc. V. Luxury hotel in a circular tower overlooking Knightsbridge and Hyde Park. Restaurant: **Le Trianon.** ⅰ **££££.**

▲▲▲ **Belgravia Sheraton,** Chesham Place, SW1, ☎235 6040. Tx. 919020. 89 rm. **£££** A. Ae. Dc. V. Restaurant: **£££** *Cl. Sat lunch.*

▲▲▲ **Capital,** 22 Basil St, SW3, ☎589 5171. Tx. 919042. 60 rm.

P £££ A. Ae. Dc. V. One of London's most sophisticated hotels with a famous restaurant. Restaurant: Mousseline of scallops with sea-urchin cream, rack of lamb. **£££**.

▲▲*Basil Street,* Basil St, SW3, ☎581 3311. Tx. 28379. 94 rm. **££** A. Ae. Dc. V. Edwardian hotel dedicated to gracious living. Restaurant: *Dining Room.* Roast beef carved from the trolley. **££**.

▲▲ *Hamilton House,* 60 Warwick Way, SW1, ☎821 7113. Tx. 28604. 41 rm. **£** A. Ae. V. Restaurant: **£**.

▲▲ *Willet,* 32 Sloane Gardens, SW1, ☎730 0634. 17 rm. **£**.

▲ *Elizabeth,* 37 Eccleston Square, SW1, ☎828 6812. 25 rm. 🏷 **£**. Quiet private hotel overlooking a stately square.

Restaurants

Le Suquet, 104 Draycott Avenue, SW3, ☎581 1785 **P** *Cl. 25 Dec–4 Jan.* Seafood. **£££££** Ae. Dc.

Waltons, 121 Walton St, SW3, ☎584 0204 *Cl. Bank hols.* British. 'Moneybag' of chicken and asparagus. **££££** A. Ae. Dc. V.

Daphne's, 112 Draycott Avenue, SW3, ☎589 4257 French. Soufflé Grand Marnier. **££** A. Ae. Dc. V.

La Fantaisie Brasserie, 14 Knightsbridge Green, SW1, ☎589 0509 *Cl. Sun, Bank hols.* **££** A. Ae. Dc. V.

Maroush II, 38 Beauchamp Place, SW3, ☎581 5434 *Cl. Christmas.* Middle Eastern. **££** A. Ae. Dc. V.

Menage à Trois, 15 Beauchamp Place, SW3, ☎589 4252 ♿ *Cl. Sun, 25 Dec.* Mousse with caviar, smoked salmon and scallops. **££** A. Ae. Dc. V.

Ports, 11 Beauchamp Place, SW3, ☎581 3837 *Cl. Sun, Bank hols.* Portuguese dishes, seafood. **££** A. Ae. Dc. V.

San Lorenzo, 22 Beauchamp Place, SW3, ☎584 1074 *Cl. Sun, Christmas, Easter.* Italian. **££**.

St Quentin, 243 Brompton Rd, SW3, ☎589 8005 *Cl. 1 wk Christmas.* French. Feuilletes d'escargot. **££** A. Ae. Dc. V.

Beccofino, 100 Draycott Avenue, SW3, ☎584 3600 *Cl. Bank hols, Sun.* Veal chop in Gorgonzola sauce. **£** A. Ae. V.

Dumpling House, 9 Beauchamp Place, SW3, ☎589 8240 *Cl. 25–26 Dec.* Peking duck, king prawns. **£** A. Ae. Dc. V.

Poissonnerie de l'Avenue, 82 Sloane Avenue, SW3, ☎589 2457 **P** *Cl. Sun, Bank hols.* Coquilles St Jacques. **£** A. Ae. Dc. V.

San Martino, 103 Walton St, SW3, ☎589 3833 **P** ♿ *Cl. Sun, Christmas, Easter, Bank hols.* Pasta dishes. **£** A. Ae. Dc. V.

South Kensington:

Hilaire, 68 Old Brompton Rd, SW7, ☎584 8993 *Cl. Sat lunch, Sun, Bank hols.* French. **£££** A. Ae. Dc. V.

Chanterelle, 119 Old Brompton Rd, SW7, ☎373 5522 *Cl. 4 days Christmas.* International. **£** A. Ae. Dc. V.

Golden Chopsticks, 1 Harrington Rd, SW7, ☎584 0855 ♿ *Cl. 25 Dec.* **£**.

Memories of India, 18 Gloucester Rd, SW7, ☎589 6450 **P** 🏷 *Cl. 25–26 Dec.* King prawn massala. **£** A. Ae. Dc. V.

Pun Chinese Cuisine, 53 Old Brompton Rd, SW7, ☎225 1609 *Cl. 25–26 Dec.* Szechuan, Peking, and Cantonese dishes. **£** A. Ae. Dc. V.

Daquise, 20 Thurloe St, SW7, ☎589 6117 *Cl. 25–26 Dec.* Polish and Russian dishes. **£**.

Pimlico:

Ciboure, 21 Eccleston St, SW1, ☎730 2505 ♿ *Cl. Sat lunch, Sun, 1 wk Christmas.* French. Leek and mushroom mousse, scallops. **£££££** A. Ae. Dc. V.

Pomegranates, 94 Grosvenor Rd, SW1, ☎828 6560 ⅃ *Cl. Sat lunch, Sun, Bank hols.* International. Jamaican curried goat, gravlax. **££££** A. Ae. Dc. V.

Ken Lo's Memories of China, 67 Ebury St, SW1, ☎730 7734 ⅃ *Cl. Sun, Bank hols.* Peking duck. **£££** A. Ae. Dc. V.

La Fontana, 101 Pimlico Rd, SW1, ☎730 6630 *Cl. Bank hols.* International. **££** Ae. Dc. V.

Le Mazarin, 30 Winchester St, SW1, ☎828 3366 🅿 ❀ *Cl. Sun, Christmas, Bank hols.* **££** A. Ae. Dc.

Mijanou, 143 Ebury St, SW1, ☎730 4099 ❀ *Cl. Sat, Sun, 3 wks Aug, 2 wks Christmas, 1 wk Easter, Bank hols.* French. Cailles au riz sauvage. **££** A. Ae. Dc.

Eatons, 49 Elizabeth St, SW1, ☎730 0074 *Cl. Sat, Sun.* French. Smoked salmon, fresh herrings. **£** A. Ae. Dc. V.

Chelsea
(Map: Inner London; itinerary 9)

Restaurants:

Tante Claire, 68 Royal Hospital Rd, SW3, ☎352 6045 ⅃ *Cl. Sat, Sun, 1 wk Christmas, 1 wk Easter, 3 wks Aug.* Galette de foie gras. **£££££** Ae. Dc. V.

English Garden, 10 Lincoln St, SW3, ☎584 7272 *Cl. 25–26 Dec.* Quail egg patty. **££££** A. Ae. Dc. V.

Bagatelle, 5 Langton St, SW10, ☎351 4185 *Cl. Sun, Bank hols.* Rack of lamb with mustard sauce. **£££** A. Ae. Dc. V.

English House, 3 Milner St, SW3, ☎584 3002 *Cl. Good Fri, 25–26 Dec.* Lamb in salt crust. **£££** Ae. Dc. V.

Meridiana, 169 Fulham Rd, SW3, ☎589 8815 ❀ Home-made gnocchi. **£££** A. Ae. Dc. V.

Le Francais, 259 Fulham Rd, SW3, ☎352 4748 *Cl. Sun, Christmas.* French regional cuisine. **££** Ae. V.

Monkeys, 1 Cale St, SW3, ☎352 4711 *Cl. 1 wk Feb, 3 wks Aug, 25–26 Dec.* Anglo-French. Game **££.**

Ponte Nuovo, 126 Fulham Rd, SW3, ☎370 6656 ❀ *Cl. Bank hols.* Linguine al cartoccio. **££** A. Ae. Dc. V.

San Frediano, 62 Fulham Rd, SW3, ☎584 8375 *Cl. Sun.* **££** A. Dc. V.

Thierry's, 342 King's Rd, SW3, ☎352 3365 ⅃ *Cl. Sun, last 2 wks Aug, Bank hols.* French. Rack of lamb. **££** A. Ae. Dc. V.

Tandoori, 153 Fulham Rd, SW3, ☎589 7749 🅿 *Cl. 25–26 Dec.* Indian/Nepalese. King prawn bhuna massala. **£** A. Ae. Dc. V.

Fulham:

Le Gastronome, 309 New King's Rd, SW6, ☎731 6993 *Cl. Sat lunch, Sun, 25 Dec–1 Jan, Bank hols.* Desserts. **££** A. Ae. Dc. V.

Barbarella, 428 Fulham Rd, SW6, ☎385 9434 *Cl. Sun, Bank hols.* **£** A. Ae. Dc. V.

The Garden, 616 Fulham Rd, SW6, ☎736 6056 *Cl. Sun, 2–3 wks Aug, Bank hols.* No red meat. Chicken and artichoke pie, vegetarian dishes. **£** A. Ae. Dc. V.

Hiders, 755 Fulham Rd, SW6, ☎736 2331 *Cl. Sat lunch, Sun, 2 wks Aug.* French. Crab terrine, noisette of lamb. **£** A. Ae. V.

Windmill, 486 Fulham Rd, SW6, ☎385 1570 ⅃ Vegetarian. Spinach and feta cheese pie. **£.**

Bayswater and Paddington
(Map 1, Inner London; itinerary 9)

Hotels

▲▲▲▲ **Royal Lancaster** (Rank), Lancaster Terrace, W2, ☎262

6737. Tx. 24822. 435 rm. ◘ **££££** A. Ae. Dc. V. Restaurant: *La Rosette.* **££.**

▲▲▲ *Colonnade,* 2 Warrington Crescent, W9, ☎289 2167. Tx. 298930. 51 rm. ◘ **££** A. Ae. V. Dc.

▲▲▲ *London Embassy,* 150 Bayswater Rd, W2, ☎229 1212. Tx. 27727. 192 rm. ◘ **££** A. Ae. Dc. V. Restaurant: **£.**

▲▲▲ *Pembridge Court,* 34 Pembridge Gardens, W2, ☎229 9977. Tx. 298363. 35 rm. ◘ **££** A. Ae. Dc. V. Restaurant: *Cap's* (at 64 Pembridge Rd) ☎229 5177 **£** *Cl. lunch Sun, Bank hols.*

▲▲▲ *White's* (Mount Charlotte), Lancaster Gate, W2, ☎262 2711. Tx. 23922. 61 rm. ◘ **££** A. Ae. Dc. V. Restaurant: **£.**

▲▲ *Coburg* (Best Western), 129 Bayswater Rd, W2, ☎229 3654. Tx. 268235. 125 rm. ♿ **££** A. Ae. Dc. V. Restaurant: **£.** *Cl. 1 wk Christmas.*

▲▲ *Hospitality Inn* (Mount Charlotte), Bayswater Rd, W2, ☎262 4461. Tx. 22667. 175 rm. ◘ **££** A. Ae. Dc. V. Restaurant: **£.**

▲▲ *Mornington* (Best Western), 12 Lancaster Gate, W2, ☎262 7361. Tx. 24281. 65 rm. **££** A. Ae. V. Dc.

Restaurants

Didier, 5 Warwick Place, W9, ☎286 7484 ♿ *Cl. Sat, Sun, Bank hols.* **££** A. Ae. V.

Al Khayam, 27 Westbourne Grove, W2, ☎727 2556 ♿ *Cl. 25 Dec.* Indian. Murag musala (chicken). **£** A. Ae. Dc. V.

Kalamaras, 76 Inverness Mews, W2, ☎727 9122 ✸ ♿ *Cl. lunch, Sun, Bank hols, 24 Dec.* Greek. Seafood in filo pastry. **£** A. Ae. Dc. V.

Knoodles, 30 Connaught St, W2, ☎262 9623 *Cl. Sun, Bank hols.* International. Home-made pasta dishes. **£** A. Ae. Dc. V.

Maroush, 21 Edgware Rd, W2, ☎723 0773 *Cl. Christmas.* Middle Eastern. **£** A. Ae. Dc. V.

▬▬ *Inner London*

Battersea

Restaurants

Chez Nico, 129 Queenstown Rd, SW8, ☎720 6960 ♿ *Cl. Mon & Sat lunch, Sun, Bank hols, 3 wks summer, 1 wk Christmas.* **££££** A. Dc. V.

Di's Larder, 62 Lavender Hill, SW11, ☎223 4618 ◘ ♿ *Lunch only. Cl. Sun, 2 wks Aug, Bank hols.* Vegetarian. **£.**

Jason's Taverna, 50 Battersea Park Rd, SW11, ☎622 6998 ◘ *Cl. lunch, Sun, 1st & 2nd wks Aug, Bank hols.* Greek. **£.**

La Preferita, 163 Lavender Hill, SW11, ☎223 1046 *Cl. Sun, 26–30 Dec.* Italian. **£** A. Ae. Dc. V.

Twenty Trinity Gardens, 20 Trinity Gardens, SW9, ☎733 8838 ◘ *Cl. Sat lunch, Sun, 25 Dec, 1 Jan.* Anglo-French. **£** V.

Camden Town

Restaurants

Koto, 75 Parkway, NW1, ☎482 2036 ♿ *Cl. Sun.* Japanese. Yose nabe, sushi. **£££** A. Ae. Dc. V.

Odette's, 130 Regent's Park Rd, NW1, ☎586 5486 ◘ *Cl. Sat lunch, Sun, Christmas, Bank hols.* International. Roulade of salmon and brill, parfait of scallops. **££** A. Ae. Dc. V.

Le Bistroquet, 173 Camden High St, NW1, ☎267 4895 ✸ *Cl. 25–27 Dec.* **£** Ae. Dc. V.

Daphne, 83 Bayham St.,NW1, ☎267 7322 ✤ ⑁ *Cl. Sun.* Greek. Charcoal-grilled swordfish. **£** A.

Lemonia, 154 Regent's Park Rd, NW1, ☎586 7454 ✤ ⑁ *Cl. 1st & 2nd wks Aug, 3 days Christmas, Bank hols.* Greek. **£.**

Nontas, 16 Camden High St, NW1, ☎387 4579 *Cl. Sun, Bank hols, Christmas.* Greek. Meze: 14 different dishes. **£** A. Ae. Dc.

Kentish Town:
The Bengal Lancer, 253 Kentish Town Rd, NW5, ☎485 6688 ⑁ *Cl. 25–26 Dec.* Lamb Pasanda. **£** A. Ae. Dc. V.

Hammersmith
Hotel

▲▲▲ **London West,** Lillie Rd, SW6, ☎385 1255. Tx. 917728. 499 rm. 🅿 **££.** A. Ae. Dc. V. Restaurant: **£.**

Restaurants

Light of Nepal, 268 King St, W6, ☎748 3586 *Cl. 25–26 Dec.* North Indian dishes. **£** A. Ae. Dc. V.

Paulo's, 30 Greyhound Rd, W6, ☎385 9264 *Cl. lunch, Sun, 2 wks Aug, Bank hols.* Brazilian dishes, feijáo, vatapa. **£.**

Shepherd's Bush:
Balzac Bistro, 4 Wood Lane, W12, ☎743 6787 ⑁ *Cl. Sun, 10 days Christmas.* French. **££** A. V.

Rajput, 144 Goldhawk Rd, W12, ☎740 9036 *Cl. 25–26 Dec.* Chicken tikka. **£** A. Ae. Dc. V.

Shireen, 270 Uxbridge Rd, W12, ☎749 5927 ⑁ *Cl. 25–26 Dec.* Tandoori dishes. **£** A. Ae. Dc. V.

Hampstead and St John's Wood
Hotels

▲▲▲▲ **Holiday Inn Swiss Cottage,** 128 King Henry's Rd, NW3, ☎722 7711. Tx. 267396. 291 rm. 🅿 ⑁ ⟟ **££** A. Ae. Dc. V. Restaurant: ⑁ Surf and Turf (chicken fillets and scampi with saffron rice). **£.**

▲▲▲▲ **Ladbroke Westmoreland,** 18 Lodge Rd, NW8, ☎722 7722. Tx. 23101. 347 rm. 🅿 **£££** A. Ae. Dc. V. Restaurant: **£.**

▲▲▲ **Charles Bernard,** 5 Frognal, NW3, ☎794 0101. Tx. 23560. 57 rm. 🅿 **££.** A. Ae. Dc. V. Restaurant: **£.**

▲ **Sandringham,** 3 Holford Rd, off East Heath Rd, NW3, ☎435 1569. 14 rm. 🅿 **£.** Small hotel adjoining Hampstead Heath.

Restaurants

Keats, 3 Downshire Hill, NW3, ☎435 3544 ⑁ *Cl. lunch, Sun.* French. Chateaubriand with three sauces. **£££** A. Ae. Dc. V.

Peachey's, 205 Haverstock Hill, NW3, ☎435 6744 ⑁ *Cl. Sat lunch, Sun eve, 24 Dec–2 Jan.* French. Beef fillet with anchovies. **££** Ae. Dc. V.

Green Cottage II, 122a Finchley Rd, NW3, ☎794 3833 *Cl. Tue, 25–26 Dec.* Vegetarian. **£** A. Ae. Dc.

St John's Wood:
Don Pepe, 99 Frampton St, NW8, ☎262 3834 🅿 *Cl. 24–25 Dec.* Spanish. Merluza a la Gallega. **££** A. Ae. Dc. V.

Lords Rendezvous, 24 Finchley Rd, NW8, ☎722 4750 *Cl. 25–26 Dec.* Peking cuisine. **££** A. Ae. Dc. V.

West Hampstead:
Sheridans, 351 West End Lane, NW6, ☎794 3234 ⑁ *Cl. Mon, 1–14 Jan, last 2 wks Aug.* Fillet of trout stuffed with prawns and crab. **££** A. Ae. Dc. V.

The Lantern, 23 Malvern Rd, NW6, ☎624 1796 🅿 *Cl. Christmas.* International. Pork escalope stuffed with Roquefort and mushroom sauce. **£** V.

Viareggio, 332 West End Lane, NW6, ☎794 1444 *Cl. Sun.* **£** A. Ae. Dc. V.

Vijay, 49 Willesden Lane, NW6, ☎328 1087 🅿 *Cl. 25–26 Dec.* South Indian dishes. **£** A. Ae. Dc.

Islington

Restaurants

Frederick's, Camden Passage, NW1, ☎359 8728 🕸 *Cl. Sun, 24 Dec, 1 Jan, Bank hols.* Beef fillet with Stilton sauce. **££** A. Ae. Dc. V.

Portofino, Camden Passage, NW1, ☎226 0884 *Cl. Sun, Easter, Christmas, Bank hols.* Italian. **££** A. Ae. Dc. V.

Upper Street Fish Shop, 324 Upper St, NW1, ☎359 1401 *Cl. Sun, 2 wks Christmas, Bank hols.* Poached halibut with herb sauce. **£.**

Canonbury:
Anna's Place, 90 Mildmay Park, NW1, ☎249 9379 🕸 ⅊ *Cl. Sun, Mon, Easter, 2 wks Christmas, Aug.* Swedish dishes, gravlax. **£.**

Hodja Nasreddin, 53 Newington Green Rd, NW1, ☎226 7757 *Cl. Christmas.* Turkish. Saté in mushroom and wine sauce. **£** A. Ae. Dc. V.

━━ *Outer London*

East

Hotel

Woodford Green, 1m NW of A406/A104 roundabout:
▲▲▲ **Woodford Moat House,** Oak Hill, ☎505 4511. 99 rm. 🕸 **££** A. Ae. Dc. V. Restaurant: **£.** *Cl. 25 Dec eve.*

Restaurants

At Ilford:
Da Umberto, 361 Ley St, ☎553 5763 *Cl. Sat lunch, Sun, 3 wks Aug, Bank hols.* Italian. Boeuf aux clute Napoléon. **££** A. V.

South Woodford:
Ho-Ho, 20 High Rd, E1 ☎989 1041 🅿 ⅊ *Cl. 25–26 Dec.* Scallops, prawns and squid in spicy sauce. **£** A. Ae. Dc. V.

North

Hotel

Enfield:
▲▲▲ **Holtwhites,** 92 Chase Side, ☎363 0124. Tx. 299670. 28 rm. 🅿 **££** A. Ae. Dc. V. Restaurant: **££.**

Restaurants

Highgate:
One Hampstead Lane, 1 Hampstead Lane, N6, ☎340 4444 🕸 ⅊ *Cl. Mon, Tue–Fri lunch, Sun eve.* French. Salmon with champagne sauce. **££** A. Ae. Dc. V.

San Carlo, 2 High St, N6, ☎340 5823 🅿 🕸 ⅊ *Cl. Mon, Bank hols.* Italian. **££** A. Ae. Dc. V.

Hornsey:
M'sieur Frog's Bistro, 36 Hornsey High St, N8, ☎340 2116 *Cl. 3 wks Aug, 1 wk Christmas.* £ Ae. V.

East Finchley:
Quincy's '84, 675 Finchley Rd, NW2, ☎794 8499 *Cl. Mon, 3 wks from 24 Dec.* Anglo-French. ££ A. V.

Muswell Hill:
Kuo Yuan, 217 High Rd, NW10 ☎459 2297 ◘ ఈ *Cl. lunch, 25–26 Dec.* Chinese. ££.

North-west

Hotels

Old Redding, 2m N of Harrow off A409:
▲▲▲ **Grim's Dyke** (Best Western), ☎954 7666. Tx. 8954958. 48 rm. ◘ ✿ Modern comfort amid the spectacular Victoriana of the former home of W.S. Gilbert, designed in the Tudor style by Norman Shaw. ££ A. Ae. Dc. V. Restaurant: Salmon coulibiac, confit of duckling with chanterelles. ££. *Cl. 25–30 Dec.*

Scratchwood Service Area, M1:
▲▲ **Travelodge** (Trust House Forte), NW7, ☎906 0611. Tx. 8814796. 100 rm. ◘ ✿ ఈ £ A. Ae. Dc. V. Restaurant: ఈ Carvery. £. *Cl. lunch.*

Restaurants

Golders Green:
Il Cavaliere, 14 North End Rd, NW11, ☎455 3849 ◘ ఈ *Cl. Mon, 2 wks summer.* Linguine al frutti di mare. £ A. Ae. Dc. V.
La Madrague, 816 Finchley Rd, NW11, ☎455 8853 ◘ ఈ *Cl. Sun, 3 wks Jan, Bank hols.* Civet de canard aux olives. £ Ae. V.
Peking Duck, 30 Temple Fortune Parade, NW11, ☎455 9444 *Cl. Tue, 25–26 Dec.* £ A. Ae. Dc. V.

Wembley:
Moghul Brasserie, 525 High Rd, ☎903 6967 ◘ Mughlai Thali. ££ A. Ae. Dc. V.

Hatch End :
Swan, 322 Uxbridge Rd, ☎428 8821 ◘ ✿ Peking-style cuisine, grilled dumplings. £££ A. Ae. Dc. V.

Mill Hill:
Good Earth, 143 Broadway, NW7, ☎959 7011 ఈ Steamed sea bass. £ A. Ae. Dc. V.

South-east

Hotels

Blackheath:
▲▲▲ **Clarendon,** 8 Montpellier Row, SE3, ☎318 4321. Tx. 896367. 215 rm. ◘ ✿ ఈ ££ A. Ae. Dc. V. Restaurant: ఈ £.

Addiscombe, 1m E of Croydon off A232:
▲▲ **Briarley,** 8 Outram Rd, ☎654 1000. Tx. 8813271. 25 rm. ◘ £ A. Ae. Dc. V. Restaurant: ఈ £.
▲▲ **Oakwood,** 69 Outram Rd, ☎654 2835. 14 rm. ◘ £ A. Ae. Dc. V. Restaurant: £.

Sanderstead, 2½m SE of Croydon on A2022:
▲▲▲▲ **Selsdon Park** (Best Western), ☎657 8811. Tx. 945003. 150 rm. ◘ ✿ ✓ Luxury hotel in a period country house, offer-

ing extensive sporting and leisure facilities. **££** A. Ae. Dc. V.
Restaurant: **£** Tournedos farci, suprême de pintade.

St Mary Cray, 3½m E of Bromley off A224:
▲ **Mary Rose,** 40 High St, ☎(0689) 71917. 8 rm. 🄿 **£** A. Ae.
Dc. V.

Restaurants

Rotherhithe:
Rogues Kitchen, St Marychurch St, SE16, ☎237 7452 ✽ *Cl.
Sun–Tue, 25 Dec, 1 Jan.* American. Jambalaya. **£.**

Greenwich:
Treasure of China, 10 Nelson Rd, SE10, ☎858 9884 *Cl. Sun,
25–26 Dec.* Szechuan prawn. **£** A. Ae. Dc. V.
Mandalay, 100 Greenwich South St, SE10, ☎691 0443 *Cl.
Sun–Wed, Thu–Sat lunch, 25 Dec–1 Jan.* Burmese. **£** A. V.

Norwood:
Luigi's, 129 Gipsy Hill, ☎670 1843   🄿 *Cl. Sat lunch, Sun, 3 wks
Aug.* **££** A. Ae. Dc. V.

Thornton Heath:
Mamma Adele, 23 Brigstock Rd, ☎683 2233   & *Cl. Sat lunch,
Sun.* Fresh home-made pasta with smoked salmon, brandy and
cream sauce. **£** A. Ae. Dc. V.

Abbey Wood:
L'Auberge, 44 Forest Hill Rd, SE22 ☎299 2211   & *Cl. Mon, 3
wks Aug.* Thin strips of calf's liver sautéed in herbs. **££** A. V.

Bromley:
Carioca, 239 High St, ☎460 7130   & *Cl. 25–26 Dec.* International. Thali. **£** A. Ae. Dc. V.

Croydon:
Chateau Napoleon, Coombe Lane, ☎686 1244 🄿 ✽ & *Cl. Sun
eve.* Fresh home-made pasta and ice creams. **££** A. Ae. Dc. V.
Hockneys, Arts Centre Complex, 98 High St, ☎688 299   🄿 *Cl.
Sun, Mon, 2 wks Aug, Christmas.* Vegetarian. **£** A. Ae. Dc. V.
Kelong, 1b Selsdon Rd, ☎688 0726 *Cl. Sun, 1st 2 wks Aug.* Chilli
crab. **£** A. Ae. Dc. V.

South-west

Hotels

Richmond-upon-Thames:
▲▲▲ **Richmond Gate,** Richmond Hill, ☎940 0061. Tx. 928556.
50 rm. 🄿 ✽ **££** A. Ae. Dc. V. One of London's 'country hotels',
adjoining Richmond Park. Restaurant: **£.** *Cl. Fri eve, Sat, Sun.*

Wimbledon:
▲ **Worcester House,** 38 Alwyne Rd, SW19, ☎946 1300. 9 rm.
£.

Restaurants

Putney:
Wild Thyme, 96 Felsham Rd, SW15, ☎789 3323 *Cl. Sun, Bank
hols.* French cuisine with oriental influence. **££** A. Ae. V.

Barnes:
Barnaby's, 39b High St, SW13, ☎878 4750   & *Cl. Sun, Sep,
Bank hols.* French regional. Suprême de volaille à l'avocat. **££.**
Il Bellamore, 5 White Hart Lane, SW13, ☎876 3335   & *Cl.
25–26 Dec.* Fillet of beef Garibaldi. **£** A. Ae. Dc. V.

Mortlake:

Crowthers, 481 Upper Richmond Rd, SW14, ☎876 6372 *Cl. Sun.* French. **££** A. Ae.

Janine's, 505 Upper Richmond Rd, SW14, ☎876 5075 ⅋ *Cl. Mon–Sat lunch, Sun and Mon eve, 2 wks Feb–Mar, Sep.* Beef Wellington. **££** A. Ae. Dc. V.

Mr Lu, 374 Upper Richmond Rd West, SW14, ☎876 2531 ⅋ *Cl. Mon lunch, 25–26 Dec.* Peking cuisine. **£** A. Ae. Dc. V.

Richmond-upon-Thames:

Madeleine, 122 Sheen Rd, ☎London 948 4445 **P** *Cl. Sun & Mon lunch, Sep.* Chicken stuffed with crab meat and crab sauce. **£** Ae. V.

Mrs Beeton's, 58 Hill Rise, ☎940 9561 *Cl. eves Sun–Tue.* Housewives commune with different chefs each day. **£.**

The Refectory, 6 Church Walk, ☎940 6264 ⊛ *Cl. Mon, 25–26 Dec, Easter.* English regional and traditional dishes. **£.**

Kew:

Lichfield's, 13 Lichfield Terrace, Sheen Rd, ☎940 5236 *Cl. Sun, Mon, 2 wks Sep, 1 wk Christmas.* Mille feuille of crab with cardamon. **£££** A. Ae.

Jasper's Bun in the Oven, 11 Kew Green, ☎940 3987 **P** ⊛ *Cl. Sun, Bank hols.* Fillet de boeuf Dijon. **£** A. Ae. Dc. V.

Twickenham:

Cézanne, 68 Richmond Rd, ☎892 3526 *Cl. Sat lunch, Sun, Bank hols.* **£** A. Ae. V.

Tooting:

Sree Krishna, 192 Tooting High St, SW17, ☎672 4250 ⅋ *Cl. 25–26 Dec.* South Indian dishes, Masala Dosai. **£** A. Ae. V.

Norbury:

Malean, 1585 London Rd, SW16, ☎764 2336 *Cl. Sun lunch, 25–26 Dec.* Bang-bang chicken. **£** A. Ae. Dc. V.

Wimbledon:

Village Restaurant, 8 High St, SW19, ☎947 6477 *Cl. Sat & Mon lunch, Sun eve, last 2 wks Aug.* Duck with passion fruit, lobster glazed with shrimp sauce and cucumber. **££** A. Ae. V.

Village Taverna, 28 Ridgeway, SW19, ☎946 4840 ⅋ *Cl. Sun, Bank hols.* Souvla, kebabs. **£** A. V.

Surbiton:

Chez Max, 85 Maple Rd, ☎399 2365 *Cl. Sat lunch, Sun, Mon, 1st 2 wks Jan, 1 wk summer, 25–26 Dec.* **£££** A. Ae. Dc. V.

Sutton:

Partners 23, 23 Stonecot Hill, ☎644 7743 ⅋ *Cl. 2 wks Aug, Christmas, New Year.* **££** A. Ae. Dc. V.

West

Hotels

Ealing:

▲▲▲**Kenton House,** 5 Hillcrest Rd, W5, ☎997 8436. Tx. 8812544. 51 rm. **P £** A. Ae. Dc. V. Restaurant: Salmon en croute. **£.** *Cl. 3–4 days Christmas.*

Ruislip:

▲▲▲**Barn,** West End Rd, ☎(08956) 36057. Tx. 892514. 56 rm. **P** ⊛ ⅋ **££** A. Ae. V. Restaurant: ⅋ **£.** *Cl. Sun eve, Christmas–New Year.*

Heathrow Airport:
▲▲▲▲ *Holiday Inn,* Stockley Rd, West Drayton, ☎(0895) 445555. Tx. 934518. 400 rm. 🅿 & ✔ **ff** A. Ae. Dc. V. Restaurant: & **f.**
▲▲▲▲ *Sheraton Heathrow,* Bath Rd, West Drayton, ☎759 2424. Tx. 934331. 405 rm. 🅿 ❀ ✔ **ff** A. Ae. Dc. V. Restaurant: **ff.**
▲▲▲ *Ariel* (Trust House Forte), Bath Rd, Hayes, ☎759 2552. Tx. 21777. 177 rm. 🅿 ❀ & **ff** A. Ae. Dc. V. Restaurant: Carvery. **f.**
▲▲▲ *Arlington,* Shepiston Lane, Hayes, ☎573 6162. 80 rm. 🅿 & **ff** A. Ae. Dc. V. Restaurant: **f.** *Cl. Sat & Sun lunch.*
▲▲▲ *Master Robert,* 366 Great West Rd, Hounslow, ☎570 6261. 64 rm. 🅿 ❀ & **ff** A. Ae. Dc. V. Restaurant: **f.**
▲▲▲ *Post House* (Trust House Forte), Sipson Rd, West Drayton, ☎759 2323. Tx. 934280. 597 rm. 🅿 **ff** A. Ae. Dc. V. Restaurant: **f.**

Restaurants

Ealing:
New Leaf, 35 Bond St, W5, ☎567 2343 *Cl. Sun lunch, 25–26 Dec.* Aromatic and crispy duck. **f** A. Ae. V.
Sinar Matahari, 146 The Broadway, W13, ☎567 6821 *Cl. Mon, Sat lunch.* Indonesian dishes, satay, rendang. **f** Ae.

Southall:
Brilliant, 72 Western Rd, ☎574 1928 & *Cl. 3 wks Aug.* Indian. Butter chicken, masala, king prawns. **f** A. Ae. Dc. V.

▬ *OTHER ACCOMMODATION*

Hostels

The long-established foundations such as the **YMCA, YWCA** and **YHA** have a number of locations in London for people to stay.
YHA (Youth Hostels Association): The centre is at 14 Southampton Street, WC2, ☎836 8541 (⊖ ⇌ Charing Cross). It will arrange membership (necessary for use of hostels) and provide addresses of London hostels. A bed in a dormitory is inexpensive, and there are hostels well-placed in the centre of town (maximum stay 4 nights).
YMCA London Central Hotel and Hostel, George William House, 112 Great Russell Street, WC1, ☎637 1333 (⊖ Tottenham Court Road). This is the largest YMCA centre in London, offering single or double rooms for both men and women – most other hostels only accept men. For information concerning YMCA, contact the central London office at 31 Craven Terrace, W2, ☎723 0071.
Central YWCA (women only), 16 Great Russell Street, WC1, ☎636 7512 (⊖ Tottenham Court Road). The administration office at 2 Weymouth Street, W1, ☎631 0654 (⊖ Regent's Park), offers the booklet 'Hostels in London'.

Camping

Tents are not provided, but all sites offer toilet facilities and many have a general shop.
Crystal Palace Caravan Harbour, Crystal Palace Parade, SE19. ☎778 7155 ⇌ Crystal Palace.
Tent City, Old Oak Common Lane, W3, ☎743 5708 – Summer only. ⊖ North Acton ⇌ Willesden Junction.
Picketts Lock Sports and Leisure Centre, Picketts Lock Lane, N9, ☎803 4756 ⇌ Angel Road.

LONDON IN HISTORY

In London's Guildhall are the wooden images of two strange mythical figures, named Gog and Magog. Originally they were Gogmagog and Corineus, an ancient Briton and a Trojan warrior, whose legendary combat was said to have led to the foundation of London in 1000 BC. London's true beginnings are not so clear. There was a Celtic settlement – at the first easy crossing place of the Thames inland from the sea – perhaps as early as 400 BC. But of this, virtually nothing remains.

ROMAN LONDON

London's story really begins with the Romans, who arrived in Britain in force around AD 40, just before the reign of the Emperor Claudius. They established a township by the same crossing place, on the north bank of the Thames around two low hills (Ludgate Hill and Cornhill). Not long after, it was devastated during Queen Boudicca's revolt. It was rebuilt and soon became the main commercial and political link between Roman Britain and the rest of the Empire. It was known as Londinium, a name probably derived from the Celtic words

---

Roman Buildings

Sections of the 3rd-century **Wall** stand within the precincts of the Tower of London, across Tower Hill in Trinity Square Gardens and along the south side of the Barbican (London Wall), where it was built on to an existing fortress. Otherwise, the only traces are the sites of various buildings and public places – all within the area of the City – which from time to time are temporarily revealed during building work and then covered again. Such has been the case with the **Temple of Mithras** (near the Mansion House), the **Governor's Palace** (by Cannon Street station), the **Baths** (near Cheapside) and, most recently (1986), the **Forum** (by Leadenhall Market). In addition, there are the foundations of a large Roman house in the crypt of St Bride's church (off Fleet Street) and some timbers of a Roman wharf by the entrance to St Magnus the Martyr (Lower Thames Street). A so-called 'Roman Bath' in Strand Lane, outside the City, is of doubtful authenticity. Much of the statuary, sections of mosaic floor and other treasures of Roman London are on display in the Museum of London.

Railings outside the Houses of Parliament

'Llyn Din' (fortress by a lake). The city flourished between AD 200 and 400. A wall was built around it, and the names of the gateways are commemorated in such place-names as Aldgate, Cripplegate and Ludgate. The city, which occupied a site of roughly half a square mile (1.3km^2), boasted some of the finest public buildings and monuments of any town or city north of the Alps, and had an estimated population of 50,000 – more than any other English city was to record until the 18th century.

With the recall of the legions around AD 410 to defend other parts of the Empire from Barbarian invasions, Londinium was mostly abandoned, its great wall and buildings inspiring awe in the invading Anglo-Saxons.

ENGLAND'S CAPITAL (900–1600)

The so-called 'Dark Ages' of European history – the break-up of the Roman Empire and its aftermath – were marked in England by the invasion of Angles and Saxons, Vikings and Danes. For most of this period of over four centuries, the story of London marked time. Its revival dates from the time of the Saxon king Alfred (849–900), who restored London as a major city and defensive bastion against the Danes. The later Saxon king, Edmund Ironside, and then the Danish king Canute, based much of their power on London.

The city's future, as England's capital, was assured by the last important Saxon king, Edward the Confessor (1002–66), who established his court a mile upstream at Westminster, so creating the division – more and more significant as time went by – between the original walled township (the City of London) and the rest of the capital.

Saxon England ended with the Norman Conquest (1066), when Duke William of Normandy secured the throne. As William I, he built the original **Tower of London,** both to protect the city and to emphasize his authority. At the same time, William and his successors, Henry I and King John, granted the citizens of London a large degree of independence, including the right to elect their own Lord Mayor (civic privileges still enjoyed by the City of London). King John's reign is also celebrated for his signing of the **Magna Carta** (15 June 1215), a charter which limited the powers of the monarch and safeguarded the life, liberty and property of his subjects through the supremacy of English law, and which is regarded as the foundation-stone of the English constitution. In the centuries which followed, London merchants and bankers further increased their power by lending money to Edward III and Henry V to fight the Hundred Years' War with France.

London's own wealth, reflected in its rich and colourful craftsmen's guilds, came from its growing maritime trade, notably with the powerful German Hanseatic League. The arrival from Europe of such useful people as the Lombard merchants and bankers also contributed to the city's prosperity. Its most famous Lord Mayor, Richard Whittington, lived at this time.

The Tudor period brought upheaval. Henry VIII quarrelled with the Pope and in 1536 created his own Church of England, abolishing the monasteries shortly afterwards. The sudden end of these institutions changed the whole character of English life, not least in London, where new hospitals and schools had to be built to replace the monasteries' traditional functions; while religious war in France brought an influx of Protestant Huguenots, who added to the overcrowding of the city but also brought new prosperity.

During the long reign of Henry's daughter Elizabeth I, Sir Francis Drake, Sir Walter Raleigh and her other 'sea dogs' explored the New World and defeated the Spanish Armada (1588), so laying the foundations of British sea power and empire. England, and especially London, also flourished culturally, with the music of Thomas Tallis, William Byrd and the madrigalists, as well as the plays of Christopher Marlowe, Ben Jonson and, above all, William Shakespeare, which were performed at the celebrated Globe Theatre in Southwark.

Medieval Architecture

Hardly anything remains of Saxon London. The Norman or Romanesque style, which spread across western Europe, reached England during the 10th or 11th century. Rounded arches and massive columns were its strongest features. The finest of London's Norman buildings are William I's **White Tower** (1097) and the adjoining **St John's Chapel** – the earliest parts of the **Tower of London**. The cupolas on the four towers, which give the Tower an almost toy-like aspect, were added in the 14th century. Other Norman landmarks, dating from the 11th and 12th centuries, include large sections of the **Temple Church** (between Fleet Street and the Embankment), the City church of **St Bartholomew-the-Great**, the crypt of **St John's Gate,** Clerkenwell, and **Old St Pancras Church,** which at that time was miles out in the country.

The succeeding Gothic style took specific English forms, progressing from Early English through Decorated to the Perpendicular style, the most obvious change being that the windows increased in size and that the design became more elaborate. The main part of **Westminster Abbey** dates from the 13th century, built at the instigation of Henry III, who was inspired by the Gothic cathedrals of northern France. **Southwark Cathedral,** which has a few remains of an earlier Norman church, is part of a priory of the same period. Nearly three centuries later, Henry VII added his **Chapel** to the existing Westminster Abbey, creating one of the finest examples of the Perpendicular style with its intricate fan vaulting. Secular buildings include **Westminster Hall** (1394), with its massive wooden hammerbeam roof; the elegant 15th-century **Guildhall** in the City (much restored after World War II bombing); grandiose **Hampton Court Palace**; and, on a smaller scale, **St James's Palace, Eltham Palace** in south-east London, and parts of **Lambeth Palace.** A row of half-timbered shops and houses fronting **Staples Inn** in Holborn, although heavily restored, is London's best surviving example of Elizabethan domestic architecture.

Great Fire of London 1666, (Dutch School).

During the four centuries from the Conquest to the Tudors, London suffered some reverses, notably at the time of the plague known as the 'Black Death' (1349) and during Wat Tyler's Peasants' Revolt (1381). By the end of Elizabeth's reign (1603), it was a city of over 200,000 people, stretching far beyond its original City limits, around the Thames upstream to Westminster, downstream to Wapping, and across the river to the districts of Southwark and Lambeth. Its two outstanding landmarks were the Norman-Gothic cathedral of St Paul's and its single bridge (London Bridge) cluttered with buildings.

WAR, PLAGUE AND FIRE (1600–1700)

Elizabeth left England strong, but religiously divided, between

Catholics, upholders of the new Church of England and various Protestant sects. During the reign of her successor, James I, Catholic involvement in the Gunpowder Plot to blow up the King and Parliament (1605) and the sailing of the Puritan Pilgrim Fathers to America (1620) underlined these divisions. With the accession of Charles I, religious dispute, as well as the monarch's more personal quarrel with Parliament, led to Civil War in 1642. London was the strategic goal of the war, and although most of the fighting took place elsewhere, it was the capital which saw the trial (in Westminster Hall) and execution (outside his own Banqueting House) of Charles I by the victorious Parliamentarians in 1649.

Oliver Cromwell ruled as Lord Protector until his death in 1658. His Commonwealth, however, did not long survive him, and in 1660 the exiled Charles II was restored to the English throne. There was a great revival of English theatre during the Restoration period, following the Puritan gloom of the Commonwealth, and the indefatigable diarist Samuel Pepys recorded the more racy side of London life. This was also the age of England's greatest composer, Henry Purcell. Two major catastrophes specifically affecting London also marked Charles II's reign. In 1664–5 there was the last but very serious outbreak of the plague (the Great Plague), which killed probably half the population and brought the city's life to a standstill. Hard on its heels, in 1666, came the Great Fire (said to have started in Pudding Lane and ended at Pie Corner), which destroyed most of the City of London and made homeless as many people as were earlier killed by the Plague.

Though a disaster for those involved, the Great Fire was something of a blessing in disguise, as it cleared away much ramshackle and insalubrious property (a prime cause of the plague and other epidemics). Within days, Charles had summoned the architect Christopher Wren to plan an entirely new city, with broad streets and a riverside quay. Rapid and piecemeal reconstruction wrecked the plan's chances, but it did result in the building of Wren's new **St Paul's Cathedral** and many other churches in the city – a unique concentration of one great architect's work.

The religious question, at least at national level, was finally settled in 1688, when the Catholic King James II was deposed in favour of the Protestant Dutchman William of Orange (William III). This bloodless revolution, known as the 'Glorious Revolu-

---

Inigo JONES and Christopher WREN

The English Jacobean style – represented by **Charlton House** in south-east London and the remains of **Holland House** in Holland Park – was a transition between the Tudor period and the entirely different styles of English Renaissance architecture, whose Italian and French models were themselves inspired by the monuments of Classical Greece and Rome.

Inigo Jones's **Queen's House** at Greenwich (1616), modelled on the work of the Italian architect Andrea Palladio, is one of the first and finest of English Renaissance buildings. The **Banqueting House,** Whitehall, the **Queen's Chapel,** facing St James's Palace, and **Covent Garden piazza,** including **St Paul's Church,** are also by Inigo Jones. Some of London's other early squares – **Bloomsbury, Leicester** and **Soho** – followed soon after.

Sir Christopher Wren's most famous Renaissance-style building is **St Paul's Cathedral** (1675–1711); but each of his other City churches – among them **St Mary-le-Bow, St Bride's** and **St Magnus the Martyr** – merits a visit. Other buildings in London by Wren include his handsome **Monument** to the Great Fire in the City, built as a Roman column with a flaming urn at its top; his magnificently sited **Royal Naval College,** Greenwich; the **Royal Hospital,** Chelsea; **Kensington Palace;** and the east wing he built on to **Hampton Court Palace. Lincoln's Inn** and **Gray's Inn** (two of the Inns of Court) contain good examples of late 17th-century domestic architecture.

tion', was followed quickly by the even more significant Bill of Rights, which defined the roles of monarch and Parliament and so established a constitutional monarchy.

LONDON IN THE 18TH CENTURY

The 18th century saw Britain emerge as a world power. During the reign of Queen Anne (1702–14), the War of the Spanish Succession brought victories for the Duke of Marlborough at Blenheim and elsewhere, and prevented Louis XIV of France from dominating Europe. British policy thus succeeded in maintaining a European balance of power. In the Seven Years' War (1756–63), Britain and France clashed again, as colonial powers. In India, General Clive advanced the cause of a British India with his victory at Plassey. Soon after, General Wolfe won Canada for Britain with the capture of Quebec. In the American War of Independence (War of the Revolution), Britain lost her other North American territories; but Captain Cook's Pacific explorations secured Australia and New Zealand.

At home, the long-standing feuds between England and Scotland were settled by the political Act of Union (1707), which survived the two Catholic-Stuart Jacobite Rebellions of 1715 and 1745. Queen Anne and then the Protestant Hanoverian monarchs presided over the growth of British parliamentary government. A two-party system emerged with the Whigs and Tories. Sir Robert Walpole, who came to prominence for his successful handling of a big financial scandal known as the 'South Sea Bubble', was the first to assume the role of prime minister, at the head of an inner government or cabinet.

In the course of the century, merchants, bankers and land-owners grew rich, thanks to Britain's burgeoning overseas trade and to the beginnings both of the Industrial Revolution and of new farming methods. As a consequence, there was a building boom throughout the country. London itself doubled in area and recorded a population rise from around 600,000 to over one million. New bridges also spanned the Thames, ending the centuries-old monopoly of London Bridge.

The capital's social and cultural life flourished. It was the age of Swift, Fielding, Defoe and Sterne, pioneers of the new literary form of the novel; of Goldsmith and Sheridan and the heyday of the theatre; and of Boswell and Johnson, Addison and Steele, habitués of London's coffee shops and founders of modern journalism. The German-born composer George Frideric Handel dominated the worlds of opera and oratorio in the first half of the century. Reynolds and Gainsborough shone as portrait painters for the well-to-do, while Hogarth depicted the seamier side of London life.

The century ended with the opening rounds of the Napoleonic Wars, and Britain's prime minister, William Pitt the Younger, trying once more to maintain a continental balance of power.

Georgian Architecture

Whole districts of London commemorate the 18th century, notably the squares of the west-central areas – **Cavendish, Hanover, Grosvenor, Berkeley, Portman, Bedford, Manchester** and **Fitzroy Square** – and neighbouring streets. Many of the Georgian brick terraces of regular height and plan which form the sides of these squares have survived.

Notable London churches of the period, broadly following the English Renaissance style, are: **St George,** Hanover Square (John James); **St George,** Bloomsbury, **Christ Church,** Spitalfields, and **St George-in-the-East,** Shadwell (all by Nicholas Hawksmoor, who also added the twin west towers to **Westminster Abbey**); and **St Mary-le-Strand** and **St Martin-le-Fields** (James Gibbs).

Secular buildings outnumber the churches. **Greycoat School** and the smaller building of the old **Bluecoat School,** both on the fringes of Westminster, belong to the early 18th-century 'Queen Anne' period. The **Mansion House**, in the City (George Dance the Elder), the **Horse Guards**, Whitehall (William Kent), the **Albany**, Piccadilly and **Somerset House**, Victoria Embankment (Sir William Chambers, with later additions), are notable landmarks from later in the century.

Outside central London there are some even finer monuments of the period: Lord Burlington's **Chiswick House,** a tribute to Palladio's famous 'Rotonda'; Robert Adam's superb remodelling of **Osterley Park,** of **Syon House,** Isleworth, and **Kenwood House,** Hampstead; and the **Paragon,** at Blackheath. There is also Horace Walpole's **Strawberry Hill,** Twickenham, a fanciful precursor to the Gothic Revival school.

THE INDUSTRIAL GIANT (1800–1900)

The British Empire reached its zenith in the 19th century. People spoke of a 'Pax Britannica', since no other nation could seriously challenge British mercantile and naval power around the world. It was the time when Britain's prime minister Lord Palmerston could, with impunity, fight the Opium Wars, forcing China to continue its imports of the drug from British India and grabbing Hong Kong as a trading post. 'Gunboat diplomacy' was a less complimentary name for such a policy.

Britain was also the 'workshop of the world', the first fully industrialized nation. Iron and steel, shipbuilding and textile industries relied upon abundant coalfields. First canals and then railways, pioneered by George and Robert Stephenson and I.K. Brunel, carried manufactured goods swiftly to ports for export all over the world.

The effect of all this on London was tremendous. With the accession of Queen Victoria in 1837, it began to change almost beyond recognition. The coming of the railways had much to do with it. The railway companies brought their terminus stations as close to the centre of the city as possible, turning whole

Military band by Tower Bridge.

districts into smoky industrial surburbs. Railways also served the docks, which expanded enormously, from the Pool of London (by the City) for miles downstream on both sides of the broadening river estuary. The docks and railways between them created other new industries. In less than a century, London quadrupled in area and population, to become the world's largest city.

The brightest side of the picture was the Great Exhibition of 1851, housed in Joseph Paxton's amazing Crystal Palace of iron and glass on a site in London's Hyde Park. The Exhibition itself was a showcase for British industry. The spirit of pride and confidence it engendered gave rise to some of London's grandest public buildings.

Two other industrial projects London could take pride in were the construction of the first tunnel beneath the Thames, between Wapping and Rotherhithe (the world's first under-river tunnel); and, in 1863, the opening of the first ever underground railway, a dark and sooty line between Paddington and Farringdon Street, but very popular from the start.

Other aspects of Victorian London were not so happy. While the wealthy new banking and merchant classes moved into the fashionable districts around Regent's Park and Hampstead, Hyde Park and Kensington Gardens, those lower down the social scale were crowded around the railways, and east and south-east along the line of the docks, spawning large areas of slums and destitution. The plight of millions of London's poor was highlighted by Charles Dickens and other writers of the time, and raised such philanthropists as Elizabeth Fry, prison and hospital reformer, American-born George Peabody, who financed new working class housing, and William Booth, founder of the Salvation Army. Prime minister W.E. Gladstone and other reformist politicians of the century consolidated upon their work.

Regency and Victorian Architecture

The early years of the 19th century saw a refinement of Georgian domestic building in the Regency style of John Nash. **Regent Street** and his grand and gracious terraces bordering **Regent's Park, Park Terrace** and the **Mall** formed part of an overall plan for West London, built under the aegis of George IV (formerly the Prince Regent). Decimus Burton's **Athenaeum** by Pall Mall and Thomas Cubitt's **Belgrave** and **Eaton** Squares are similar in character.

For the rest of the century, architectural styles in London, as elsewhere, proliferated. The **British Museum** (Robert Smirke) and the **National Gallery** (William Wilkins) are in the Classical Revival style. The **Houses of Parliament** (Charles Barry and Augustus Welby Pugin) represent the Gothic Revival style, more exuberant examples of which are the hotel (now offices) attached to **St Pancras Railway Station** (George Gilbert Scott), and the **Royal Courts of Justice** in the Strand (G.E. Street). A blend of Italianate styles inspires the massive **Royal Albert Hall** (Captain Francis Fowke) and the neighbouring **Royal College of Organists** (Lieutenant H.H. Cole). Not far away is the superb Neo-Romanesque **Natural History Museum** (Alfred Waterhouse). At the end of the century came the Neo-Byzantine **Westminster Cathedral** (J.F. Bentley) and the Art Nouveau **Whitechapel Art Gallery** (C.H. Townsend).

The Victorians were at their most original as engineers. The huge span of **St Pancras Station** roof, I.K. Brunel's triple-arched iron and glass **Paddington Station** and Decimus Burton's **Palm House** in Kew Gardens give some idea of the imaginative scope of the **Crystal Palace** (which in 1854 was moved to a new site in south London, but burned down in 1936). Some of the Victorian bridges, such as **Albert** and **Hammersmith**, combine fine construction with elegant design. **Tower Bridge**, a masterpiece of 19th-century engineering, is dignified by Gothic Revival towers.

There were other, unforeseen consequences for the huge city. One of these was fog. This had always been a seasonal nuisance, but the sulphurous smoke from thousands of domestic and factory chimneys turned it into what Londoners called 'pea-soupers'. Though glamourized in books and films, such 'smogs' were a serious health hazard and a continuing menace until well into the 20th century.

More serious still was the problem of sanitation. Sewage and water services had continually been overtaken by population growth since Roman times. By the 1850s, river pollution and inadequacy of water supplies and sewers resulted in the great public works programmes of Sir Joseph Bazalgette, who also radically changed and improved much of London's riverside with the construction of the **Victoria, Albert** and **Chelsea Embankments.** Other important civic works included the creation of large new cemeteries around what was then the city's perimeter – now romantic havens of Victorian funerary art and sentiment.

Queen Victoria's Diamond Jubilee was celebrated in 1897, almost at the end of the century. By then the nation's worst social problems were being tackled, and London, the imperial capital, was the scene of splendid celebrations.

A NEW RENAISSANCE

The two world wars have dominated the story of Britain, and of London, in this century. Britain was on the winning side in both, but the enormous economic cost accelerated an industrial decline that had already begun by the turn of the century. The main reason for this was growing overseas competition, but the decline was punctuated by the General Strike of 1926 and by a world slump and mass unemployment in the succeeding years. British industry was rapidly geared to the needs of World War II but declined again afterwards.

Winston Churchill, the nation's leader during World War II, was anxious to halt a corresponding decline in the British Empire, but Clement Attlee, Britain's new prime minister at the end of the war, realistically granted independence to India. Successive governments continued the peaceful dismantling of the Empire and created a Commonwealth of Nations – a 'family' of independent states which had once been part of the Empire, bound more by sentiment than by politics.

London was not so affected by industrial decline as many other towns and cities. Indeed, between the two world wars there was a noticeable shift of new industry from other parts of the country to London and south-east England, resulting in yet another huge building boom in and around the capital, to produce a conurbation of almost nine million people by 1939.

London was worst hit by the bombing of World War II. The City, especially, was devastated. Post-war proposals for a planned reconstruction were largely unfulfilled, although the idea of a 'Green Belt', to halt further unplanned growth, was accepted. The 1951 Festival of Britain, intended to celebrate both the nation's post-war recovery and the centenary of the Great Exhibition of 1851, involved the clearance of a large, derelict site on London's South Bank and the beginning of a new arts centre. The **Barbican,** in the City itself, combined an ambitious housing development (to restore a resident population to the City) with major new cultural facilities.

Such developments have marked yet another dramatic change in London's character and appearance. The miles of dockland and the older industries have disappeared. A renaissance in the arts has taken place, and there has been a huge growth in the 'service' industries such as travel, tourism and catering. Only the City retains its traditional role as a world centre of banking and finance.

The evidence of these changes is supplied by the dramatic new skyline, the cleaning of major public buildings, and thanks to legislation and the passing of the old industries, a cleaner atmosphere and a cleaner Thames than London has enjoyed for centuries. It is no longer the world's largest city, nor the heart of a mighty empire, but it is, in many respects, a far more pleasant place to live in or to visit.

20th-Century Architecture

Two of London's largest stores, **Harrods** of Knightsbridge and **Selfridges** of Oxford Street, date from the early years of this century, as does the **Old Bailey** (Central Criminal Court) in the City, which is crowned by its celebrated gilded figure of Justice.

Following World War I, London broke away from traditional architecture and design. The new 'Jazz Age' produced the Art Deco **Daily Express Building** in Fleet Street and the **Odeon Cinema,** Leicester Square. Less flamboyant but notable buildings of the period include the **Dorchester Hotel,** Park Lane, **Broadcasting House,** Portland Place, and – in line with the best international architecture of the period – two stores, **Simpson** in Piccadilly and **Peter Jones** in Sloane Square. Many London Transport stations of the 1920s and 1930s were also built to a high standard (although recent face-lifts have changed their character), as were **Battersea Power Station** and the new **Waterloo Bridge,** both designed by Sir Giles Gilbert Scott. The buildings of the **South Bank Arts Centre,** beginning with the **Royal Festival Hall** (1951), reflect changing architectural styles over 25 years.

Telecom Tower (formerly the Post Office Tower), which is more of an engineering feat than a building, and **NatWest Tower** in the City (Britain's tallest structure at the time of writing) are two important landmarks on today's skyline. **Lloyd's** new City headquarters (by Richard Rogers, architect of Paris's Pompidou Centre) is the capital's most striking 'High Tech' building.

CHRONOLOGY

c.43   Roman invaders build Londinium and construct a bridge across the Thames.

61   Queen Boudicca's rebel army burns the city.

410   As Roman forces leave Britain, the Saxons seize London.

9thC   The Danes pillage London. King Alfred drives them out.

1066   William the Conqueror becomes king and starts building the Tower of London.

1215   King John signs the Magna Carta.

1294   An Eleanor Cross is set up at Charing Cross to commemorate the Queen.

1348–9   The Black Death (bubonic plague) kills nearly half the population.

1381   In the Peasants' Revolt, 100,000 men occupy London. The peasants' leader, Wat Tyler, is killed with a dagger.

1397   Richard Whittington, a wealthy merchant, is elected Lord Mayor.

1401   Piped water is brought from Tyburn.

1450   Jack Cade's rebellion of 30,000 Kentish men briefly occupies London.

1455   The Wars of the Roses begin. In 1461 Edward of York is proclaimed king.

1476   Caxton sets up the first printing press in England, near Westminster Abbey.

1483   Edward V, still a child, is imprisoned in the Tower by his uncle, who is proclaimed King Richard III. Edward and his brother disappear, apparently murdered.

1485 Henry VII defeats Richard at Bosworth and establishes the Tudor dynasty.

1509   Henry VIII comes to the throne and marries the first of his six wives.

1536 Henry establishes the Church of England with himself as its head.

1553   Londoners welcome Mary Tudor as queen. Lady Jane Grey, the 'Nine Days' Queen', is executed. Protestants are persecuted for several years.

1558–88   Elizabeth I comes to the throne, with plots against her encouraged by Spain until the defeat of the Armada in 1588. The arts flourish with playwrights Shakespeare, Marlowe, and Jonson, and the composers Tallis, Byrd, and Dowland.

17thC   London expands across the Thames to Southwark and Lambeth.

1605   The Gunpowder Plot, to blow up King James I and Parliament, fails when Guy Fawkes is discovered with the explosives.

1642–60   Parliamentary forces under Oliver Cromwell are supported by London during the Civil War. In 1649, King Charles I is executed at Whitehall and Cromwell becomes Protector, but in 1660 the monarchy is restored under Charles II.

1665   The Great Plague kills a quarter of London's 400,000 inhabitants.

1666   The Great Fire of London destroys much of the city.

1675   A new St Paul's Cathedral is begun by Sir Christopher Wren.

1685–9   James II attempts to impose absolute rule, but is deposed in the Glorious Revolution. The Bill of Rights limits the powers of future monarchs.

1694   City merchants establish the Bank of England.

1730   The Fleet River, by now an open drain, is covered over.

1780   In the Gordon Riots against Roman Catholics a mob overruns London.

19thC   London's population passes 1,000,000. Industrial growth transforms London with the building of canals and railways, expansion of the docks, construction of embankments along the Thames and the opening of the first tunnel underneath it.

1847   The new British Museum is opened.

1851   The Great Exhibition, encouraged by Prince Albert, is held in Hyde Park.

1858   The Royal Opera House opens at Covent Garden.

1863   The first Underground uses special steam trains from Paddington to the City.

1882   The Law Courts are completed in the Strand.

1894   Tower Bridge is opened.

1907   The Central Criminal Court (Old Bailey) is built on the site of Newgate prison.

1914–18   World War I. Bombing from planes and airships causes 2,600 casualties.

1939–45   During World War II London suffers fierce air raids and rocket attacks which destroy much of the Dockland area and the City. People shelter in Underground stations, but 30,000 are killed, 50,000 injured, and many left homeless.

1948   The Olympic Games are held in London.

1951   The Festival of Britain is held on the South Bank. Royal Festival Hall is opened.

1953   Queen Elizabeth II is crowned in Westminster Abbey.

1960 s   The controversial Centre Point building, towering over the West End, is completed and three towerblocks are opened at the Barbican.

1981   Prince Charles is married to Lady Diana Spencer in St Paul's Cathedral. The tallest building in the City is opened for the National Westminster Bank.

1982   The Thames Flood Barrier is completed at Woolwich.

FROM TRAFALGAR SQUARE TO WESTMINSTER

Almost the whole area, from Trafalgar Square at the north end of Whitehall to the Houses of Parliament at the south end, was once covered by the old royal palace of Whitehall, and it is still the centre of government today, with many of the ministries along Whitehall, the prime minister's residence in Downing Street and Parliament in the 'Palace of Westminster'. Up the river on Millbank is the Tate Gallery, London's gallery of British and modern art, while towards Victoria Station is Westminster's Roman Catholic Cathedral, lying behind Victoria Street. This leads back to Westminster Abbey, the greatest of London's medieval buildings and Britain's national shrine.

▬ *TRAFALGAR SQUARE* ★★

MAP IV B4   ⊖ Charing Cross, Leicester Square   ⇌ Charing Cross

Trafalgar Square is the true hub of central London, linking the government quarter of Whitehall, the ceremonial stretch of the Mall, and the commercial West End. It was envisaged by John Nash on the site of the old royal stables as part of his overall plan for west London, but the detailed planning was carried out by Sir Charles Barry in 1840, with the recently completed National Gallery on the north side of the square.

The square's most famous feature is **Nelson's Column,** commemorating the naval hero who died while winning victory in the Battle of Trafalgar (1805). The actual Corinthian column is 145ft (44m) high, and the figure of Nelson adds another 17ft (5m). The bronze reliefs round its base, cast from captured cannon, celebrate that and other victories. The famous lions, also of bronze, are by Sir Edwin Landseer. The fountains, which were not part of the original scheme, were remodelled in 1939 as memorials to two later admirals, Beatty and Jellicoe. The square also has statues to George IV, General Napier, and, just to the south facing Whitehall, Hubert le Sueur's equestrian statue of Charles I with its pedestal reputedly designed by Wren and carved by Grinling Gibbons. In the terrace wall on the north side are displayed metal measures of the standard inch, foot and yard.

The **National Gallery** (*see page 185 for detailed description*) was built by William Wilkins in 1832–8. It has since been considerably enlarged, and a further extension, designed by the American, Robert Venturi, is now in the planning stage. To the east is the **National**

Vaulting of Henry VII's Chapel, Westminster Abbey

Portrait Gallery, containing a fascinating selection of portraits – politicians, kings and queens, scholars and writers are all represented. To the north-east of the square is the church of **St Martin-in-the-Fields,** the burial place of Nell Gwynne, highwayman Jack Sheppard, William Hogarth, Sir Joshua Reynolds and Thomas Chippendale. It was built in 1722–4 by James Gibbs, and has an elegant steeple set centrally above a Classical portico. Today St Martin's is noted for its charity work and for its association with the London orchestra of the same name.

▬ *WHITEHALL* ★★

MAP IV C4–5   ⊖ Charing Cross, Westminster

The Old Palace of Whitehall, which stretched almost the whole way from Trafalgar Square to Parliament Square, was largely created by Henry VIII and continued to serve as a royal residence up to the time of William and Mary, who preferred Kensington Palace. Not long after that, in 1698, most of it was burned down, except for the Banqueting House, which now stands mid-way down the modern thoroughfare of Whitehall.

Completed by Inigo Jones in 1622, the **Banqueting House** was central London's first Renaissance-style building, modelled on Sansovino's Library in Venice. The **painted ceiling** (1635) by Rubens, which celebrates the benefits of wise rule, was commissioned by Charles I – and it was on a scaffold outside the Banqueting House that the king was beheaded in 1649. (*Open Tue–Sat 10am–5.30pm, Sun 2–5.30pm; closed 1 Jan, Good Fri, 24–26 Dec and Bank hols.*) Directly opposite is the Palladian-style but appropriately military looking **Horse Guards** building of 1745 by William Kent. It is guarded by sentries of the Horse Guards Cavalry regiments (*parades Mon–Sat 11am, Sun 10am, 4pm*). On the far side is the broad expanse of **Horse Guards Parade** (flanked to the north by the Admiralty building and to the south by the rear of Downing Street), where the Trooping of the Colour ceremony (originally intended to familiarize troops with their regimental flag before a battle) takes place each June. There are statues to Field Marshals Kitchener, Wolseley and Roberts, and the **Cadiz Memorial,** a huge French mortar mounted on a cast-iron dragon, captured in 1812 during the Peninsular War.

Apart from the **Whitehall Theatre** at the Trafalgar Square end, the rest of Whitehall is given over almost entirely to government buildings, of which the **Treasury** (built in 1733 by William Kent, with later alterations by Sir John Soane) and the **Home** and **Foreign Offices** (built in 1868 by Sir George Gilbert Scott) are suitably weighty and dignified in their different styles. Downing Street is on a more domestic scale, with houses dating from between 1680 and 1766, although they have been greatly modified since. **No. 10 Downing Street** has been the official home of prime ministers since 1731. The Cabinet, composed of leading government ministers, regularly meets there. No. 11 is the home and office of the Chancellor of the Exchequer. At the far end of King Charles Street are the World War II underground **Cabinet War Rooms,** preserved exactly as they were when used by Winston Churchill and his wartime government. (*Open Tue–Sun 10am–5.50pm; closed 1 Jan, Good Fri, May Day, 24–26 Dec.*) Across Whitehall is the **Norman Shaw Building**, named after its architect and dating from 1890. It was formerly New Scotland Yard, one-time headquarters of the Metropolitan Police, standing on that part of the old Whitehall Palace which was once used as a residence by visiting Scottish monarchs. In the centre of Whitehall stands the **Cenotaph** (by Sir Edwin Lutyens, 1919), a national memorial to the dead of two world wars and the focal point for an annual service of remembrance on the nearest Sunday to World War I Armistice Day (11 Nov). Statues to Field Marshals Haig and Montgomery are nearby.

THE PALACE OF WESTMINSTER ★★

MAP IV D5   ⊖ Westminster

The Palace of Westminster, which is occupied now by the Houses of Parliament, was originally a royal palace, created by Edward

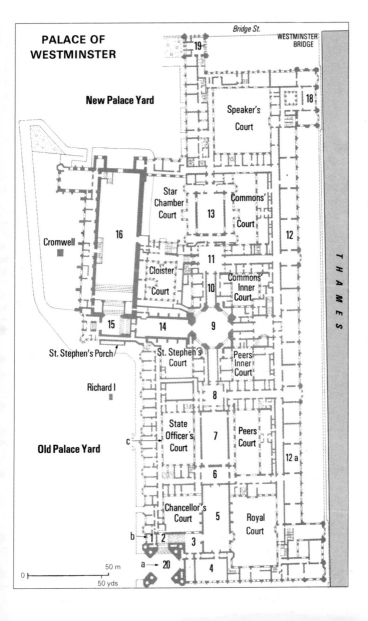

PALACE OF
WESTMINSTER

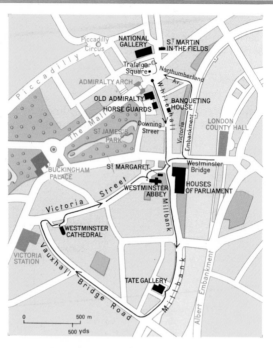

From Trafalgar Square to Westminster

the Confessor in the years before the Norman Conquest of 1066, and gradually enlarged by successive monarchs. Almost from the start it was also a place of debate (a parliament) and legislation,

---

Big Ben

The name 'Big Ben' really refers to the largest bell in the chime of the clock on the Houses of Parliament, although the name is used for both the clock and its bell tower by Westminster Bridge, London's most famous landmark. The clock itself took fifteen years (1844–59) to complete, and became not only England's largest clock, but also its most accurate. The weights hang down a shaft 160ft (48m) deep and the pendulum is 13ft (nearly 4m) long, weighing 685lb (over 300kg). The clock requires winding up only once a week, but before automatic winding-gear was installed in 1913 it took two men 32 hours to complete the operation. The familiar chime, the length of which increases at each quarter until it is sounded complete on the hour, is played on four bells which were made and hung in the belfry without problems, but the fifth bell, which strikes the hour, created enormous difficulties. The first bell made, weighing 16 tons, cracked during trials, and the second cracked after it had been put in place, though it was possible to repair it. The name itself remains something of a mystery, but it seems to have been coined by *The Times*, who announced that 'Big Ben has cracked' in October 1857, playing also upon the news of the retirement, after an epic 60-round fight, of the boxer Benjamin Caunt, a huge man who was landlord of a nearby pub.

Westminster Hall

by stages becoming the main seat of government. In 1843 fire destroyed most of the area, and the present Gothic Revival building (1837–60), with 1,000 rooms and two miles of corridors, rose in its place to designs by Sir Charles Barry and Augustus Welby Pugin, who was responsible for the decorative scheme. It was damaged in World War II and restored by Sir Giles Gilbert Scott but remains one of the finest examples of 19th-century architecture and a potent symbol of the British constitution.

The two main external features of the Houses of Parliament, best seen from Westminster Bridge or from across the river, are the **Victoria Tower** (*20*), which is 336ft (102m) high, and the Clock Tower (*19*), 316ft (96m) high, known as **Big Ben** after the famous bell, which weighs nearly 14 tons and first chimed in 1858. A light at the top of the tower remains lit as long as the Commons is in session. In **Old Palace Yard** is a statue to Richard I (the Lionheart); facing the Victoria Tower is the **Jewel Tower,** a part of the old palace built in 1366 by Edward III, which houses a small museum; and beyond the Tower are the **Victoria Tower Gardens,** with a cast of Rodin's 'Burghers of Calais', inspired by an event in Anglo-French history.

Westminster Hall (*16*) is the major surviving part of the old palace. It was rebuilt for Richard II in 1394–1402 by the king's master mason Henry Yevele and the carpenter Hugh Herland, who were responsible for the magnificent oak hammerbeam roof. On the wall at the south end are six 14th-century statues of kings. The hall has seen royal banquets, the trials of Sir Thomas More, Anne Boleyn, Guy Fawkes and Charles I, the proclamation of Oliver Cromwell as Lord Protector (his statue stands outside), and, in more recent times, the lying-in-state of Sir Winston Churchill. Below Westminster Hall is the **Crypt Chapel,** another medieval survival dating from around 1300. A lobby (*15*) leads to the Neo-Gothic **St Stephen's Hall** (*14*). The Visitors' entrance to

the building is by the **Norman Porch** (*3*) beside the Victoria Tower. The
Robing Room (*4*) with its sumptuous fireplace and carved wooden
ceiling shows Pugin's taste for lavish decoration, and the frescoes by
William Dyce, which use stories from the legend of King Arthur to
represent royal virtues, are very fine. The **Royal Gallery** (*5*) and
Prince's Chamber (*6*) are also richly decorated, with gilt statues of
kings and queens and many royal portraits. The **House of Lords** (*7*)
with the magnificent Gothic throne for State Openings of Parliament
and the woolsack for the Lord Chancellor, is Pugin's masterpiece, and
the rich effect of carved wood and gilding is enhanced by the red
leather of the seats. The **Peer's Lobby** (8) leads to the **Central Hall** (*9*),
beyond which the rooms were reconstructed after air-raid damage in
1941. A corridor with the **Churchill Arch** (*10*) leads to the **Commons
Lobby** (*11*) and the **House of Commons** (*13*), with the Speaker's
Chair, which comes from Australia, and the Table of the House, on
which stands the Mace, symbol of parliamentary authority. Here the
seating is covered in green leather. Tours by order of an M.P. For
admission to Strangers' Galleries of House of Commons (*Mon–Thu
4.15pm, Fri 9.30am*) and House of Lords (*Tue–Wed 2.30pm, Thu 3pm,
Fri 11am*) queue at St Stephen's Porch, when houses are in session.

The Gunpowder Plot

The years following the establishment of the Church of England
under Henry VIII saw much conflict between English Protestants
and Catholics. During the reign of Henry's daughter Mary Tudor,
Catholicism was briefly restored, and over 300 Protestants were put
to death; but for most of the next 150 years Catholics were regarded
as public enemies and could be severely punished for not attending
the Anglican Church. There were a number of Catholic uprisings,
including a conspiracy in 1586 to murder Elizabeth I and put
Catholic Mary Queen of Scots in her place. But the most famous
plot of all was to have taken place on 5 November 1605, at the State
Opening of Parliament, and was intended to kill the king, his
ministers and all the members of both Houses of Parliament. The
plot was organized by Robert Catesby, but it was Guy Fawkes who
was to set off the explosion. The conspirators rented a building next
to the House of Lords in December 1604 and began tunnelling
through the cellars. After 11 months they had reached the vaults of
Parliament and managed to store 36 barrels of gunpowder.
However, the plot was betrayed when an anonymous letter was
sent to one of the peers. A search was made and Guy Fawkes was
discovered with his lantern, matches and tinder box (the plan had
been for him to light the explosive with a slow-burning match and
then to escape in a boat waiting on the River Thames). Fawkes was
arrested and later tortured and executed – along with those of the
other conspirators who had not been killed while attempting to
escape. Ever since then festivities have taken place on 5 November
in his name. The burning of the effigy of Guy Fawkes was a most
important and portentous ceremony and today, on Guy Fawkes or
Bonfire Night, 'Guys' are still burnt on bonfires throughout the
country and fireworks are lit. Children display their home-made
Guys in the streets, and beg passers-by for 'A penny for the Guy',
while before every annual State Opening, the cellars of the Houses
of Parliament are searched.

MILLBANK AND VICTORIA

MAP IV DEF 2–5   ⊖ Pimlico, Victoria, St James's Park   ≉ Victoria

The name of the street that runs past Victoria Tower Gardens along the Thames to Vauxhall Bridge is a reminder of the old Abbey Mill, but the buildings on Millbank all date from this century, including the 32-storey **Millbank Tower** (1965) and the **Tate Gallery** (*for details of collections and opening times see pp.191–6*).

At the top of Vauxhall Bridge Road is **Victoria Station,** the point of arrival for many visitors to London, since it serves both the Channel ports and Gatwick Airport. Nearby, separated from Victoria Street by a small piazza, is the Neo-Byzantine Roman Catholic **Westminster Cathedral** (1895–1903) by John Francis Bentley. Its most striking external feature is the 280ft (85m) domed bell tower, built like the rest of the building of red brick with white stone bands and dressings. The building is 360ft (110m) long and has the widest nave in England. The rich interior decor of marble and mosaics, although impressive, is only half finished. The **Stations of the Cross** (1913–18) are by designer and sculptor Eric Gill. A giant rood or crucifix hangs from the main arch of the nave.

Among all the gleaming new office buildings of Victoria Street is **New Scotland Yard** (1967), headquarters of London's Metropolitan Police. The corner of Victoria Street and Great Smith Street marks the site of William Caxton's first British printing press (1476). Just behind, approached through a gateway from Broad Sanctuary, is **Dean's Yard,** part of the abbey precinct, with **Church House,** used during World War II by both houses of parliament, and **Westminster Abbey Choir School.** The buildings of historic **Westminster School** start in Dean's Yard, although the most interesting of them, **Ashburnham House**, stands in Little Dean's Yard. This house dates from the 1660s and is the finest of its period in London, with a superb staircase. (*Open school Easter hols, Mon–Fri 10am–4pm, closed Good Fri, Easter Mon.*) A few minutes' walk away is **Smith Square** (1726), where the national headquarters of the Conservative Party may be found. In the middle of the square is the baroque **St John's Church** (1714) by Thomas Archer, which was restored after World War II bombing and is now a public hall, frequently used for concerts.

PARLIAMENT SQUARE

MAP IV D4   ⊖ Westminster

Despite the presence of both the Whitehall and Westminster palaces, much of the surrounding district was for centuries slum property until the 1860s, when it was finally cleared and Sir Charles Barry laid out **Parliament Square** as a suitable approach to his new Houses of Parliament. It was replanned earlier this century, making the centre of the square into a large traffic island.

There are statues to British prime ministers Lord Palmerston, George Canning, Sir Robert Peel, Benjamin Disraeli and Sir Winston Churchill; others are to Field Marshal Smuts (by Epstein) and to United States President Abraham Lincoln (a copy of a statue in Chicago). On the west side of the square is the Neo-Gothic **Middlesex Guildhall** (1906); behind this are the **Methodist Central Hall** (1905), used also for public gatherings, and the new **Conference Centre** (1985). On the south side is **St Margaret's,** parish church of the House of Commons. Dating from the 15th century with restorations in the 18th and 19th centuries, it has Tudor monuments and some fine stained glass, including the east window made to commemorate the projected marriage of Catherine of Aragon to Prince Arthur, elder brother of Henry VIII, and the south aisle windows (1967) by John Piper. Samuel Pepys, John Milton, Sir Walter Raleigh and Admiral Blake are buried here. Overshadowing St Margaret's is **Westminster Abbey**.

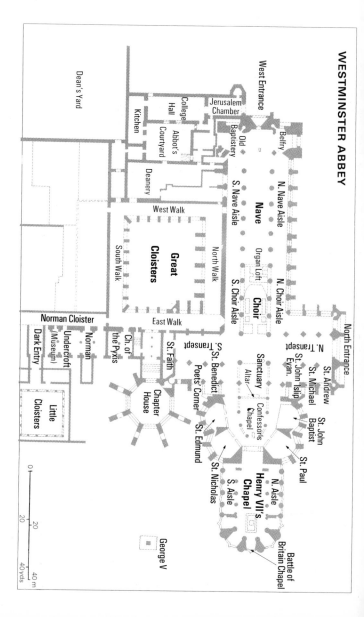

WESTMINSTER ABBEY

Dean's Yard

College Hall
Kitchen
Abbot's Courtyard
Deanery

Jerusalem Chamber
West Entrance
Old Baptistery
Belfry

West Walk
S. Nave Aisle
Nave
N. Nave Aisle

Great Cloisters
South Walk
North Walk
Organ Loft
S. Choir Aisle
Choir
N. Choir Aisle

Norman Cloister
East Walk

Dark Entry
Norman Undercroft (Museum)
Ch. of the Pyxis
St. Faith
S. Transept
St. Benedict
Poets' Corner
N. Transept
Sanctuary Altar
St. John Evan.
St. John Islip
St. Andrew
St. Michael
North Entrance

Little Cloisters
Chapter House
Confessor's Chapel
St. John Baptist
St. Edmund
St. Nicholas
St. Paul

Henry VII's Chapel
S. Aisle
N. Aisle
Battle of Britain Chapel

George V

0 20 40 yds
0 20 40 m

Effigy of Elizabeth I, Westminster Abbey

WESTMINSTER ABBEY ★★★

MAP IV D4   ⊖ Westminster

The first abbey on the site was built in the 7th–8th centuries, but Edward the Confessor started to rebuild the church c.1050–65. Only a few fragments of this church and monastery remain, and the present church was begun in 1245 by Henry III to contain the shrine of his saintly predecessor and as a royal coronation and burial church. The tombs of Henry, his family and descendants are among the Abbey's greatest treasures. The church was completed by the end of the 14th century under the supervision of the master mason Henry Yevele, and in 1503 **Henry VII's Chapel** was begun, a tour de force in Perpendicular style built to replace Henry III's Lady Chapel. The west towers were added by Hawksmoor in 1735. The Abbey has seen the coronation of every English or British monarch since William I in 1066, and many of the nation's most famous men and women are either buried within its precincts or commemorated there.

The most authentic parts of the exterior (which was virtually recased in the drastic 19th-century restoration) are at the east end, in particular the **Chapter House** (1245–50), with its imposing flying buttresses, and **Henry VII's Chapel**, whose curved buttresses have creatures crawling down towards the turrets, which are capped with Tudor domes.

Inside, the nave is impressive for the unity of the 13th- and 14th-century work and for the great height of the vault. The pillars have shafts of dark Purbeck marble, and there is much fine sculptural decoration. Facing the west entrance, in the centre of the nave, is the

Tomb of the Unknown Soldier, commemorating the dead of World War I. Next to it is a commemorative plaque to Sir Winston Churchill, and nearby another to President Roosevelt.

The **Sanctuary** has an Italian mosaic pavement (1268) and contains the wooden sedilia (c.1308) with over-lifesize paintings of kings and saints. On the north side are three great medieval tombs, of Edward I's brother, Edmund Crouchback, Earl of Lancaster (d.1296), and his countess, Aveline (d.1272), and of the king's cousin Aymer de Valence (d.1324). They have large gabled canopies over the effigies and tomb-chests with little figures of 'weepers', originally all painted. Beyond the Sanctuary is **Edward the Confessor's Chapel** containing Edward's shrine and the tombs of eight other kings and queens. The shrine was commissioned in 1241 by Henry III before he had started rebuilding the church. The high base, which contains the tomb, is Italian marble inlay of 1270, but the richly jewelled upper part of the shrine was stolen during the Reformation. This chapel also houses the **Coronation Chair,** made in 1300–01 by Master Walter, the king's painter, to contain the **Stone of Scone** (stone of destiny) which Edward I had taken from the Scots: it stands against a 15th-century stone screen with a frieze of scenes from the life of Edward the Confessor. Close to the chair is the tomb of Edward I (d.1307), a large undecorated chest of black Purbeck marble with no effigy. His queen, Eleanor of Castile (d.1290), is commemorated by an outstandingly beautiful gilded bronze effigy by William Torel on her Purbeck tomb-chest, a companion piece to the effigy of her father-in-law Henry III (d.1272), also made by Torel in 1291. On the south side of the chapel are the tombs of Edward III (d.1377), with an effigy of gilded bronze showing an almost hieratic figure with long hair and beard on a tomb-chest by Yevele, and of his queen, Philippa of Hainault (d.1369), sculpted in marble by Hennequin de Liège with touching realism; also the double tomb of Richard II and his queen, Anne of Bohemia, made in 1394–5. **Henry V's Chantry Chapel** (finished c.1460) is at the east end, with a tomb (1422–c.1430), but only the wooden core of the silver effigy of the king survives. Notable among the many monuments in the ambulatory chapels are the Limoges engraved and enamelled effigy of William de Valence (d.1296) and the elegant alabaster effigy and tomb-chest of John of Eltham (d.1337), both in **St Edmund's Chapel,** and the enormous (37ft/11m-high) tomb of Lord Hunsdon (d.1596) and his wife in the **Chapel of St John the Baptist.**

At the east end of the Abbey is **Henry VII's Chapel** with its magnificent fan vaulting (built by Robert and William Vertue) and the flamboyant Gothic stalls (c.1520) of the Knights of the Order of the Bath, above which hang their banners. In the main body of the chapel is the tomb of Henry VII and Elizabeth of York by Pietro Torrigiani (completed 1518). The gilded bronze figures, in contrast to the architectural sculpture of the chapel, are in full Renaissance style, with realistic effigies and beautiful angel figures at each corner. In the north aisle is the powerfully naturalistic effigy of Queen Elizabeth I (d.1603) on her quite modest tomb by Maximilian Colt, and the **Innocents' Corner** with Colt's tomb of the infant daughters of James I. In the south aisle are Torrigiani's tomb (1513) of Lady Margaret Beaufort, Henry VII's mother, and Cornelius Cure's grand monument (c.1607–12) to Mary Queen of Scots, mother of James I, which has a glorious marble effigy. In the apsidal chapels are three wonderful allegorical monuments by Hubert Le Sueur to James I's cousin, the Duke of Lennox and Richmond (d.1624) and his wife (d.1639), and to the king's favourite, George Villiers, Duke of Buckingham (d.1628). The **Battle of Britain Chapel** at the far end (founded 1947) includes the tombs of RAF leaders Lords Trenchard and Dowding. **Poet's Corner** (in the south transept) has the tombs of Chaucer, Ben Jonson (buried upright), Dryden, Samuel Johnson, Sheridan, Browning and Tennyson; and memorials to Shakespeare, David Garrick, Blake, Milton, Keats, Shelley, Byron, Wordsworth, Dickens, Hardy, Kipling, Dylan Thomas, and, alone among composers, Handel. Others buried in the Abbey or commemorated there are, among scientists and inventors, Sir Isaac Newton, Michael Faraday, Lords Rutherford and Lister, Robert Stephenson and James Watt; and prime ministers Pitt the Elder and Younger, Palmerston, Disraeli, Gladstone, Asquith, Lloyd George and Attlee. Particularly notable among the many elaborate memorials are those of Sir Francis Vere (1609) in the north transept, with his armour on a slab supported by four kneeling knights, the famous **Nightingale Monument** (1761, by Roubiliac) showing Joseph Nightingale trying to protect his young wife from the lance wielded by a gruesome figure of Death, and, at the west end of the north aisle, the monument to Charles James Fox (1810–15), by Westmacott.

The 13th-century **Chapter House** has Gothic vaulting which springs from a single slim central pier, an equally fine tiled floor and 13th- and 14th-century sculptures and paintings. The **Cloisters,** which date from the same period, have a brass rubbing centre. The **Abbey Museum** in the Norman undercroft (separate entrance and admission charge) has wooden or wax funerary effigies of several monarchs, Henry V's shield and helmet from Agincourt, and other treasures. The **Jerusalem Chamber** by the west door of the Abbey contains tapestries and seven medallions of 13th-century stained glass.

PLACES TO STOP

Around Trafalgar Square:

National Gallery Restaurant (*daily 10am–5pm, Sun from 2pm*).
Sherlock Holmes (Whitbreads), 10 Northumberland St; pub with restaurant celebrating the famous fictional detective.

Near Victoria:

Goring Hotel – lounge, 15 Beeston Place, Grosvenor Gardens (*daily 10am–6pm; tea 4–5.30pm*).
Ebury Wine Bar, 139 Ebury St.
Costa Coffee Shop and Café, 324 Vauxhall Bridge Rd (*Mon–Sat 8.30am–6pm*).
Orange Brewery, 37 Pimlico Rd; lively pub with home-brewed beer.

Near Parliament Square and Victoria Street:

Methuselah's – wine bar and brasserie, 29 Victoria St (*Mon–Fri*).
Carriages – wine bar, 43 Buckingham Palace Rd (*Mon–Fri & summer weekends*).
Tapster – wine bar, 3 Brewers Green, Buckingham Gate (*Mon–Fri to 8.30pm*).
Wilkins – vegetarian café, 61 Marsham St (*Mon–Fri 8am–5pm*).
Buckingham Arms (Youngs) – pub, 62 Petty France; lunchtime snacks.

SHOPPING

Trafalgar Square:

National Gallery Shop (*daily 10am–5.40pm, Sun from 2pm*); gifts, stationery, reproductions and art books.

Near Victoria:

Tate Gallery Shop (*daily, 10am–5.30pm, Sun from 2.30pm*).
Inca, 45 Elizabeth St (*Mon–Sat 10am–6pm, Sat to 2pm*): Peruvian and other ethnic fashions.

Itinerary 2

ROYAL LONDON: ST JAMES'S
AND MAYFAIR

S t James's Palace, built by Henry VIII, was one of the
principal residences of the English monarchs until the
early 19th century, and St James's Park was always a favourite place for royal recreation. Buckingham Palace became
the official London residence of the reigning sovereign during Victoria's reign, and the surrounding area has assumed a
certain regal and gracious aspect of its own, so that today this
whole district may quite aptly be called 'Royal London'.

THE MALL *

MAP IV B4 C3–4   ⊖ St James's Park, Charing Cross

The Mall, which takes its name from a once-fashionable ball
game, runs in a broad, straight line for half-a-mile between
Trafalgar Square and **Buckingham Palace.** After the Restoration
of 1660 it became a popular, tree-lined promenade on the north
side of **St James's Park.** John Nash's terraces, which were built
in the early 19th century, added grandeur to the scene, and the
Mall was replanned in 1910 by Sir Aston Webb as a processional
route for important state occasions.

Admiralty Arch, part of the 1910 reconstruction, marks the Mall's
eastern end leading to Trafalgar Square. On the south side is the rear of
the **Admiralty,** and the **World War II Citadel,** a bomb-proof communi-
cations centre. There is also a statue to the explorer Captain James
Cook. On the north side is Nash's **Carlton House Terrace** (1837), the
last and grandest of his Regency projects. Once the home of prime
ministers Palmerston and Gladstone, the Terrace now houses various
institutions, including the **Mall Galleries** (*open daily 10am–5pm during
exhibitions*) and the **Institute of Contemporary Arts** (*open daily
10am–11pm*), which has a gallery (*10am–8pm*), cinema, video library
and restaurant. Both have changing exhibitions. **St James's Park,**
which borders the south side of the Mall, was inaugurated by Henry
VIII in 1532 and is the oldest of London's royal parks. It was a particular
favourite of Charles II, who created the lake, which is famous for its
wild fowl. There was also a large aviary, from which **Birdcage Walk**
takes its name. The view from across the lake, eastwards to Whitehall
and westwards to Buckingham Palace, is one of the most picturesque
in London. At the end, facing Horse Guards Parade, is the **Guards
Memorial** (1926). By Birdcage Walk are the renovated **Wellington
Barracks** (1833) and new **Guards Chapel** (1963). Just behind Birdcage
Walk and the bronze *Mother and Child* by Henry Moore, is **Queen
Anne's Gate,** a beautifully preserved enclave of 18th-century houses,
with a statue to the monarch.

Buckingham Palace from St James's Park

▬ BUCKINGHAM PALACE *

MAP IV D2 ⊖ St James's Park, Victoria, Hyde Park Corner
⇌ Victoria

The original early 18th-century Buckingham House, home of the
Duke of Buckingham, was bought by George III in 1762. But it
was his son, the Prince Regent (later George IV), who began its
conversion into a real palace, employing his favourite architect,
John Nash. Crises over the expense of the enterprise meant that
the building work was far from finished when Queen Victoria
came to the throne in 1837 and took up residence in the Palace.
During her reign the Palace was enlarged several more times,
by Edward Blore and Sir James Pennethorne. Sir Aston Webb
added the weighty, Neo-Georgian east front, facing the Mall, in
1913. The present building has some 600 rooms, and there is a
large garden, with a lake, at the rear. The royal standard flies
over the Palace when the sovereign is in residence.

The **Queen's Gallery** in Buckingham Palace Road, once the
Palace chapel, has changing exhibitions from the Royal Collection of
paintings and drawings, including works by Leonardo da Vinci. (*Open
Tue–Sat & Bank hol Mon 11am–5pm, Sun 2–5pm; closed Mon except
Bank hols, Good Fri, 25–26 Dec and between exhibitions.*) The **Royal
Mews,** also in Buckingham Palace Road, was built by Nash and is
separate from the Palace itself; it houses the various royal coaches,
including the Gold State Coach (1762), used at coronations. (*Open
Wed & Thu 2–4pm; closed Ascot Week and during State visits.*) The
Changing of the Guard ceremony is usually performed at 11am (some

---

Maundy Money

The ritual of Maundy is one of the longest preserved customs in
which the British monarch still takes part. The word 'maundy'
comes from the Latin 'mandatum' meaning 'command', and it is
associated with the command Jesus gave his disciples as he symbo-
lically washed their feet before the Last Supper. The command was
that they should love one another. From the time of Edward III in
the 14th century, it was the custom for the king of England to wash
the feet of poor people in remembrance of that command. Every
Maundy Thursday (the day before Good Friday) some of London's
poor people would have their feet cleaned in warm scented water
by the Yeomen of the Laundry; the monarch would then carry out a
ceremonial washing, and food and clothing would be distributed.
Queen Elizabeth I, at the age of 39, performed this ceremony at her
palace at Greenwich, attended by 39 ladies and gentlewomen,
washing the feet of 39 poor people. Since 1689, the giving of money
has taken the place of foot washing, and this has become known as
Maundy Money. Each person receives specially minted silver pen-
nies equalling in value the age of the king or queen. The money is
contained in small leather purses which are distributed by a Yeoman of the Guard. Bunches of sweet-scented flowers and herbs are
carried, and the clergy carry linen towels over their shoulders as a
reminder of the washing ceremony that used to take place. Since
1953 the ceremony, which used to be held at Westminster Abbey,
takes place in cathedrals around the country.

The Game of Pall Mall

On 2 April 1661, Pepys entered in his diary, 'In St James's Park, where I saw the Duke of York playing at Pelemele, the first time that I ever saw the sport.'

The Duke's brother, King Charles II, had recently formed what is called the Mall in St James's Park for the playing of this game. There had previously existed a walk for this purpose (lined with trees) on the ground now occupied by the street called Pall Mall. The game was introduced from France, probably about the beginning of the 17th century; but the derivation of the name appears to be from the Italian *Palamaglio*, i.e. *palla*, a ball, and *maglio*, a mallet. The aim of the game was to drive a ball some 2½ ins (6cm) in diameter along a straight alley and through a ring at the end which was raised on a post – a kind of elevated golf-hole. The mallet was about 3ft 8ins (110cm) in length. The alley was hardened and covered with pounded shells so as to provide a perfectly smooth surface, and the sides seem to have been boarded, to prevent the ball from going off the straight line. Charles II was clearly an excellent player, but the craze for the game was short-lived and seems to have died out by the end of the 17th century.

times 11.30am) on alternate days in the Palace forecourt (*telephone 246 8041 for details*). The regiments of ceremonial Foot Guards who perform the ceremony – Grenadier, Coldstream, Scots, Irish and Welsh Guards – all wear the familiar dark blue trousers, scarlet tunic and black bearskin hat but are distinguished by the different colours of the plumes in their bearskins and by the distribution of buttons on their tunics. In front of Buckingham Palace, the **Queen Victoria Memorial** (1910) marks the west end of the Mall.

ST JAMES'S PALACE *

MAP IV C3   ⊖ Green Park, St James's Park

Between the Mall and Pall Mall stands **St James's Palace,** Henry VIII's 16th-century Tudor residence and the last royal palace in London to be built as such. Later modified by several famous architects and craftsmen – Wren, Grinling Gibbons, Hawksmoor, Kent – its east wing was destroyed by fire in 1809.

Although no longer a royal residence, the Palace retains some ceremonial functions – newly arrived ambassadors are 'accredited to the Court of St James'. Facing it, on Marlborough Road, is Inigo Jones's **Queen's Chapel** (1627), built for Charles I's queen, Henrietta Maria, and London's earliest Renaissance-style church (*open Sun for services at 8.30 and 11.15am*). Beside the chapel is the 18th-century **Marlborough House,** formerly a royal residence, now a Commonwealth Centre; its principal salon is decorated with paintings of the Battle of Blenheim by Louis Laguerre. On the other side of the Palace are Nash's **Clarence House** (1828), still a royal residence, and **Lancaster House** (1824–41), with splendid interior decor, now a government reception and conference centre (*limited public access*).

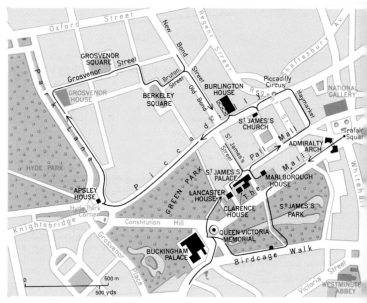

Royal London: St James's and Mayfair

▬ *PALL MALL AND ST JAMES'S STREET*

MAP IV B2–4 C3   ⊖ Green Park, Piccadilly Circus

Taking its name from the same game that was later played on – and gave its name to – the Mall, **Pall Mall** was laid out in the time of Charles II. In the 18th century both streets were famous for their coffee-houses, and are now known for their clubs.

These include, in St James's Street, **Boodle's** (1765), **Brooks's** (1778) and **White's** (1788), and in Pall Mall, the **Royal Automobile, Junior Carlton, Reform** and **Travellers,** the last two in Renaissance-style palazzi by Barry (*no public access*). At the corner with Lower Regent Street, leading back to the Mall, are **Waterloo Place** and the **Duke of York Steps** and **Memorial Column** (1834). The Duke of York was George IV's brother, a popular but profligate soldier, of whom it was said that the Tuscan-style column had to be tall enough to keep him from his creditors! It stands 124ft (38m) high. In **Waterloo Place,** which marks the southern end of Nash's **Regent Street** (*see p.153*), is the **Guards Crimea Memorial,** partly made from captured Russian cannon, which includes a statue of Florence Nightingale, and a statue of polar explorer Captain Robert Falcon Scott. A commemorative plaque marks General de Gaulle's World War II Free French headquarters in Carlton Gardens. The **Athenaeum** (1828, Decimus Burton) in Classical Revival style, is considered to be London's most distinguished club.

▬ *THE HAYMARKET AND PICCADILLY CIRCUS* ★

MAP IV A3 B4   ⊖ Piccadilly Circus

The Haymarket, which runs parallel to Lower Regent Street, was indeed once a hay, straw and cattle market. The **Theatre Royal** (1831, Nash) with its Corinthian portico, is one of London's most handsome buildings. Facing it is **Her Majesty's Theatre,** the fourth one on that site, behind which is the **Royal Opera Arcade** (1818, Nash), London's oldest shopping arcade. Piccadilly Circus is no longer a 'circus' as such, due to a changed traffic scheme, which required the re-siting of the statue and fountain of **Eros** (by Sir Alfred Gilbert). This was erected in 1893 as a memorial to the philanthropist Lord Shaftesbury and was originally intended, not as a pagan god of love, but as an angel of Christian Charity!

PICCADILLY *

MAP IV B2–3 C1   ⊖ Piccadilly Circus, Green Park, Hyde Park Corner

Piccadilly owes its name to a 17th-century dressmaker who created a type of frilly collar called a 'picadil' and built a house in the vicinity. The thoroughfare, with **Green Park** on the south side for much of its length, was largely developed during the 18th century, and was the site of some of London's most palatial homes. It is now one of the main commercial arteries of the West End. Green Park itself has seen some famous events, including the fireworks display celebrating the Peace of Aix-la-Chapelle (1748), for which Handel wrote his 'Royal Fireworks' music.

St James's Church (1684, Wren), on the south side of Piccadilly, has a large handsome interior, with reredos, font and organ case by Grinling Gibbons. It organizes excellent series of lunchtime and evening concerts. Attached to it is the **London Brass Rubbing Centre** (*open Mon–Sat 10am–6pm, Sun noon–6pm*), with replicas of memorial brasses from many churches. On the corner of Duke Street is the oldest-established shop in Piccadilly, now a fashionable department store, **Fortnum and Mason,** founded in 1705. Jermyn Street, south of and parallel with Piccadilly, also contains some of London's oldest shops. Piccadilly Arcade connects the two streets. On Piccadilly's north side is **Burlington House** (1717, with extensions), home of the **Royal Academy,** the nation's oldest fine arts society, founded in 1768. Its permanent collection includes paintings by Reynolds, Gainsborough, Stubbs, Turner and others, with sculpture by Michelangelo. It holds changing exhibitions throughout the year, including the famous Summer Exhibition. (*Open daily 10am–6pm; closed Good Fri, 25 Dec.*)

Behind Burlington House, in Burlington Gardens, is the **Museum of Mankind,** a branch of the British Museum, with ethnic exhibits from around the world. The collections of sculpture from Nigeria, Ghana and other African countries and of Oceanic and Native American art are outstanding. (*Open Mon–Sat 10am–5pm, Sun 2.30–6pm; closed 1 Jan, Good Fri, May Day, 24–27 Dec.*) The **Albany** (1774), on the east side of Burlington House, is one of Piccadilly's original residences and the address of many celebrities. On the other side is **Burlington Arcade** (1819), one of several elegant West End shopping arcades, based on continental models, all dating from about the same time. At the north-east corner of Green Park is the **Ritz Hotel** (1906), in opulent French Empire style, the first steel-framed building in London.

HYDE PARK CORNER

MAP III CD6   ⊖ Hyde Park Corner

Hyde Park Corner, where both Decimus Burton's Greek-Corinthian **Constitution Arch** (1827), surmounted by a bronze Chariot of Victory, and his Greek-Ionic **Screen** were originally intended as a ceremonial link between Buckingham Palace and Hyde Park, is now central London's busiest traffic intersection.

Next to the Screen stands **Apsley House,** built by Robert Adam in 1771, though much altered externally when it became the Duke of Wellington's home in 1828. It is now the **Wellington Museum,** preserving many of his apartments, his household and military effects, mementoes of his great adversary Napoleon, and a fine collection of paintings, with canvasses by Correggio, Vermeer, Brueghel, Rubens, Velasquez and Goya. At one time, it was known as No. 1 London, being the first building within the boundaries of the city, next to the Hyde Park turnpike.(*Open Tue–Thu & Sat 10am–6pm, Sun 2–6pm, closed Bank hols.*) Facing Apsley House is the **Achilles Statue** (1822), cast in bronze from captured French cannon, another tribute to the 'Iron Duke'.

▬▬ MAYFAIR *

MAPS III AB6; IV ABC1–2   ⊖ Marble Arch, Bond Street, Green Park

North of Piccadilly is Mayfair. The name comes from a cattle market or fair held each May until the early 18th century, although the district, one of London's most prestigious, extends far beyond the vicinity of the old market.

Mayfair is bounded on the west by Park Lane, today a very busy thoroughfare, with some famous hotels – **Grosvenor House**, the **Dorchester,** the tall **London Hilton** and the **Inn on the Park** overlooking Hyde Park. A few surviving town houses are a reminder of more leisurely days. Curzon Street has Georgian terraced houses; also **Crewe House** (1730) in its own grounds; and almost opposite, **Shepherd Market,** named after architect Edward Shepherd, an enclave of small shops, restaurants and pubs. The **Church of the Immaculate Conception** (1844), Farm Street, headquarters of the English Jesuits, has a notable Gothic Revival interior and high altar by Pugin, while Berkeley Square has 18th- and 19th-century houses on its west side. **Grosvenor Chapel** (1739), South Audley Street, is in American Colonial style, and **Grosvenor Square** (1731), one of London's largest squares and for a long time Mayfair's most exclusive address, has strong US connections. In World War II No. 20 was General Eisenhower's headquarters. The US Embassy (1959, Saarinen) occupies the whole of the west side, and there is a statue to President Roosevelt (1948).

Bond Street (Old and New), named after Sir Thomas Bond, a 17th-century court financier, is an exclusive centre for luxury goods and antiques. **Sotheby's** of New Bond Street, world-famous fine art auctioneers and valuers, was founded in 1744 and moved to its present address in 1917. The sculpture over the door is Egyptian (c.1600 BC). The **Royal Arcade** (1879), patronized by Queen Victoria, connects Old Bond Street with Albemarle Street, where the **Royal Institution** houses the **Michael Faraday Museum**, with a reconstruction of the scientist's laboratory. (*Open Tue–Thu 1–4pm; closed Bank hols.*)

▬▬ PLACES TO STOP

The Mall and St James's:

ICA Restaurant and Bar, Nash House, The Mall (*Tue–Sun noon–9pm*).
Two Chairmen (Courage) – pub, 1 Warwick House St, Cockspur St.
Red Lion (Ind Coope) – pub, 2 Duke of York St.
Red Lion (Watney Combe Reid) – pub, 23 Crown Passage, Pall Mall.
Green's Champagne and Oyster Bar, 36 Duke St (*Mon–Fri to 8pm*).
Crowns Wine and Coffee Bar, 3 Crown Passage (*Mon–Fri 9.30am–8pm*).

Piccadilly Circus:

Bentley's – wine and oyster bar, 11 Swallow St (*Mon–Fri to 11pm, Sat to 3pm*).
New Piccadilly Hotel – lounge, Piccadilly (*daily 8am–midnight, tea 3–5.30pm*).

Piccadilly:

Brown's Hotel – lounge, Dover St (*daily 9am–12.30am, tea 3–6pm*).
Ritz Hotel – Palm Court, Piccadilly (*daily 10am–2pm, tea 3.30–5.30pm, 6–10.30pm*).
Richoux – pâtisserie, 172 Piccadilly (*daily 8.30am–11.30pm, Sun from 10am, Sat 9am–midnight*).
Dover Street Wine Bar, 8 Dover St (*Mon–Fri lunchtime, Mon–Sat 6.30pm–2.30am*).

Hyde Park Corner and Park Lane:

Dorchester Hotel – Promenade and Cocktail Bar, Park Lane (*daily, 9am–1am, tea 3–6pm*).
Inn on the Park – lounge, Hamilton Place (*daily 9am–2am*).

Grosvenor Square and Mayfair:

London Marriott Hotel – Regent Lounge, Grosvenor Square (*daily 24 hrs, teas*).
L'Autre – wine bar, Shepherd St (*Mon–Fri lunchtimes, Mon–Sat 5.30–11.30pm*).
Down's – wine bar, 5 Down St (*daily*).
Audley (Clifton) – pub, 41 Mount St; bar and restaurant food.
Bunch of Grapes – pub, 16 Shepherd Market; lunches.

Bond Street:

Westbury Hotel – lounge, New Bond St (*daily 24 hrs, teas*).

▬ SHOPPING

Most shops in this area open at 9 or 9.30am and close at 5.30pm, Mon–Fri, often earlier Sat.

St James's Street (*Sat to 1pm*).

James Lock, No. 6; famous hatter.

Jermyn Street (*Sat to around 4pm*).

Turnbull & Asser, No. 71; shirtmakers.
Foster & Son, No. 83 (*Sat to noon*); bootmaker.
Paxton & Whitfield, No. 93; old-established speciality cheese shop.

Piccadilly (*Sat to around 5pm*).

Fortnum & Mason, No. 181; historic department store famed for its food halls. Plus Fountain Restaurant.
Hatchards, No. 187; best general bookshop in town.
St James's Church – craft market (*Fri–Sat 10am–6pm*).

Burlington Arcade (*Sat to 1pm*) – *speciality shops.*

Haymarket:

The Design Centre, No. 28 (*Mon–Sat 10am–8pm, Mon to 6pm, Sun 1–6pm*); products which have received Design Centre approval for safety and good design. Plus café.
Burberry's, No. 18 (*Mon–Sat 9am–5.30pm, Thu to 7pm*).

New Bond Street (*Sat to 1pm; many fashion shops Thu to 7.30pm, Sat to 5.30pm*) – *art galleries, high fashion, jewellery and antiques:*

White House, No. 51; finest household linens.
Smythson, No. 54; bespoke stationery, diaries.
Asprey's, No. 165; London's grandest gift shop.

Itinerary 3

FROM CHARING CROSS TO THE TOWER OF LONDON

The Strand, which once ran along the north bank of the Thames, leads from Westminster to the City of London, the boundary being marked by Temple Bar, near the Law Courts and the Temple. There its name changes to Fleet Street, still the home of some of London's newspapers. At Ludgate Circus, site of one of the ancient city gates, the road climbs to St Paul's Cathedral, the supreme masterpiece of Sir Christopher Wren, and continues parallel to the river as far as the Monument, also by Wren, which commemorates the end of the Great Fire of London in 1666. The eastern boundary of the City is marked by the Tower of London – built just outside the city walls by William the Conqueror – which recalls some of the bloodiest incidents in English history.

▄▄▄ CHARING CROSS AND THE STRAND

MAP IV AB5 ⊖ Embankment, Charing Cross ⇌ Charing Cross

Dr Johnson said that 'the full tide of human existence is at Charing Cross.' At different times it served as a place of execution, the site of a puppet theatre and the place of arrival and departure for millions of soldiers in World War I, but its fame today rests on its railway station, which houses what was one of Victorian London's most palatial hotels. In the station forecourt stands a replica of the Gothic cross marking the final resting place, on the way to Westminster Abbey, of Edward I's dead queen, Eleanor of Castile.

The **Strand,** meaning a stretch of beach or sandy bank, was originally a bridle path when the course of the Thames was wider still. It was the main road between the City and the Palace of Westminster from the Middle Ages right up to the creation of the Embankment, and for a long time it was graced by large houses for the nobility and the clergy. It remains one of London's busiest thoroughfares, devoted equally to commerce and entertainment.

On the north side of the Strand are the **Adelphi** and **Vaudeville Theatres** and the **Strand Palace Hotel,** while on the south is the **Savoy Hotel.** This was London's most prestigious hotel when it was opened by the impresario Richard D'Oyly Carte in 1889, with the celebrated Auguste Escoffier as chef. One of his creations was 'Pêche

Melba' for the singer Dame Nellie Melba. The adjoining **Savoy Theatre** (opened 1881, refurbished 1929) was also promoted by D'Oyly Carte and is forever associated with the first productions of the 'Savoy Operas' of W.S. Gilbert and Sir Arthur Sullivan. The adjacent **Savoy Chapel,** dedicated to the Royal Victorian Order, dates back to the 16th century, but most of the building is more recent. **Savoy Hill,** first premises of the BBC, from 1922 to 1932, is commemorated by a plaque (No. 2 Savoy Place).

Somerset House by Sir William Chambers, dating from 1776, stands to the east of Waterloo Bridge. It is one of London's grandest Georgian buildings, much enhanced by its position, which is best appreciated from Waterloo Bridge or from the South Bank Arts Centre across the river. The massive stone arcade supporting the main part of the building, like the York Watergate (*see p.121*), indicates the river-front before the construction of the Embankment. Most of Somerset House is used for government offices; while the east wing, added in 1835 by Sir Robert Smirke, houses **King's College,** a part of London University. The eastern end of the Strand is marked by two well-known churches, both on island sites surrounded by traffic. **St Clement Danes** (1682) is a Wren church, badly damaged in World War II and afterwards restored as an RAF Memorial Chapel. A bronze statue of Dr Samuel Johnson, a regular member of the congregation in his time, faces Fleet Street. The steeple was built by James Gibbs, who had recently completed the companion church of **St Mary-le-Strand** (1717).

The **Aldwych** (derived from an Anglo-Saxon word meaning 'Old Settlement') is the main part of a big development carried out in the early years of this century, a broad crescent that connects the Strand with **Kingsway,** and London's closest equivalent in scale to Hauss-mann's Paris boulevards. The **Strand** and **Aldwych Theatres** are here, as well as the **Waldorf Hotel. Bush House,** home of the BBC's overseas services, is flanked by **India House** and **Australia House,** all in grandiose style.

Frost Fairs

On several recorded occasions part of the River Thames has frozen solid and Londoners have taken advantage of this to turn it into a sort of pleasure ground. In the winter of 1564 lively games of football took place there and in 1684 the diarist John Evelyn recorded how all sorts of booths were arranged in 'streets' upon the ice. During the winter of 1715–16, the river was thickly frozen for a distance of several miles, and entertainments to be enjoyed included the roasting of a whole ox on the ice. For weeks in January 1740 people lived in temporary 'towns' on the frozen water; whilst at the 'frost fair' of 1814, a sheep was cooked and sold in slices as 'Lapland mutton'. There was also music, dancing, merry-go-rounds and skittle games. The ice, which was solid between London and Blackfriars bridges, lasted for nearly a week; unfortunately the thaw, when it came, was sudden. Some of the traders, reluctant to lose customers, stayed longer than was wise; three people were drowned, vast numbers got soaked, and a strange assortment of tents, merry-go-rounds and printing presses could be seen stranded on blocks of ice which floated down the river. In 1832 old London Bridge, with its narrow arches, was replaced by a new bridge which allowed the water to flow more freely: the River Thames never again froze in the same way.

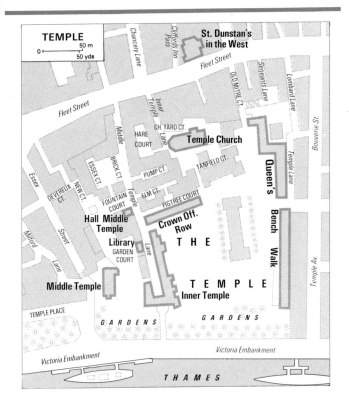

THE TEMPLE AND THE LAW COURTS **

MAP V BC1 ⊖ Temple

The **Temple,** situated between Fleet Street and the Thames, takes its name from the Knights Templar, the medieval paramilitary order who owned the land until the 14th century. It then became the domain of lawyers, and has remained so, forming the Inner and Middle Temple, two of the Inns of Court. It has retained its cloistered air, and the quiet courtyards have the atmosphere of a university rather than a bustling city centre.

The **Temple Church,** built by the Templars in the 12th century (with 19th- and 20th-century restoration), is a blend of Norman and Gothic styles, with a rare circular nave, modelled either on the Church of the Holy Sepulchre or the Dome of the Rock, Jerusalem. Inside are stone effigies of Templar Knights, a tiny penitential cell, a fine 17th-century carved reredos, and windows bearing the crests of the Inner and Middle Temples. (*Open Apr–Oct, Mon–Sat 10am–5pm; Nov–Mar, 10am–4.30pm, Sun 2–4pm; Christmas Day, services only; closed 26 Dec.*) **Middle Temple Hall** (14th–16th centuries) has an oak double-hammerbeam roof and Tudor furnishings, as well as royal portraits and suits of armour. The hall is rich in history; Shakespeare's *Twelfth Night* was played here at Candlemas (2 Feb) 1601. (*Open Mon–Fri 10am–noon, 3–4.30pm, Sat 10am–4pm by appointment; closed Sun and Bank hols.*) **King's Bench Walk** (Inner Temple) has terraces built

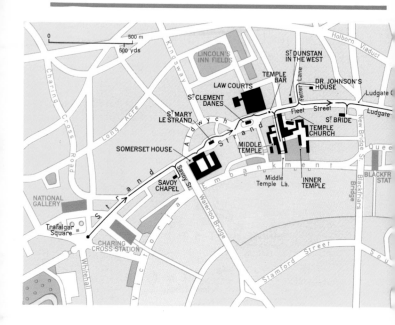

mainly to designs by Wren; playwright Oliver Goldsmith lived at No. 3. **Inner** and **Middle Temple Gardens** extend to the Victoria Embankment.

Across the Strand are the **Law Courts** (Royal Courts of Justice), built in 1874–82 to the design of G.E. Street and London's last major essay in the Gothic Revival style. The complex of buildings, with over 1,000 rooms and four miles of corridors, deal mainly with civil cases. Although Street's plans were not fully carried out, it is a superb building. The **Main Hall** (*usually open to the public*) is rich in statuary and decoration, while over the main entrance are statues of Christ, King Solomon and King Alfred. There is also a museum of legal costume.

▬▬ *FLEET STREET*

MAP V B1–2   ⊖ Temple, Blackfriars   ⇌ Blackfriars

Most of the area surrounding Fleet Street was incorporated into the City of London as it expanded westwards beyond the original Roman Wall during the Middle Ages. The street itself takes its name from the River Fleet, which ran its course from Hampstead, down Farringdon Street and into the Thames at Blackfriars. It was channelled underground during the 18th century. The western end of **Fleet Street** is at **Temple Bar,** where there was a gate marking the limit of the City from the 13th century. Traditionally the sovereign, when visiting the City, stops here to ask permission of the Lord Mayor to enter. The Lord Mayor offers his sword as a sign of loyalty, and this is then carried in front of the royal procession to show that the monarch is under his protection. The gate was rebuilt by Wren but removed in 1870 to Theobalds Park (Hertfordshire) to ease traffic congestion, and replaced by a memorial surmounted by a griffin, one of the emblems of the City.

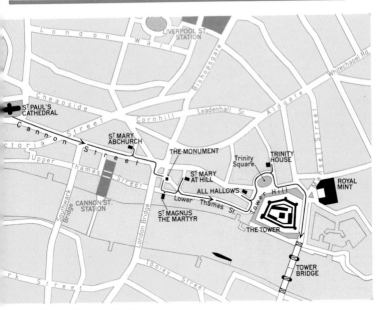

From Charing Cross to the Tower

Coffee Houses

An exotic new drink was brought to England in the 17th century: this had arrived in Europe from Arabia and was an infusion of coffee beans. The first coffee house was actually set up in Oxford, but in 1652 London's Cornhill had its own establishment in St Michael's Alley. Soon there were many coffee houses in the City – along the Strand and Fleet Street. The new drink was supposed to be beneficial to the health and to cure the effects of too many hours spent in a tavern; it certainly appeared to encourage conversation. In the club-like atmosphere of the coffee houses, men would meet to discuss politics, literature and gossip. Chocolate, imported from the West Indies, was soon drunk in similar surroundings. Distinguished men of the day such as Dr Johnson, David Garrick, Joseph Addison and Richard Steele frequented such places; and in time the coffee and chocolate houses developed their specialist interests from the subjects discussed there. *The Tatler* magazine, founded by Steele in 1709, first reported 'entertainment' from White's Chocolate House, 'poetry' from Will's Coffee House, and 'foreign and domestic news' from St James's Coffee House. *The Spectator* was brought out by Steele and Addison shortly afterwards. Newspapers, which were printed in relatively small quantities, were circulated amongst the coffee and chocolate drinkers; and gradually newspaper offices crowded out the coffee houses in Fleet Street. Business talk at Lloyd's Coffee House became a business in itself, as Lloyd's became and remained one of the most important names in the world of insurance. Establishments in the district around Pall Mall and St James's, like White's Chocolate House, developed into the select gentlemen's clubs that are there today.

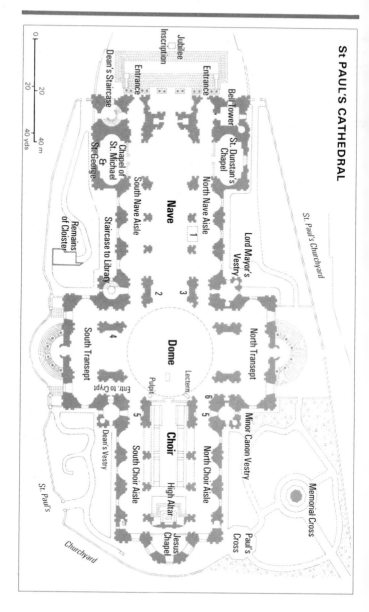

St PAUL'S CATHEDRAL

St. Paul's Churchyard

Jubilee Inscription

Dean's Staircase

Entrance

Entrance

Bell Tower

St. Dunstan's Chapel

Chapel of St. Michael & St. George

South Nave Aisle

North Nave Aisle

Nave

Lord Mayor's Vestry

Remains of Cloister

Staircase to Library

Dome

North Transept

South Transept

Minor Canon Vestry

Entr. to Crypt

Pulpit

Lectern

Choir

Dean's Vestry

South Choir Aisle

North Choir Aisle

High Altar

Jesus Chapel

Paul's Cross

Memorial Cross

St. Paul's

Churchyard

Fleet Street runs almost due east to **Ludgate Circus,** site of an even older, Roman, gateway across the Fleet river and named after the legendary Celtic King Lud. The street and its neighbourhood was the traditional home of the big national newspapers, although new printing technology is taking some of them to premises elsewhere. The two most impressive newspaper buildings are the **Daily Telegraph Building** (1928) in the best 'modernistic' style of the period, and the slightly later **Daily Express Building** (1932) in the even more flamboyant Art Deco style. Also in Fleet Street itself is **St Dunstan's Church** (St Dunstan-in-the-West), with many historical associations, though rebuilt in Gothic Revival style in the last century as part of a street widening scheme. The old bracket clock, which was mentioned in Dickens's *Barnaby Rudge* and several other novels, was restored to the new church building in 1935 and features two strange figures, probably Gog and Magog. Nearby, at No. 17 Gough Square is **Dr Johnson's House,** where he compiled much of his celebrated *Dictionary*. His household effects and a first edition of the *Dictionary* are on display. It is the only original house left in the square. (*Open May–Sep, Mon–Sat 11am–5.30pm; Oct–Apr, Mon–Sat 11am–5pm; closed Bank hols.*) On the opposite side of Fleet Street, forming part of the narrow passage leading to the area of the Temple, is **Prince Henry's Room,** with Tudor and Jacobean decoration (*open Mon–Fri 1.45–5pm, Sat 1.45–4.30pm; closed Sun and Bank hols*). Just south of Fleet Street is **St Bride's Church,** with Wren's tallest steeple (226ft/79m), looking something like an extended telescope or a wedding-cake of many tiers. World War II bombing revealed Roman remains in the crypt, which is now a museum of ancient relics. Nearby, in Bride Lane, is the **St Bride Printing Library,** with a display of early printing presses and typefaces (*open Mon–Fri 9.30am–5pm*).

ST PAUL'S CATHEDRAL ***

MAP V B3   ⊖ St Paul's

At the top of Ludgate Hill stands **St Paul's Cathedral,** which replaced the earlier Norman-Gothic cathedral burnt down in the Great Fire, and was originally conceived by Sir Christopher Wren as the centrepiece of his plan for the reconstructed City. Work began on the great Renaissance edifice in 1676 and was finished in 1711, when the last stone in the lantern above the dome was set in place by the 79-year-old architect's son. St Paul's was damaged during World War II but was saved from destruction by a special corps of fire-watchers. It has been the setting for many great state occasions, including the funerals of Admiral Lord Nelson (1806), the Duke of Wellington (1852) and Sir Winston Churchill (1965), and the wedding of Prince Charles and Lady Diana Spencer in 1981. (*Open Mon–Sat 8am–6pm [winter 5pm]; crypt and galleries, Mon–Sat 10.45am–4.15pm [winter 3.15pm]; on certain Feast Days, for services only.*)

The most striking external feature is the dome, mounted on its pillared 'drum' and surmounted by the lantern and golden ball and cross, 365ft (111m) above ground level, but the church is in fact of traditional English cathedral form — an aisled nave lit by a clerestory with vaults supported by flying buttresses, aisled transepts and chancel, with a crossing tower (replaced by Wren's dome) and two west towers. However, in order to give the building proportions adequate for the dome, Wren raised the outer walls as screens above the aisle roof to the height of the nave, so hiding the buttresses (which had no place in a classical design) and giving a more unified, massive appearance to the building. The dome, subtly elongated so as to appear hemispherical from ground level and raised high on a drum, also belies its internal arrangement, for what is seen from inside is in fact an inner dome, made of brick, the top of which scarcely reaches the base of the external dome. Between the two, and supporting the lead-covered wooden structure of the outer dome, is a huge cone of brickwork, which also serves to support the stone lantern. In its contrast of appearance and reality St Paul's is undoubtedly a masterpiece of the Baroque. The twin towers on the west front were a late addition to Wren's plan. Each Sunday a peal of bells rings out from the north tower, and the south tower has a clock and the bell known as *Great Tom*. The whole exterior is richly decorated with stone statues and reliefs by Grinling Gibbons and others.

The frescoes round the vault of the dome are by Sir James Thornhill, the choirstalls and organ-case are by Gibbons, and the wrought-iron railings, gates and screens are by the Frenchman Jean Tijou. In the nave, transepts and choir are monuments to Nelson (1808–18, with the admiral's portrait by John Flaxman), Wellington (a massive work that occupied Alfred Stevens for 55 years, 1857–1912) and John Donne, poet and Dean of Old St Paul's, portrayed in his funeral shroud by Nicholas Stone. Holman Hunt's painting *Light of the World* hangs in the south aisle. The **American Chapel,** commemorating the dead of World War II, is behind the **High Altar,** which commemorates the British Commonwealth dead of two world wars. Wren himself is buried in the **Crypt** (*closed Sun and some other days*), as well as Nelson and Wellington, whose funeral gun carriage (1852, Gottfried Semper) also reposes there. There are many other monuments or memorial plaques to famous British men and women. Access is available to the internal **Whispering Gallery** and the external galleries, a lower one around the base of the dome and, above, the **Golden Gallery,** 542 steps from the ground (*also closed Sun and some other days of the year*). Within the west towers are the **Library,** reached by a geometrical staircase, with fine panelling and original bookcases, and the **Trophy Room,** which contains Wren's successive models for the cathedral and historical material on Old St Paul's.

▬ CITY CHURCHES ★★

MAP V C3–6   ⊖ St Paul's, Monument, Tower of London

Before the Great Fire there were 87 City churches. The Fire destroyed or badly damaged 76 of them. Many were rebuilt by Wren. His close contemporaries added more. Despite the further destruction of World War II, over 30 City churches remain, some much restored, and some of outstanding interest and merit (*see also pp.122–4, 126*).

There are several fine Wren churches between St Paul's and the Tower. South of Cannon Street, on either side of Queen Street, are **St James Garlickhythe,** with a very graceful spire above a square tower and fine original woodwork in the interior, and **St Michael Paternoster Royal,** burial place of Richard Whittington, the famous Lord Mayor, who is commemorated in stained glass. A little further on, and on the north side of Cannon Street are **St Mary Abchurch** and **St Clement Eastcheap,** the first of which has a splendid interior with a dome supported on eight arches; the dome painting is by Thornhill and the magnificent carved reredos by Grinling Gibbons. Beyond the Monument are **St Magnus the Martyr,** burial place of Miles Coverdale and rich in monuments and fine carved woodwork (also with relics of a Roman wharf and old London Bridge); **St Mary-at-Hill,** whose interior is richly decorated with 18th-century plasterwork and boasts the City's finest gilded and enamelled iron sword-rests; and **St Margaret Pattens,** another church with lovely old woodwork. Close by the Tower are two medieval churches which escaped the Great Fire of 1666, though not the bombing of 1940: **All Hallows-by-the-Tower** dates back to the 8th century, and there are remains of Roman building in the crypt as well as two Saxon crosses; there are also fine monuments and brasses (14th–17th centuries). (*Open Mon–Fri 9am–5.30pm, Sat & Sun 11am–5.30pm; brass rubbing, 11am [Sun 12.30pm]–5.45pm.*) **St Olave's** dates from the 15th century with 17th-century furnishings.

Christopher WREN

Christopher Wren, England's greatest architect, was born in Wilt-
shire in 1632, but soon came to London, where he attended
Westminster School. He showed exceptional brilliance in mathematics and went to Oxford before he had turned fourteen. He
invented several mathematical instruments and in 1655 assisted, in
perfecting the barometer. Six years later he was one of the founders
of the Royal Society, which was to become a powerhouse of
scientific research in the 17th century. King Charles II then summoned Wren to give advice on architectural matters. The study of
architecture was one to which Wren had given great attention,
notwithstanding his devotion to mathematics, astronomy, chemistry, and even anatomy. In 1663 he was engaged by the Dean and
Chapter of St Paul's to make a survey of the cathedral, and he drew
up a very careful and elaborate report, but before any steps were
taken St Paul's was irreparably damaged by the fire of 1666, so
Wren was destined to be the architect of the new cathedral instead
of the restorer of the old. The first work actually built from a design
by Wren was the chapel at Pembroke College, Cambridge, in 1663,
and he undertook a number of college buildings both there and in
Oxford.

In 1665 Wren visited Paris, where he met the great Italian
architect and sculptor Bernini. In the following year he returned to
find the Royal Society earnestly engaged in searching out the
causes of the Great Plague, so soon to be succeeded by the Great
Fire which laid London in ashes. The disaster at once opened a
wide field for the exertion of Wren's genius. He formed a plan and
drew designs for the entire rebuilding of the metropolis, embracing
wide streets, magnificent quays along the banks of the river, and
other improvements. In rebuilding London, however, few of
Wren's recommendations were adopted. He was certainly chosen
to be the architect of the new St Paul's, begun in 1675, besides
which he designed more than fifty other churches in place of those
destroyed by the fire.

Wren was knighted in 1672 and in 1680 was elected President
of the Royal Society. He continued to supervise the construction of
St Paul's, and in 1710 the last stone was laid upon the lantern by his
son Christopher. He died, at the age of 90, in 1723 at his house in
Hampton Court – where some of his finest work is to be seen at the
royal palace – and was buried in St Paul's Cathedral. His tomb is
marked by the Latin inscription which says: 'If you seek my
monument, look around.'

THE MONUMENT

MAP V C5   ⊖ Monument, Bank

Wren's **Monument** (1671), a 202ft (62m) Greek-Doric column,
surmounted by a gilded image of a flaming urn, and commemorating the Great Fire, is the tallest single stone column in the
world. The view from the top platform (reached by 311 steps)
used to offer a fine panorama of the City, but this is now
diminished by the tall new buildings around it.

Close by, along Upper and Lower Thames Streets, is **Fishmongers'
Hall** (1841), a handsome Classical Revival City Livery Company build

ing (best seen from London Bridge); and the old buildings of **Billingsgate Fish Market** (1875) and the **Custom House** (1817).

▬▬▬ *THE TOWER OF LONDON* ★★★

MAP V D6   ⊖ Tower Hill   ⇒ Fenchurch Street

Marking the City's eastern limits, and technically just outside it, the **Tower of London** was begun by William I (the Conqueror) soon after the Norman Conquest of 1066, both as a symbol of his new authority and as a defence against attack from the river. It was added to by a succession of monarchs over the next 500 years and used by them as a residence, a prison (the last prisoner was Rudolf Hess in World War II), place of execution, treasury, mint, armoury, even as a menagerie. Until the 19th century it was surrounded on three sides by a broad moat. Today it is a museum of priceless relics, as well as being one of the best preserved castles in the world. It is attended by the Yeoman Warders ('Beefeaters'), originally a royal bodyguard, who still wear Tudor uniform. (*Open Mar–Oct, Mon–Sat 9.30am–5pm, Sun 2–5pm; Nov–Feb, Mon–Sat 9.30am–4pm, closed Sun.*)

The **White Tower** or keep (1077–97) was the original fortress. It was whitewashed in 1241, hence its name; and the turret cupolas

---

The Great Fire of London

On 2 September 1666 a fire broke out in London, which was to burn down two-thirds of the city. Only six people died in the blaze; but the old medieval city was burnt to the ground over an area of about 400 acres. 80,000 people (more than half the population) were made homeless, while 76 churches and 13,000 houses were destroyed.

The fire started in the house of the royal baker in Pudding Lane very early on Sunday morning. There was a strong wind blowing from the east, and the fire burned without stopping until 6 September. It spread so quickly and seemed to blaze up in places away from the main fire, that many thought it had been started deliberately by Dutch or French enemies, or papists (Catholics). The great diarist Samuel Pepys recorded how he buried his gold and silver valuables in his father-in-law's garden for safe keeping. Many took their goods to the river, which was full of boats piled high with furniture. Others escaped to the country with their belongings and the fields for miles around were strewn with tents for their temporary shelter. On 4 September the diarist John Evelyn wrote: 'The burning still rages, and it has now gotten as far as the Inner Temple, all Fleet Streete, the Old Bailey, Ludgate Hill, Warwick Lane, Newgate, Paul's Chain, Watling Streete, now flaming, and most of it reduc'd to ashes; the stones of Paules flew like granados, ye melting lead running downe the streetes in a streame, and the very pavements glowing with fiery rednesse, so as no horse nor man was able to tread on them, and the demolition had stopp'd all the passages, so that no help could be applied.' The wind finally dropped and by blowing up houses the fire was confined, ending at Pye Corner in Gillspur Street.

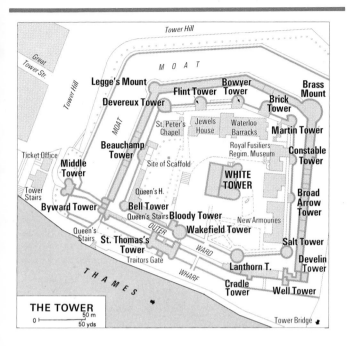

THE TOWER
0 |—————————| 50 m
|—————————| 50 yds

Tower Hill

MOAT

Great Tower Str.

Tower Hill

Legge's Mount

Devereux Tower

Flint Tower

Bowyer Tower

Brick Tower

Brass Mount

St. Peter's Chapel

Jewels House

Waterloo Barracks

Martin Tower

Beauchamp Tower

Royal Fusiliers Regim. Museum

Constable Tower

Ticket Office

Middle Tower

Site of Scaffold

WHITE TOWER

Tower Stairs

Queen's H.

Broad Arrow Tower

Byward Tower

Bell Tower

Queen's Stairs

Bloody Tower

New Armouries

Queen's Stairs

St. Thomas's Tower

OUTER

WARD

Wakefield Tower

Salt Tower

Traitors Gate

WHARF

Lanthorn T.

Develin Tower

THAMES

Cradle Tower

Well Tower

Tower Bridge

were added in the 14th century. The curtain walls with bastion towers around the central enclosure were built during the 13th century. The White Tower now houses the **Royal Armoury,** one of the greatest collections of arms and armour, and within it is **St John's Chapel,** a fine example of Norman church architecture. Several of the bastion towers contain relics of the fortress's sinister past. The **Bloody Tower** (12th century) was probably where the two young princes, sons of Edward IV, were imprisoned before their murder (1485), and where Sir Walter Raleigh was incarcerated for 12 years prior to his execution. **Traitor's Gate** and **St Thomas's Tower** (14th century) formed the main entrance from the river, leading to the **Wakefield Tower.** Other buildings within the enclosure now house museums, of which the most famous is the **Jewel House** (*closed Feb*), containing the **Crown Jewels.** These date from the Restoration and later – most earlier regalia having been sold or melted down by Cromwell – and include the Imperial State Crown, with 3,000 jewels, and the Royal Sceptre, containing the Star of Africa, the world's biggest cut diamond. The **Royal Fusiliers Museum, New Armouries** and **Waterloo Barracks** contain arms and other regalia of the regiment, and there is also an **Oriental Gallery** of arms and armour from India, Burma, China, and Japan. **Tower Green** was an execution and burial place, numbering among its victims two of Henry VIII's wives, Anne Boleyn and Catherine Howard. Many more people were executed on neighbouring **Tower Hill.** The Yeoman Warders parade each day at 11am, and perform the **Ceremony of the Keys** each evening at 10pm (*admission on application only*). The ravens which live in the grounds of the Tower of London are believed to ensure its safety.

Beyond the Tower is the leisure area that has been developed around **St Katharine's Dock,** with a marina, museum, restaurants, pubs and shops (see p.174).

The Tower of London from Tower Bridge

Tower of London

The Tower of London, Europe's oldest fortress prison, remains the most powerful reminder of the bitterness of political struggle over hundreds of years, and its walls have been witness to some of the darkest deeds of England's history. There have been countless executions, scenes of torture and long periods of incarceration. Many famous people including Henry VIII's second wife Anne Boleyn, Thomas More and Lady Jane Grey have lost their heads here, and Sir Walter Raleigh was imprisoned three times in the Tower – once for 12 years. The last man to be beheaded was Lord Lovat in 1747; but spies were shot here during both World Wars. Walls in the fortress have been inscribed by numerous unfortunate inmates: the name 'Jane' can be seen in two places in the Beauchamp Tower where Lady Jane Grey's young husband, Lord Dudley, was imprisoned before his execution. There are also said to be ghosts. In the White Tower noises of people groaning under torture have been heard; and the headless figure of Anne Boleyn, dressed in white, appears on Tower Green where royalty and nobles were beheaded (commoners met their death outside on Tower Hill). On moonlit nights Walter Raleigh patrols Raleigh's Walk – but if disturbed, will instantly disappear.

Tower Green is still inhabited by the ominous black ravens; and it is believed that if these leave, the Tower will fall and England will be doomed. In the past there was also a menagerie containing lions, dating back to the days of Henry III, in the 12th century, who received a present of three leopards (an allusion to the royal coat-of-arms) from Emperor Frederick of Germany. In the 14th century, to maintain a lion in the Tower cost sixpence a day, while human prisoners were supported for one penny. To go and see these Tower lions became an indispensable duty of all country visitors to London, insomuch as to give rise to a proverbial expression, 'the lions', which passed as equivalent to all kinds of city wonders which country people go to see. The menagerie was maintained in considerable strength as late as the 1830s, when the last Tower lions were finally removed to the Zoo in Regent's Park. About 40 Yeoman Warders, dressed in Tudor costume, guard the Tower of London; and every night at 10pm the Chief Warder locks the gates and hands the keys to the Resident Governor – as he has done for the past 700 years.

▬ PLACES TO STOP

The Strand:

Savoy Hotel – Thames Foyer (*10am–midnight*).
L.S. Grunts Chicago Pizza Co, 12 Maiden Lane (*daily, noon–11.30pm, Sun to 9pm*).

Aldwych and Law Courts:

Waldorf Hotel – Palm Court Lounge, Aldwych (*tea 3.30–6.30pm*).
Balls Brothers – wine bar, 142 Strand (*Mon–Fri to 7.30pm*).
Daly's – wine and sandwich bar, 46 Essex St (*Mon–Fri 8.30am–5.30pm*).
Lincoln's Inn Wine Bar, 49a Lincoln's Inn Fields (*Mon–Fri to 10.30pm*).

Printer's Devil (Whitbreads) – pub, 98 Fetter Lane.
Old Bell – pub, 95 Fleet St.
Olde Cheshire Cheese – pub, 145 Fleet St; traditional English menu.
Mother Bunch's Wine House, Arches F/G, Old Seacoal Lane (*Mon–Fri to 8.30pm*).

St Paul's:

Balls Brothers – wine bar, 2 Old Change Court, St Paul's Churchyard (*Mon–Fri to 7.30pm*).
Albion – pub, 2 New Bridge St; steaks in upstairs dining-room (*lunchtimes*).
Slenders – vegetarian restaurant and café, 41 Cathedral Place, Paternoster Square (*Mon–Fri 7.30am–6.15pm*).
Olde Watling (Vintage) – pub, 29 Watling St; home-made food.

London Bridge and the Tower:

Balls Brothers – wine bar, St Mary-at-Hill (*Mon–Fri to 7.30pm*).
Old Wine Shades, 6 Martin Lane.
Punters – wine bar, 5 Alchurch Yard, Alchurch Lane (*Mon–Fri to 8pm*).
Dickens (Courage) – pub, St Katharine's Way.

▬▬ SHOPPING

The Strand (*Mon–Sat 9am–5.30pm*).

Alpine Sports, No. 456 (*10am–6pm, Thu to 7pm*); everything for skiers, ramblers and mountaineers.
Fox Talbot Cameras, No. 443 (*Sat to 5pm*).
City Bag Store, No. 434 (*Mon–Fri to 6pm, Thu to 7pm*); luggage and bags of all kinds.
Stanley Gibbons International, No. 399 (*Mon from 10am, Sat 10am–1pm*); the world's largest stamp shop.
YHA Shop, 14 Southampton St (*Mon–Sat from 9.30am, Tue 10am–6pm*); equipment for walkers, cyclists and other outdoor sports enthusiasts, plus full details of Youth Hostels in Britain.

Itinerary 4
THE CITY

The City of London, close to one square mile (2.6km²) in area, is the oldest part of the capital, with its own forms of government and institutions (including its own police force), traditions and pageantry. The system of roads, though modified, notably since World War II, still conforms quite closely to that of Roman and medieval times, though the wall that once enclosed it, with its entrance gates, was mostly demolished in the 18th century. The Great Fire of 1666, and the more recent devastation of World War II, deprived the City of many buildings of real antiquity, but the monuments to the past that have survived are among London's finest, and the City's unique atmosphere endures, as does its position as a world centre of banking and finance.

▬▬ THE EMBANKMENT *

MAP IV A6 BC5; V C1–2 ⊖ Embankment, Temple, Blackfriars
⇌ Blackfriars

The **Victoria Embankment,** which follows the broad curve of the Thames from Blackfriars Bridge round to Westminster Bridge, is a link to the City of London from the almost equally venerable City of Westminster. It was part of a great 19th-century public works programme by the civil engineer Sir Joseph Bazalgette (*see also p.81*), which realigned the north bank of the Thames. It is still furnished with many of its original cast-iron lamp standards, handsomely decorated with dolphins, and with equally fanciful seats. One of its landmarks is **Cleopatra's Needle,** an Egyptian granite obelisk dating from about 1400 BC, bequeathed to the British government in 1819 and erected on its present site, after a perilous sea voyage, in 1878. Buried beneath it are several contemporary Victorian items, including coins and a copy of Bradshaw's famous *Railway Guide.*

The **Embankment Gardens,** by Hungerford rail and pedestrian bridge, contain the **York Watergate** (1626), the one-time riverside entrance to York House in the Strand. The Gardens also have a bandstand, and statues to Scottish poet Robert Burns and composer Sir Arthur Sullivan. Elsewhere along the Embankment are statues to Queen Boudicca featured with her daughters in a war chariot (by Westminster Bridge), W.S. Gilbert, poet, playwright and librettist to Sullivan (near Hungerford Bridge), Sir Joseph Bazalgette himself (also near Hungerford Bridge) and fellow engineer Isambard Kingdom Brunel (in Temple Place).

Lloyds of London building, 1986

Behind the Embankment Gardens are several important buildings: the rear of the **Savoy Hotel** (*see p.105*), **Shell Mex House** (1931), surmounted by a gigantic clock in the 'modernistic' style of the time, and the **Adelphi Building** (1938). The latter is named after, and occupies, much of the site of what was one of London's most gracious riverside façades, the **Adelphi Terrace**. Built by Robert Adam and his brothers ('adelphi' is the old Greek word for 'brothers') between the years 1768 and 1774, it was a large terrace of Georgian town houses, with an arcade beneath giving direct access to the river. After falling into gradual disrepair, most of the terrace was demolished in 1936. A few sections remain, notably the house at No. 7 Adam Street, which has portions of what was then the new decorative style of stucco plaster work.

▬▬ THE BANK OF ENGLAND AND THE GUILDHALL *

MAP V B4   ⊖ Bank

The Bank of England, reached by Queen Victoria Street (which was cut through the south-west corner of the City in the same years that the Victoria Embankment was built), is the very heart of the City, at a busy intersection where eight roads meet.

On the east side is the **Royal Exchange,** formerly the Stock Exchange, now an exhibition centre and home of the London International Financial Futures Exchange (LIFFE). A carillon plays at certain times. (*Open Mon–Fri 11am–2pm, closed Bank hols.*) On the southside is the Palladian-style **Mansion House,** built by George Dance the Elder between 1739 and 1752, the official residence of the Lord Mayor. On the front pediment is an allegory of 'London defeating Envy with Plenty, while Father Thames looks on'. Facing the Mansion House is the **Bank of England** ('The Old Lady of Threadneedle Street'), centre of the nation's finances. Little of Sir John Soane's building has survived in the extensive reconstruction. (*Visits, by special permit only, Mon, Tue, Fri 12–2pm*). The present **Stock Exchange** (1973), with a public viewing gallery and cinema, is a little further up Threadneedle Street. (*Open Mon–Fri 10am–3.15pm, closed Bank hols.*)

Westward, along Gresham Street, the **Guildhall** is the centre of the City of London's civic life. Lord Mayors have been elected there since 1192. It has also seen some famous trials, including that of the Anglican martyr Archbishop Cranmer (1553). The 15th-century building was badly damaged by the Great Fire but later restored. It was wrecked again in World War II and again restored, but parts of the 15th-century structure, including the crypt, remain. The **Main Hall** (*open Mon–Sat 10am–5pm; Sun, May–Sep only, 2–5pm; closed Bank hols*), where the annual Lord Mayor's Banquet is held, contains the coats-of-arms and banners of the twelve great City Livery Companies, statues to Nelson, Wellington and Churchill, and replicas of the large wooden figures of Gog and Magog, mythical founders of pre-Roman London. The **Library** (*open Mon–Sat 9.30am–5pm; closed Bank hols and for official functions*), which was first endowed by Richard Whittington in 1423, has manuscripts, maps and prints relating to the history of the City and of London as a whole. The **Clock Museum** (*open Mon–Fri 9.30am–5pm*), which houses the collection of the Worshipful Company of Clockmakers, has over 700 exhibits covering five centuries of horology.

▬▬ WREN CHURCHES **

MAP V B3–4, C2–4   ⊖ Blackfriars, Cannon Street

The south-western corner of the City is especially rich in churches built – or more often rebuilt – by Sir Christopher Wren

City Livery Companies

As early as the 1st century AD, a Roman historian described the city of London as a 'busy emporium for trade'. The City of London, the oldest part of the capital, with its own government (the Corporation) and its own Lord Mayor, has remained busy – though its importance now resides in the fact that it is an international centre for banking, insurance and stockbroking. Although its buildings were largely destroyed by the Great Fire of 1666, a number of the City's institutions and traditions date from medieval times. Many of these are connected with its guilds or livery companies.

Guilds were the first workers' organizations in England, and were formed to protect the interests of people practising a certain trade or craft, and to monitor the way they carried out their business. By the 13th and 14th centuries they had become very powerful, and in London they were known as livery companies because of the particular dress or 'livery' they wore. The companies also became wealthy enough to finance charities, schools and almshouses for their members, as well as churches. In outdoor performances of Mystery plays each guild would stage a biblical scene appropriate to its trade – the Fishmongers, for example, would perform Jonah and the Whale.

There are now 96 companies, each with various officials and about 20,000 members. These include the Mercers, Grocers, Drapers, Skinners, Apothecaries, Saddlers and many more. Although membership is now largely an honorary matter, the guilds often give aid to the trades with which they are connected by name and take part in activities related to their trades. For example, the Goldsmiths' Company is responsible for stamping hallmarks on gold and silver articles. In addition to the main Guildhall (the seat of the City of London's government for 1,000 years), various different livery companies have their own magnificent halls. These may be viewed by the public on certain days, and the companies hold annual banquets there. On these occasions a Loving Cup of hot mulled wine or of punch is passed from guest to guest: while each person drinks, the men on either side of him stand up until he has finished – this dates from the time when a man holding the cup would be unable to reach for his sword and defend himself if attacked, so his neighbours would act as bodyguards.

Each year the livery companies elect a Lord Mayor of London. The new Lord Mayor stages a pageant (the Lord Mayor's show) on the second Saturday in November. The following Monday there is a lavish banquet at the Guildhall, usually attended by the prime minister.

after the Great Fire, but there was great destruction again in the bombing of 1940–1. A few survived intact, others have been restored to their former glory, but many interiors have had to be entirely rebuilt.

Three churches stand on Queen Victoria Street, near the 17th-century **College of Arms** (*visit by written request*): **St Andrew-by-the-Wardrobe, St Benet** and the spireless remains of **St Nicholas Cole Abbey. St Benet,** attractively built of dark red brick and Portland stone, has one of the best preserved of Wren's interiors, with much original woodwork, including the galleries, pews, stalls, lectern and pulpit. It is the burial place of Inigo Jones.

A short walk through the streets to the west of the Bank leads past another eight churches: **St Mary Aldermary,** which Wren rebuilt in Gothic style, with a plaster fan-vaulted ceiling; **St Stephen Walbrook,** with a domed interior which is a masterpiece among all Wren's City churches, anticipating several features of St Paul's Cathedral (Sir John Vanbrugh is buried here); **St Margaret Lothbury,** where the interior furnishings, mostly brought from other Wren churches pulled down in the 19th century, include a screen designed by the architect

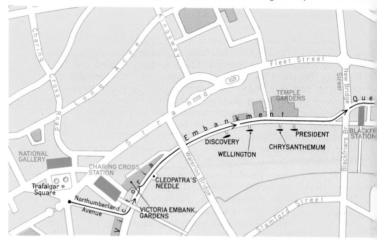

The City and Embankment

himself and a pulpit and font thought to be by Grinling Gibbons; **St Lawrence Jewry,** once richly decorated but completely burnt out in 1941; **St Botolph Aldersgate,** an old church rebuilt a century after Wren and preserving a lovely late 18th-century interior; **St Anne and St Agnes,** though small, one of Wren's finest, with a square interior vault supported on four Corinthian columns; **St Vedast-alias-Foster,** with a very baroque steeple and a beautifully restored interior furnished from other demolished Wren churches; and finally **St Mary-le-Bow,** gutted in 1941 and rebuilt (a Norman crypt survives), but boasting the most famous and elaborate of all Wren's steeples, from which the legendary **Bow Bells** ring out.

▬ AROUND CORNHILL ★

MAP V BC 4–6   ⊖ Bank

Cornhill is the highest hill in the City, where the basilica of the Roman town stood and where the medieval corn market was held; Leadenhall Street leads down to the old Aldgate; Bishopsgate leads to the former gate of the same name; and Gracechurch Street leads down to Billingsgate and London Bridge.

On the angle between Lombard Street (whose name recalls the Italian bankers who settled in London in the 12th century) and King William Street stands the church of **St Mary Woolnoth,** (1716–27), built by Wren's assistant Nicholas Hawksmoor, with a monumental exterior and – despite the restricted site – grandiose interior, which

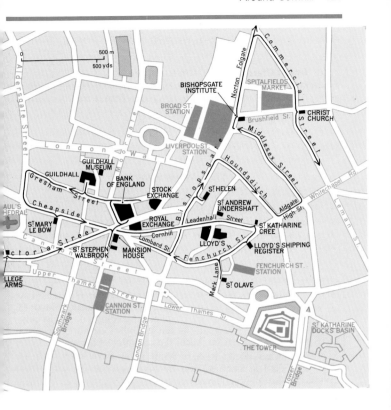

retains much original woodwork including a splendid organ case.

To the north, up Gracechurch Street, is **Leadenhall Market,** an old poultry market, housed beneath a fine Victorian arcade. It is now overshadowed by the new **Lloyd's of London** building, the capital's most remarkable new landmark (1986, Richard Rogers). It houses the Lutine Bell, which was recovered from a sunken French sailing ship. It is traditionally struck when announcements are made of the loss or safe arrival of a ship. Now the fate of space flights is announced in the same time-honoured way. **St Michael** and **St Peter** on Cornhill are two more Wren churches, but several churches in this part of the City survive from before the Great Fire: **St Katharine Cree** (1631) in Leadenhall Street, built in late Perpendicular Gothic, has a plaster-ribbed ceiling with bosses that display the badges of the City Livery Companies; **St Olave** (15th century), Hart Street, has fine woodwork and monuments; as do **St Andrew Undershaft** (mostly 16th century), which also has 17th-century stained glass and splendid ironwork (Tijou), and **St Helen Bishopsgate** (13th century), originally the church of the convent of Benedictine nuns, where there is a memorial window to Shakespeare, who lived for a time within the parish. Behind Hounds-ditch, on Bevis Marks, is the **Spanish-Portuguese Synagogue** (1701), built very much in the style of the contemporary Wren churches.

Houndsditch is on the site of the moat that ran along the city wall, the junction with Aldgate High Street standing just east of the site of Aldgate, one of the six original city gates. The area just to the north, outside the City boundaries, has for centuries been one of the busiest commercial areas of London, with many small manufacturers. It is also famous for its street markets, particularly the Sunday market around 'Petticoat Lane' (Middlesex Street). To the south is **Spitalfields Market,** East London's fruit, vegetable and flower market, and facing it stands **Christ Church** (1720), a masterpiece by Nicholas Hawksmoor, now undergoing restoration (*not regularly open to the public*). At the other side of the market, opposite **Liverpool Street Station** (the main station for trains to East Anglia), is the **Bishopsgate Institute** (1894) with a reference library devoted to the history of London.

Dick WHITTINGTON

Dick Whittington is one of England's favourite folk-heroes, still celebrated – together with his cat – in the annual pantomimes that are staged at Christmas time. The legend may be far from the truth, but it was certainly based on a real person who lived in London during the 14th century. According to the story, Dick was a poor boy who came to London to seek his fortune, having been told that the streets were paved with gold. He found a job in the house of Alderman Fitz-Warren, but was so harshly treated by the cook there that he ran away. However, as he walked up Highgate Hill he heard Bow Bells chiming 'Turn again, Whittington, thrice Mayor of London'. Encouraged by this prophecy, he returned. All he possessed in the world was a cat, but this legendary creature made him a fortune, and he married Alice, the daughter of his master.

There was indeed a Richard Whittington who was born around 1358 and died in 1423: he was no poor boy but the son of Sir William Whittington. Nevertheless, he was apprenticed to Fitz-Warren, a prosperous mercer, and married his daughter. Moreover, he did become Mayor – not just once, nor three times, but four times – as well as being a Member of Parliament. There is no specific record of his cat, but a sculptured stone of him holding a cat was discovered in the foundations of a 15th century house belonging to his family. He had no children, but left his great wealth to charity. During his lifetime he was renowned for his generosity and honesty. He was a member of the Mercers' Company, and attacked bad practice amongst City merchants; he founded libraries and almshouses, helped individuals in need, restored St Bartholemew's Hospital, entertained the king and gave him money. A stone set up on Highgate Hill in 1821 marks the spot where the young Richard is supposed to have sat when he heard Bow Bells calling him.

▄▄▄ PLACES TO STOP

Embankment:

Gordon's Wine Cellar, 47 Villiers St (*Mon–Fri to 9pm*).

Blackfriars:

Food for Health, 15 Blackfriars Lane (*Mon–Fri 8am–3pm*); old-established vegetarian restaurant and café.

Samuel Pepys (Toby - Bass) – pub, Brooks Wharf, Upper Thames St.

Black Friar – pub, 174 Queen Victoria St; home-cooked food lunchtime Mon–Fri. Opulent Edwardian and Art Nouveau decor.

Bank:

Balls Brothers – wine bar, 42 Threadneedle St (*Mon–Fri to 7.30pm*).

Greenhouse – wine bar, 16 Royal Exchange (*Mon–Fri to 7.30pm*).

Leadenhall Street/Fenchurch Street:

Five Lamps – wine bar, 3 Railway Place (*Mon–Fri to 7pm*).
New Yorker – sandwich bar, 4 Fenchurch Buildings (*Mon–Fri 7am–3.30pm*).

Cheapside and Guildhall:

Balls Brothers – wine bar, 6 Cheapside (*Mon–Fri to 7.30pm*).
Bow Wine Vaults, 10 Bow Churchyard (*Mon–Fri to 7pm*).
Old Dr Butler's Head – pub, Mason's Ave, Coleman St.

Liverpool Street/Bishopgate:

Gow's – oyster bar, 81 Old Broad St (*Mon–Fri lunchtime*).
Pavilion – wine bar, Finsbury Circus Gardens (*Mon–Fri to 8pm*).
Dirty Dick's – pub, 202 Bishopsgate.

▬▬ SHOPPING

Embankment:

Charing Cross Collectors' Market (*Sat–Sun 8.30am–5pm*); coins, stamps, magazines – anything collectable.

Leadenhall Street/Fenchurch Street (*Mon–Fri 9am–5.30pm*):

Leadenhall Market: wonderful Victorian iron and glass aisled market building with speciality food shops and stalls, sandwich bars etc.
Thomas Pink, 16 Cullum St; best shirtmakers outside the West End.

Middlesex Street (*Sun 8am–2pm*):

'Petticoat Lane' and the adjacent *'Club Row'* (Sclater St), *Brick Lane* and *Wentworth Street* (*also Tue–Fri lunchtime*) *Markets* come alive on Sunday mornings, and there are stalls set up in almost all the adjacent streets. Goods on offer include clothing, hardware, food, animals (Club Row) – just about anything new or second-hand.

Itinerary 5

LONDON WALL AND CLERKENWELL

The Roman wall around Londinium was probably built in the late 2nd century, and traces of it survive in a number of places, most visibly near the street named London Wall. Just to the north of this is the recent Barbican development of housing, shops and an ambitious Arts Centre. The northern edge of the City of London is bordered by Clerkenwell, a rural district until well into the 17th century. It was long noted for its clockmakers and other craftsmen, and also for its breweries, distilleries and local spas, all of which derived their business from the district's abundant sources of water. In 1613 Clerkenwell also provided the City with its first piped domestic water supply.

AROUND SMITHFIELD

MAP V AB1–2   ⊖ Farringdon, Barbican   ⇌ Holborn Viaduct

The fields just outside the City walls, on which London's principal meat market has been held since the 12th century, have been the scene of many dramatic events in the City's history – tournaments, the treacherous killing of the peasant leader Wat Tyler, and many executions, including the burning of over 200 martyrs in the reign of Mary Tudor – as well as the famous Bartholomew Fair. Beyond the arcades of the covered markets (1866 and later), which extend over an area of 10 acres (4ha), are **St Bartholomew's Hospital** and **Church** and, across Newgate Street, the **Central Criminal Court (Old Bailey)**.

Leading north from Holborn Circus is **Hatton Garden** (a street not a garden), London's diamond and jewellery centre, with many shops selling jewellery and gems. There is also an old **Charity School** building (1696) with the figures of two children; and in adjoining Ely Place, **St Etheldreda's Church,** with crypt (1251) and fragments of Roman wall. In the connecting passageway is the **Old Mitre** pub (1546), one of London's oldest, housing the trunk of a cherry tree which Elizabeth I is supposed to have danced around.

Joining Holborn to Newgate Street, bridging the valley of the Fleet River, is **Holborn Viaduct** (1869), a splendid monument to Victorian enterprise with ornate cast-iron work and bronze statues representing Commerce, Argriculture, Science, and Fine Art. Beside the Viaduct are the **City Temple** (1874), a large nonconformist church famous for its preachers, and **St Andrew Holborn,** a Wren church that was gutted in 1941 but has been restored with furnishings from the old **Foundling Hospital** (*see p.147*), including an organ donated by Handel and the

Spire of Christ Church, Newgate

Newgate and St Sepulchre's

Newgate Prison, where the Old Bailey now stands, was where condemned prisoners awaited execution, and nearby is the church known by the grisly name of St Sepulchre's. In 1705 Robert Dowe left instructions in his will, addressed to the vicar and churchwarden, that on the night before an execution they should ring a bell and deliver a sermon to the condemned prisoners in Newgate. For many years this request was faithfully carried out. At midnight, the sexton of St Sepulchre's came with a hand-bell to the window of the condemned cell, rang his bell and delivered this address:

'All you that in the condemned hold do lie,
Prepare you, for to-morrow you shall die:
Watch all and pray, the hour is drawing near
That you before the Almighty must appear:
Examine well yourselves, in time repent,
That you may not to eternal flames be sent:
And when St Sepulchre's bell to-morrow tolls,
The Lord above have mercy on your souls!'

On the following day, as the dismal procession set out for Tyburn (near Marble Arch), the prisoners paused at the gate of the church while the clergyman offered a prayer on their behalf, and the great bell tolled. Later, when executions took place in front of Newgate, the clergyman's address was given up, but for many years the sexton came to offer his midnight address, so the terms of Mr Dowe's bequest might be fulfilled; but the offer was always declined, because all needful services of the kind were performed by the chaplain of the prison.

tomb of Thomas Coram, the hospital's founder. Further east is **Holy Sepulchre Church,** which has associations with the Crusades, with old Newgate Prison, and now with the Royal College of Church Music. The tower dates from the 15th century and the spacious interior, rebuilt (probably by Wren) after the Great Fire, has a fine wooden gallery and organ case. On the other side of Newgate Street is the **Old Bailey,** the place of many sensational trials, which occupies the site of Old Newgate Prison. The **General Post Office** stands on the site of old Greyfriars Monastery, still marked by Wren's magnificent tower of **Christ Church.** Within the Post Office is the **National Postal Museum,** which displays mainly 19th-century British stamps. (*Open Mon–Thu 10am–4.30pm, Fri 10am–4pm; closed Bank hols.*) Nearby, there is a statue to Sir Rowland Hill, founder of the penny post.

▬ *THREE PRIORIES* ★★

MAPS V A2–3 B2; Inner London A5–6   ⊖ Farringdon, Barbican

The medieval City of London was surrounded by a whole series of monastic foundations, but all of them were secularized by Henry VIII in 1540, so that there is generally little left for the modern visitor to see. Here, however, just north of the old city walls, are extensive remains of three priories, one famed for its hospital, another, founded by the Carthusians, which later became a great public school, and the third which was founded by the crusading order of the Hospitallers of St John of Jerusalem.

Bartholomew Fair

When Rahere, minstrel and jester to Henry I, left the pleasures of court life for the quiet of the cloister, he showed much worldly prudence in arranging his future career. He delcared that he had seen Bartholomew the apostle in a vision, and been directed to found a church and hospital in his honour in the suburbs of London, at Smithfield. The land was readily granted by the king, Henry II; for it was marshy wasteland, and would be improved by the proposed foundation. The marsh was drained, and the monastery founded on its site in 1123. Rahere was made prior. St Bartholomew's shrine became very popular as many sick people claimed to have been miraculously cured. The new prior, still keeping an interest in worldly affairs, also acquired the right to hold a fair on the festival of his patron saint. This attracted traders from a wide area to Smithfield and became the chief cloth-fair in the country.

Several centuries later the trading-fair became exclusively a pleasure-fair. Its earlier associations with the cloth trade were remembered in the opening ceremony, with drapers and tailors snapping their shears.

Ben Jonson set his comedy *Bartholomew Fair* (1614) in Smithfield during the celebration of the fair, and later in the century it became a huge carnival. The licence was extended from three to fourteen days, theatres were closed during this time and the actors brought to Smithfield. The fair was enjoyed by all classes who were entertained by shows and exhibitions, jugglers and acrobats, and all manner of weird and wonderful creatures. By the end of the 18th century the fair had got out of hand. Efforts were made to restrict gambling and some of the theatrical performances, but when the Lord Mayor finally refused permission to erect booths at all, there were riots. Rents were raised so high that finally no showmen appeared and the fair came to an end in 1855.

St Bartholomew's Hospital, founded in the 12th century, still retains a collegiate atmosphere thanks to the buildings by James Gibbs (1759), which form three sides of a quadrangle, and the gatehouse (1702) from West Smithfield with its statue of Henry VIII. The great staircase has two huge paintings by Hogarth, and there are portraits of famous medical men in the Great Hall. (*Open Mon–Sat by appointment,* ☎*600 9000 ext. 3478.*) The priory church of **St Bartholomew-the-Great** (founded 1123), is one of London's loveliest medieval churches, retaining much of its original Norman structure. The circular piers around the choir with galleries above are particularly fine, and there is the canopied tomb (c.1500) of Rahere, founder of the priory and hospital. In **Cloth Fair** (which takes its name from the old Bartholomew Fair), next to the church, is an old house which, although restored, gives an idea of the houses built just after the Great Fire. North of Smithfield Market is **Charterhouse Square,** mostly Georgian, with adjacent remains of the **Charterhouse** itself, a 14th-century Carthusian priory, then a famous school (now moved from London), whose pupils included the writers Addison and Steele as well as John Wesley and William Thackeray. The chapel contains the tomb of the founder, Thomas Sutton. (*Open Apr–June, Wed only, 2–5pm.*)

St John's Gate (off Clerkenwell Road), the 16th-century gateway to a 12th-century priory, now houses the **Museum of the Order of St**

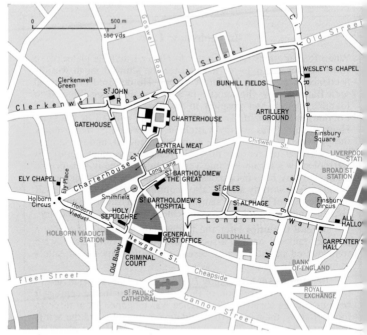

London Wall and Clerkenwell

John, with relics of the crusading order that founded it. The 12th-century crypt contains a superb monument to a Spanish nobleman who died in 1575; he lies in full armour with a young page beside him. (*Open Tue, Fri 10am–6pm, Sat 10am–4pm*).

Clerkenwell Green has the **Karl Marx Memorial Library,** where Lenin worked for a time. These associations serve as a reminder that the area was also a focal point for the Chartist reform movement during the days of 19th-century industrial unrest. To the east, the rather melancholy **Bunhill** (Bone Hill) **Fields,** a famous burial ground from the time of the Great Plague (1665), contain the tombs of John Bunyan, Daniel Defoe, William Blake and George Fox. **John Wesley's House** and Chapel is now a memorial and museum to the founder of Methodism. (*House open Mon–Sat 10am–4pm, Sun 12–3pm; Chapel open daily 9am–dusk.*) He is buried in the chapel yard.

▬ THE BARBICAN ★

MAP V A3   ⊖ Barbican, Moorgate

The area to the north of London Wall is occupied by the **Barbican**, which incorporates part of the old Roman fort, although the name is taken from a medieval watchtower. The 60-acre (24ha) site covers an area which was almost completely devastated during World War II. Plans were drawn up soon after for its redevelopment as a combined commercial, residential and recreation area; but this most ambitious of all post-war London developments was only finished in 1981.

The most striking features are the 412ft (126m) high tower blocks, part of the housing scheme and the tallest residential buildings in

Europe. The **Arts and Conference Centre,** on the north side, includes a concert hall, exhibition gallery, library, cinema and theatre (London home of the Royal Shakespeare Company). Next to it is the **Guildhall School of Music and Drama.** At the western end of the site is the **Museum of London,** presenting aspects of the city's life from pre-historic times to the present day. It also houses the Lord Mayor's coach (1757) which takes to the streets once a year in the Lord Mayor's Show (*full details of opening times and collections on p.210*). The 16th-century church of **St Giles Cripplegate** is also within the Barbican complex. John Milton is buried in the churchyard.

▬ *EAST END* *

MAPS V AB6; Inner London AB6   ⊖ Whitechapel, Bethnal Green

For centuries the 'East End' has been the home of immigrants, the Protestant Huguenot refugees in the 17th century, later many Jews, and more recently people from Asia, Africa and the West Indies – who have contributed so much to the com-

---

Cockneys

Strictly speaking, the only true Cockneys are those Londoners who are born within the sound of Bow Bells. In days gone by the street traders and other working people in the East End evolved a language of their own which made them unintelligible to outsiders. This 'rhyming slang' was developed, it is said, to confuse the police, who were always ready to pounce on the market traders for obstruction and other forms of public nuisance. Two or three words would be substituted for the word intended – the only connection being that they rhymed. Thus 'apples and pears' stood for 'stairs', 'Hampstead Heath' for 'teeth' and 'bacon and eggs' for 'legs'. To make matters more confusing, only the first word of the phrase would be used in conversation: so if a man commented on a girl's lovely bacons, he would be referring to her legs; and if he said he'd lost his uncle, he would really mean he couldn't find his shirt (from 'Uncle Bert'). 'Hat' was abbreviated to 'Titfer' (from 'Tit for tat'). While the East End community is not as tightly knit as it was and rhyming slang is no longer a private code, many of the words and phrases have been more universally adopted. Many people for example, frequently say that somebody talkative 'rabbits on', without realizing that they are actually using the short form of 'Rabbit and pork' (i.e. 'talk').

Cockney traders had their own ceremonial dress too. This was quite unlike everyday market wear and consisted of suits of clothes decorated with thousands of mother-of-pearl buttons, sewn over-lapping each other to make patterns. With these costumes the men would wear silk mufflers, and the women, enormous ostrich feather hats. Those entitled to sport such finery were called pearly kings and queens, and were elected by the different boroughs from amongst the important members of the street-trading community. In the past these 'kings' and 'queens' did charity work for the old and poor in their areas and once a year would attend a special harvest festival service in the Old Kent Road. Although the service still takes place (now the Costermongers' Harvest Festival in St Martin-in-the-Fields), there are few 'pearlies' left. However, the Pearly King of the City of London still attends Petticoat Lane market every Sunday.

merce and life of London, though the poverty and overcrowding, particularly in the 19th century, were appalling. Many of the most harrowing descriptions in Charles Dickens's novels are of this part of London. The East End consists of the districts of **Whitechapel**, once famed for coaching inns and markets by the main road from the east coast and later given notoriety by the murders of Jack the Ripper; **Shoreditch,** with old theatrical connections (England's first playhouse – known originally as 'The Theatre' – was erected here in 1576 before being moved and re-erected as the Globe Theatre in Southwark); and **Bethnal Green,** the poorest district of Victorian London, noted for its Labour Yard, where men broke stones for a bowl of soup.

Among the most interesting sites for the visitor in Whitechapel are the **Whitechapel Art Gallery** (1897, C.H. Townsend), a striking building in Art Nouveau style, which has changing exhibitions throughout the year, mainly of modern art (*open Wed, Fri–Sun 11am–5.50pm, Tue, Thu 11am–7.50pm);* **Whitechapel Bell Foundry,** founded 1420, a distinguished survivor of the district's old industries, where Big Ben and the bells for Westminster Abbey were cast; the **Trinity Almshouses** (1695), Mile End Road, originally built for retired seamen or their widows, with a handsome chapel at one end; and **St George-in-the-East** (1714, Hawksmoor) an imposing church restored after bomb damage, with windows by Sir Joshua Reynolds. In Shoreditch the **Geffrye Museum** (Kingsland Road), housed in former almshouses built in the early 18th century for the Ironmongers Company, displays a series of rooms demonstrating the different styles of English furniture and furnishings from Tudor times to the present day; there is also a reconstructed Georgian street and the original chapel of the almshouses. (*Open Tue–Sat 10am–5pm, Sun 2–5pm; closed 24–26 Dec, 1 Jan, Good Fri.*) The **Bethnal Green Museum of Childhood,** part of the Victoria and Albert Museum, has a marvellous collection of dolls, dolls' houses, puppets and toy theatres, as well as displays devoted to the history and craft of the famous Huguenot silk-workers of Spitalfields. (*Open Mon–Thu, Sat 10am–6pm, Sun 2.30–6pm; closed 25 Dec, 1 Jan, May Day.*)

▬▬ PLACES TO STOP

Holborn Circus:

Olde Mitre (Allied) – pub, Ely Court, Hatton Garden.
Old Bottlescrew – wine bar, 52 Bath House, Holborn Viaduct (*Mon–Fri to 8.30pm*).
Nosherie – salt beef bar, 12 Greville St (*Mon–Fri 8am–5pm*).

Smithfield:

Cock – pub, Poultry Market; breakfast 5.30am, lunch and evening snacks.
Three Compasses (Trumans) – pub, 66 Cowcross St.
Fox & Anchor (Ind Coope) – pub, 115 Charterhouse St; breakfast 6–11am, lunches.
Hand & Shears (Courage) – pub, 1 Middle St.

Clerkenwell:

Café St Pierre, 9 Clerkenwell Green (*daily, breakfast 7.30–10am, lunch Sun–Fri, eve Mon–Sat to 11pm*).
Pheasant & Firkin (Bruce's) – pub, 166 Goswell Rd.

Around Old Street:

Windmill (Charringtons) – pub, 27 Tabernacle St.

East West, 188 Old St (*Mon–Sat 11am–10pm, Sat to 3pm*); macrobiotic restaurant and cafeteria.

Barbican/London Wall:

Chiswell Vaults (Whitbreads) – pub, Chiswell St; bar food and restaurant.
Balls Brothers – wine bar, Moor House, London Wall (*Mon–Fri to 7pm*).

Stepney:

Hollands – pub, 9 Exmouth St.

Whitechapel:

Grave Maurice (Trumans) – pub, 265 Whitechapel Rd.

Homerton:

Falcon & Firkin (Bruce's) – pub, 274 Victoria Park Rd.

Wapping:

Prospect of Whitby (Watneys) – pub, Wapping Wall; restaurant and bar food.

Plaistow:

Black Lion (Imperial) – pub, 59 High St; steak and kidney pudding, fish and chips.

Limehouse:

Grapes (Taylor Walker) – pub, 76 Narrow St; seafood specialities.

▬ SHOPPING

Holborn Circus:

Hatton Garden – street which is the gold, silver and diamond centre of London. Auctions are held at No. 36 each Thu (viewing Fri 9.30am–4.30pm).
London Silver Vaults, 53–64 Chancery Lane (*Mon–Fri 9am–5.30pm, Sat to 12.30pm*); underground arcade of shops selling new and antique silver.
Leather Lane Market (*Mon–Fri noon–3pm*); clothes, leather and hardware.

Clerkenwell:

David Joseph, 33 Clerkenwell Rd (*Mon–Fri 10am–6pm*); designer jewellery.
Farringdon Road Market (*Mon–Fri 11.30am–2pm, Sat 9.30am–1pm*); books.

Old Street:

Clearspring, No. 196 (*Mon–Sat 10.30am–7pm, Sat to 5pm*); health foods, beauty preparations and household products.
Whitecross Street Market (*Mon–Fri noon–2pm*); lunchtime market for food and clothes.

Bethnal Green:

Bethnal Green Market (*Mon–Sat 8am–5pm, Thu to 1pm*); food, hardware and general goods.
Columbia Road Market (*Sun 8am–noon*); flowers, plants and everything for the garden.
Friends Foods, 15 Roman Rd (*Mon–Sat 10am–6pm, Thu to 2pm, Fri to 7pm*): wholefood co-operative with women's café.

Itinerary 6

THE SOUTH BANK

The establishment of Roman London and then of West—minster on the north bank of the Thames, set a pattern for the main development of the capital north of the river for the next six or seven centuries. Yet today, nearly half the people of London live south of the Thames, and the large area encompassed by the broad bend in the river from the region of Lambeth Palace to Southwark Cathedral is a vital part of the city.

SOUTHWARK *

MAP V D3–4 E4–5   ⊖ ⇌ London Bridge

Southwark, or South Work, is the oldest part of London south of the Thames, commanding the main route from Dover and the Continent into the City over London Bridge. Hence its many coaching inns, including the now-demolished Tabard, where Chaucer's pilgrims met in the *Canterbury Tales*. Also, with more space than the City itself, it became a place of entertainment (Shakespeare's Globe Theatre and the Bear Garden) and, more unhappily, of prisons (notably the Clink and Marshalsea). There is still much evidence of this colourful past in the bustling south London district today.

Just across London Bridge from the City, at the start of Borough High Street is **Guy's Hospital,** founded in 1722, with large modern extensions. The old operating theatre in Thomas Street may still be visited (*open Mon, Wed, Fri 12.30–4pm*). Under the arches of London Bridge railway station, by Tooley Street, is the **London Dungeon**, an unusual museum of the macabre (*open Apr–Sep, daily 10am–5.45pm; Oct–Mar, daily 10am–4.30pm*). In Borough High Street itself is the **George Inn** (1676), one of the very few galleried inns left in the country. It is owned and preserved by the National Trust, and Shakespeare's plays are performed in the cobbled courtyard during the summer. The church of **St George the Martyr** (founded 1122, rebuilt 1736) has an interesting interior, including memorials to the City Livery Companies and to Dickens's novel *Little Dorrit,* which was inspired by the nearby Marshalsea debtors' prison.

Southwark Cathedral (St Saviour's) was founded as a priory in 1106, but most of the edifice dates from the 15th century, the square tower being of a later date. The church became a cathedral only in 1905. The interior is rich in decoration and in monuments, including the wooden effigy of a knight (c.1275), the memorial to John Gower (a friend of the poet Chaucer), and another to Shakespeare (1912). There is also the **Harvard Chapel,** in honour of John Harvard, who was

The National Theatre from the Victoria Embankment

William SHAKESPEARE

Shakespeare was born in Stratford-upon-Avon in Warwickshire in 1564, traditionally on St George's Day, 23 April. He came to London in his early twenties, and it was there that the greater part of his career was to be played out. The commercial theatre was in its infancy, its development stimulated – paradoxically – by a ban enacted in 1576 by the Corporation of London on the performance of plays in public within the bounds of the city, in the interests of morality and hygiene. This ban, in fact, led to the erection in Shoreditch, outside the city limits, of a theatre with the first fixed stage and with professional management. It was called the Theatre and was run by James Burbage. Shakespeare acted here and was a friend of Burbage's son Richard, who, after the Theatre was closed down (1592) because of the plague, managed the Lord Chamberlain's Company of actors, for which Shakespeare became actor-dramatist. Richard Burbage dismantled the Theatre after his father's death and rebuilt it on Bankside, Southwark, in 1599 as the Globe.

Southwark – again outside the city limits – was already an area of entertainment, with a bear-garden and other amusements as well as the Rose and Swan theatres. Many of Shakespeare's plays were acted at the Globe, including *Hamlet, King Lear, Macbeth, Richard III, As You Like It, A Midsummer Night's Dream* and *Twelfth Night*. His plays were also performed at the Curtain, another Shoreditch theatre, and at Burbage's Blackfriars Theatre, in which Shakespeare had a share. There were special performances before the Queen at Greenwich Palace (Christmas 1594), and, in a building which still survives, Middle Temple Hall, a memorable performance of *Twelfth Night* at Candlemas (2 Feb) 1601. In 1613 the Globe burnt down as a result of a cannon being used for stage effects, but Shakespeare had by now returned to Stratford, although he bought a house in Blackfriars for his visits to London. He died in Stratford on St George's Day 1616.

baptized in the church and was the founder of Harvard University. Between London and Blackfriars bridges is **Bankside,** redeveloped as a riverside walk with excellent views across the Thames to St Paul's and the City. Although dominated by Giles Gilbert Scott's 1929 power station (no longer in use, like his larger one at Battersea), there are smaller interesting local sites. Close to Southwark Cathedral are the remains of 12th-century **Winchester House** and, beyond it, **St Mary Overie Dock,** now containing an old merchant ship, and the 18th-century **Anchor Inn,** with cubby holes which hid fugitives from the notorious Clink prison nearby. Also on display are manacles and other relics from the prison itself. On the other side of Southwark Bridge, on the site of the **Globe Theatre,** stands the **Shakespeare Globe Museum,** tracing the history of Elizabethan theatre, with models of the Globe and Cockpit playhouse. (*Open Tue–Sat 10am–5.30pm, Sun 2–6pm; closed 25–26 Dec, 1 Jan.*) The 18th-century **Hopton Almshouses,** behind the power station, are still used as old people's homes.

▬ LAMBETH ★

MAPS IV C6 DEF 5–6; V E1 F1–2; Inner London CD 4–5 ⊖ Lambeth North

Most of Lambeth was empty marshland until the 18th century, except for the Palace, which stands in splendid isolation across the river from Westminster, and was long served by a special ferry. A number of industries grew up near the river, and in the 19th century much of the area decayed into slums, which have been replaced since World War II with municipal housing, including many tower-blocks.

St George's Roman Catholic Cathedral (1841), at the top of Blackfriars Road, was designed by Pugin but never completed, and was badly damaged by bombing. A little way down Waterloo Road from St George's Circus is the **Old Vic Theatre** (1818, reconstructed 1870 and again in 1927). During the 1930s it was closely associated with Sadler's Wells opera and ballet companies and renowned for drama productions with such noted actors as Laurence Olivier and John Gielgud. In 1963 it was the temporary home of the newly-formed National Theatre, until that company's new theatres were opened on the South Bank. Closed down in 1981, it was restored and re-opened in 1983.

The **Imperial War Museum,** founded in 1917 and devoted mainly to British Empire and Commonwealth involvement in two world wars, is housed in what was a part of the old Bethlehem Royal Hospital known as 'Bedlam'. The dome and portico were added in 1838 by Sydney Smirke, architect of the British Museum Reading Room. At the time of writing, a major renovation programme is in hand, but large parts of the exhibition remain on display, including a World War I tank and a Sopwith Camel combat aircraft; World War II Spitfire fighter aircraft, an Italian manned torpedo, and a German V1 Flying Bomb; also a major collection of drawings, paintings and cartoons by Henry Moore, Paul Nash, John Piper, Laura Knight, Augustus John and other British war artists. (*Open Mon–Sat 10am–5.50pm, Sun 2–5.50pm; closed*

Bedlam

The Bethlehem Hospital for the insane was founded in King Henry VIII's reign in the buildings of the suppressed priory of Our Lord of Bethlehem (which also had a hospital attached) and could accommodate 50 or 60 patients. It was moved in 1675, and again in 1815 to the building now occupied by the Imperial War Museum in Lambeth, which was later enlarged so that some 400 patients could be accommodated. Some idea of the horror of Bedlam in the 17th century can be gained from two statues (later moved to the Guildhall) carved by C.G. Cibber to adorn the entrance to the hospital, and described by Alexander Pope as 'Great Cibber's brazen brainless brothers'. They were modelled upon two patients at the hospital, one apparently a servant of Oliver Cromwell, and depict 'Melancholy' and 'Raving Madness'. They lie naked, with shaven heads, on mattresses of rushes. Spectators were admitted to the hospital, which became one of the sights for the curious and heartless visitor to London.

Two hundred years later conditions had improved, and a guide to London of that time commends 'the way in which the comfort of the patient is studied by everyone connected with the Hospital . . . The women have pianos, and the men billiard and bagatelle-tables. There are indeed few things to remind you that you are in a mad-house beyond the bone knives in use, and a few cells lined and floored with cork and indian-rubber, and against which the most insane patient may knock his head without the possibility of hurting it.' The hospital was finally moved to Surrey in 1930.

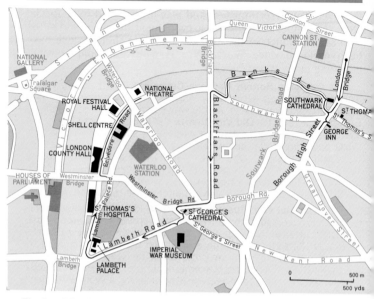

The South Bank

24 – 26 Dec, 1 Jan, Good Fri and Bank hols.) The museum also maintains the **Cabinet War Rooms** in Whitehall and **HMS Belfast,** moored by Tower Bridge.

  Lambeth Palace has been the London residence of the Archbishops of Canterbury since the 12th century and, perhaps because of its long-exposed situation, has had quite a stormy history, including attack during the Peasants' Revolt of 1381, and again by Gordon Rioters in 1780. Its most interesting features are a 13th-century vaulted **Crypt,** the **Tudor Gatehouse, Great Hall** and **Lollards' Tower,** although its aspect is now somewhat diminished by all the other buildings round about. It is not generally open to the public, being still regularly used for church affairs. Next to it is the church of **St Mary-at-Lambeth,** (mainly dating from the 19th-century Gothic Revival, but with a 14th-century tower), which now houses the **Museum of Garden History.** The **Tradescant Garden,** commemorating Charles I's gardener John Tradescant, who is buried in the churchyard, has been planted with shrubs and flowers of the period (*open Mar–mid-Dec, Mon–Fri 11am–3pm, Sun 10.30am–5pm*).

  The Albert Embankment leads southwards from Lambeth Palace to the area of **Vauxhall,** site of the once famous 18th-century Pleasure Gardens, which featured in many period plays, novels and pictures. Today a huge traffic concourse, with the **Oval Cricket Ground** nearby, replaces them. To the east is the huge traffic intersection of **Elephant and Castle,** which takes its name from a pub (probably originally the 'Infanta of Castile'). The library next to Southwark Town Hall, in Walworth Road, houses the **Cuming Museum,** one of London's most interesting local history museums, with special collections devoted to the scientist Michael Faraday, who was born in nearby Newington Butts, and to the Lovett collection of London superstitions. With Lambeth Palace once more a starting point, the riverside view of the Houses of Parliament from across the road is particularly fine. Northwards, past **St Thomas's Hospital** and beyond Westminster Bridge is **County Hall** (1919), a massive Neo-Classical edifice, whose future is currently in doubt following the 1986 abolition of the Greater London Council.

Vauxhall Gardens

London's most celebrated pleasure gardens were situated in Lambeth, opposite Millbank, near a manor called Fulke's Hall (once the residence of Falkes de Breauté, a follower of King John in the 13th century) – hence Vauxhall. The fame of the gardens was such that this name entered the Russian language (by a somewhat devious route) to mean 'railway station'. The gardens, known as New Spring Garden, opened soon after the restoration of Charles II, and Pepys, writing in 1667, described the 'abundance of roses' and the 'cakes and powdered beef and ale', finding the entertainments 'mighty devertising'. Like all visitors until the mid-18th century, Pepys had to come across the Thames by boat to visit the gardens.

Vauxhall's greatest period was in the 18th century, when not only were there water cascades and fireworks, but excellent concerts in the splendid rococo music-room. A statue of Handel was erected, and visitors who came to hear the music included Dr Johnson, Oliver Goldsmith and their friends, the Mozart family during their visit to London, and Joseph Haydn, who wrote that 'the grounds and its variety are perhaps unique in the world. There are 155 little dining booths in various places, most charmingly situated, each comfortably sitting 6 persons. There are very large alleys of trees, which form a wonderful roof above, and are magnificently illuminated. Tea, coffee and almond-milk all cost nothing. The entrance fee is half a crown per person. The music is fairly good...' The first part of the 19th century saw many spectacular shows, including balloon ascents and a re-enactment of the Battle of Waterloo, but the gardens ran into financial difficulties, and they closed, after a final gala, in July 1859.

THE SOUTH BANK ARTS CENTRE *

MAP IV B6   ⊖ Waterloo, Embankment   ⇌ Waterloo

The genesis of the Arts Centre was the 1951 Festival of Britain, when a semi-derelict industrial area of the Lambeth riverside, around Hungerford railway bridge and Waterloo Bridge, was chosen as the Festival's main exhibition site. A new concert hall, the **Royal Festival Hall**, was included, and from this the rest of the Arts Centre, unified by a large pedestrian precinct, has grown.

The **Royal Festival Hall,** which was modified and enlarged in 1965, has year-round concert and ballet seasons, as well as a riverside restaurant, cafeterias and bars, bookshop, art exhibitions, and there is a fine panorama of London across the river. The **Queen Elizabeth Hall** and **Purcell Room** (1967) complement the Festival Hall as smaller concert or recital rooms. The **Hayward Gallery** (1968), in the same building complex, stages major art exhibitions. The **National Film Theatre,** beneath Waterloo Bridge (first opened in 1951 and enlarged in 1970), has two cinemas, and a cinema museum in preparation. On the other side of Waterloo Bridge, the **National Theatre** complex (1977) has three theatres, the **Olivier** (the largest, named after Lord Olivier, the company's first artistic director), **Lyttelton** and **Cottesloe,** as well as bookshops, a restaurant and cafeterias. Tours of the building, including backstage and workshops, are available Mon–Sat 10am–1pm. From here, too, there are more striking views across the Thames. Sometimes included in the South Bank area is the **Shell Centre** (1962) with its 351ft (107m) tower block and surrounding offices.

Charles DICKENS

Our view of Victorian London is inevitably shaped by Charles Dickens (1812–70) since his experiences – particularly the difficulties of his youth – and his observations are so vividly relived in his novels. The Dickens family came to London when Charles was nine years old after his father had lost his job, and he soon experienced the deepest misery when his father was imprisoned for debt and he himself had to work in a blacking factory – events that reappear in *David Copperfield* and *Little Dorrit*. He became a shorthand writer at Doctor's Commons, working among lawyers, and lived for a time in Furnival's Inn, Holborn – where he wrote *Pickwick Papers* (1837), his first great success – then in Doughty Street and later in Devonshire Place (Marylebone) and Tavistock Square (Bloomsbury) before returning to his native Kent, the most successful and admired writer of his age.

Dickens's works are full of memorable London characters, from Jo the crossing-sweeper (*Bleak House*) or the Artful Dodger (*Oliver Twist*) to the benevolent clerk Newman Noggs (*Nicholas Nickleby*), the drunken nurse Mrs Gamp (*Martin Chuzzlewit*) or the ever-optimistic Mr Micawber (*David Copperfield*).

Among his most memorable descriptions of London are the rookeries of Seven Dials and St Giles in *Oliver Twist*, the building of the railway in *Dombey and Son*, many of the scenes on the river Thames and the masterly description of a London fog in the opening of *Bleak House;* 'Implacable November weather . . . Fog everywhere. Fog up the river . . . fog down the river, where it rolls defiled among the tiers of shipping, and the waterside pollutions of a great (and dirty) city. Fog on the Essex marshes, fog on the Kentish heights. Fog creeping into the cabooses of collier-brigs; fog lying out on the yards, and hovering in the rigging of great ships; fog dropping on the gunwales of barges and small boats . . . Chance people on the bridges, peeping over the parapets into a nether sky of fog, with fog all round them, as if they were up in a balloon, and hanging in the misty clouds.'

▬▬ *PLACES TO STOP*

Southwark/London Bridge:

Cuddeford's – wine bar, 20 Duke St Hill (*Mon–Fri lunchtime*).
Skinker's – wine bar, 42 Tooley St (*Mon–Fri to 8pm*).
Anchor (Courage) – pub, 1 Bankside; restaurant and barbecue food.
Market Porter, 9 Stoney St; pub food and restaurant.
Founders Arms (Youngs) – pub, 52 Hopton St, Bankside.
George (Whitbread Fremlins), 77 Borough High St; the last of London's galleried coaching inns.

Bermondsey (east of Southwark):

Angel – pub, Bermondsey Wall East; bar food and full restaurant menu.

Lambeth:

Boot & Flogger – wine bar, 10 Redcross Way (*Mon–Fri to 8.30pm*).
Rebato's – Spanish wine bar, 169 South Lambeth Rd (*Mon–Sat to 11pm, closed Sat lunchtime*).
Cooke's Eel and Pie Shop, 84 The Cut (*Mon–Sat 10.30am–2.30pm, Fri–Sat to 3.30pm*).
Pizzeria Castello, 20 Walworth Rd (*Mon–Sat noon–11pm, Sat from 5pm*).
Goose & Firkin (Bruce's) – pub, 47 Borough Rd.

Kennington:

Windmill Fish Bar, 211 Kennington Lane (*daily 11.30am–2.30pm, 5pm–midnight*).

South Bank:

Archduke – wine bar, Concert Hall Approach (*Mon–Sat to 11pm, closed Sat lunchtime*).
Royal Festival Hall – riverside café, buffet, sandwich and salt beef bars (*daily 8am–8pm, Fri–Sun to 10pm*).

▬ SHOPPING

Southwark/London Bridge:

London Bridge Auctions, 6 Park St, Borough Market (*Sun: viewing 10am, sales 2pm*); antiques, silver and jewellery.

Bermondsey:

Bermondsey (New Caledonian) Market, off Tower Bridge Rd (*Fri 5am–noon*); unique antiques market, the best bargains are to be had early.

Lambeth:

Imperial War Museum Shop (*daily 10am–5.50pm, Sun from 2pm*); posters.
 The Cut Market (*Mon–Fri 11am–2pm*); food, hardware and general goods.
Baldwin's, 173 Walworth Rd (*Tue–Sat 9am–5.30pm*); herbs and herbal preparations.
Percival Cameras, 11 Lower Marsh (*Mon–Sat 8.30am–5.30pm, Sat to 12.30pm*); discount new and second-hand cameras and photographic equipment.

South Bank:

W.H. Smith's Computer Shop, Waterloo Station (*Mon & Wed–Fri 8am–8pm, Tue 9.30am–5.30pm, Sat 9am–6pm*).
South Bank Craft Centre, 164–7 Hungerford Arches (*Tue–Sun noon–7pm*); collection of craft workshops open to visitors, with textiles, ceramics, jewellery, prints etc. for sale.

SOHO, BLOOMSBURY AND HOLBORN

The eastern part of the City of Westminster contains some of London's liveliest areas, including the theatre, restaurant and entertainment district of Soho, the bustling activity around the former fruit and vegetable market in Covent Garden, as well as Bloomsbury, the home of the British Museum, London University and many publishing houses. Bloomsbury's development began in the late 17th century, with the creation of Southampton (later Bloomsbury) Square – the first London square so named. In the course of the 18th and 19th centuries, the squares in this district – Bedford (the best preserved), Bloomsbury itself, Fitzroy (with work by Robert Adam), Gordon, Russell, Tavistock, Torrington and Woburn – made Bloomsbury London's social centre. Earlier this century, the district attracted many writers and philosophers – Leonard and Virginia Woolf, Clive and Vanessa Bell, Roger Fry, E.M. Forster, Lytton Strachey, J.M. Keynes and Bertrand Russell – who became known as 'The Bloomsbury Group'.

▬ *SOHO* ∗

MAP II DE 3–4 ⊖ Tottenham Court Road, Piccadilly Circus, Leicester Square

The name of this most compact and cosmopolitan London district is probably derived from an old hunting cry 'So-Ho!', although it was already a built-up area by the 17th century. French Huguenots were among the first to settle there, followed by Italians, Greeks and Chinese. The Chinese community is centred on colourful **Gerrard Street.**

Soho is bisected by **Shaftesbury Avenue** at the heart of theatre land, with the **Shaftesbury, Cambridge, Palace, Lyric, Apollo, Globe,** and **Queens** theatres all within a stone's throw of each other. The avenue itself, named after the great 19th-century reformer, the Earl of Shaftesbury, dates from the 1870s when, with Charing Cross Road, it formed part of a scheme to improve the road system of the area and to do away with some of the capital's worst slums. **Leicester Square,** once the home of Hogarth and Reynolds, is a pedestrian precinct, with statues that include Shakespeare and Charlie Chaplin, and several large cinemas. Just behind it is the church of **Notre Dame de France** (1955), of unusual circular plan, with interior decoration, including an Aubusson tapestry, by Jean Cocteau. Among other interesting Soho churches are the **French Protestant Church** and **St Patrick's,** both in Soho Square,

Telecom Tower from Fitzroy Square

and the **Church of Our Lady of the Assumption,** Warwick Street. Nearby **Carnaby Street** is a pale shadow of its former 'Swinging Sixties' self. **Wardour** and **Dean Streets** are commercial centres of the cinema industry. Otherwise, Soho is a colourful conglomerate of restaurants, cinemas, night clubs and sex shops. Of the night clubs, one of the most distinguished is **Ronnie Scott's,** Frith Street, London's premier jazz club. Soho Square also has the **House of St Barnabas,** now a hostel for homeless women, which contains the finest example of a rococo interior in London, with rich plasterwork and a splendid staircase. (*Open Wed 2.30–4.15pm, Thu 11.30am–12.30pm, or by special arrangement.*)

   Charing Cross Road and **St Martin's Lane** form another impor-tant area of London's theatre-land. In the former are the **Garrick, Wyndham's** and **Phoenix** theatres, as well as many secondhand bookshops. In St Martin's Lane stand the **Duke of York's** theatre and the **Coliseum,** London's largest theatre auditorium, built in florid Edwardian style in 1904 as a variety theatre, now the home of the English National Opera. To the north of the area, once notorious for the thieves' dens of Seven Dials, is **St Giles High Street,** with the Georgian church of **St Giles-in-the-Fields** (1731, Flitcroft), and across New Oxford Street is Bloomsbury.

▬▬ THE BRITISH MUSEUM ★★★

MAP II C4 ⊖ Holborn, Tottenham Court Road, Goodge Street, Russell Square

This museum, housing one of the world's great collections of historical treasures, was founded in 1753 (*see also p.177*). The main part of the present building, with its massive Ionic portico and colonnade facing Great Russell Street, was constructed between 1823 and 1847 to designs by Sir Robert Smirke. Later additions include the circular, copper-domed **Reading Room** (1857) by Sydney Smirke, the **Edward VII Galleries** (1914) and the **Duveen Gallery** (1938). Major bequests include George IV's library of 65,000 volumes and the Parthenon sculptures known as the **Elgin Marbles.**

   Just to the south of the museum in Bloomsbury Way, is **St George's Church** (1716, Hawksmoor) with an imposing Classical portico and unusual tower in the form of a stepped pyramid, crowned by a statue of George I posing as St George. In complete contrast is nearby **Congress House** (1958), headquarters of the Trade Union Congress (TUC), with a sculpture by Epstein. West of busy Tottenham Court Road, in the district known as **Fitzrovia,** Bloomsbury borders on Oxford Street and the fringes of Soho. **Pollock's Toy Museum** and shop in Scala Street (*open Mon–Sat 10am–5pm*) contains an enchant-ing collection of mainly Victorian toy theatres, dolls and dolls' houses. Not far away, **Telecom Tower** (1963), until recently London's tallest structure (580ft, 177m), looms above elegant and previously secluded **Fitzroy Square.**

▬▬ LONDON UNIVERSITY AND BLOOMSBURY ★

MAP II BC 4–5 ⊖ Tottenham Court Road, Russell Square

Behind the British Museum, extending almost as far north as Euston Road, are the various institutions connected with **London University**, dominated by **Senate House** (1932), headquarters of the University, which was for many years the capital's tallest building.

The **Courtauld Institute Galleries,** Woburn Square, house an important collection of Renaissance, Impressionist and Post-Impressionist paintings, including major works by Degas, Manet, Gauguin, Van Gogh and Cézanne. (*Open Mon–Sat 10am–5pm; Sun 2–5pm.*) The **Percival David Foundation,** in adjoining Gordon Square, has a representative collection of Chinese ceramics. (*Open Mon 2–5pm, Tue–Fri 10.30am–5pm, Sat 10.30am–1pm; closed Bank hols.*) No. 46 Gordon Square, the home of Virginia and Vanessa Stephen before their marriages, was for some time the headquarters of the Bloomsbury Group. **University College,** founded in 1826 to provide a higher education for those at that time excluded from Oxford or Cambridge on religious grounds, stands on Gower Street. The main building, set back in its own precinct or quadrant, is by William Wilkins, architect of the National Gallery, and is in similar Classical Revival style. It contains the John Flaxman collection of sculptures, and the somewhat macabre clothed skeleton of economist and philosopher Jeremy Bentham, who bequeathed himself to the College. Across Gower Street is the associated **University College Hospital,** founded in 1828, where Lord Lister and others did much pioneer work in the fields of antiseptics and anaesthetics. The present idiosyncratic building, by Alfred Waterhouse, dates from 1897.

In Bloomsbury's north-east corner, by Upper Woburn Place, stands the **Jewish Museum,** displaying ritual objects and antiquities of Jewish life and worship. (*Open May–Sep, Tue–Fri 10am–4pm, Sun 10am–12.45pm; Oct–Apr, Tue–Thu 10am–4pm, Fri and Sun 10am–12.45pm.*) At the corner of Upper Woburn Place and Euston Road is **St Pancras New Church** (1819), a remarkable building in Greek Revival style, with transepts modelled closely on the Temple of the Erechtheion in Athens.

HOLBORN *

MAPS II BCD 5–6; V AB 1   ⊖ Holborn, Chancery Lane

The old borough of Holborn takes its name from Hole Bourne, a tributary of the Fleet River, and includes much of Bloomsbury; but its early development came with the spread northwards of the lawyers from the Temple, into **Lincoln's** and **Gray's Inns.** Following the construction of many of the elegant squares from the Restoration period on, the 18th century saw the establishment of the **Foundling Hospital** and the building of the New Road (Euston Road). Today the area has a typical central London mix of residential and commercial building.

Coram Fields is the site of the **Foundling Hospital** for abandoned children, founded by Thomas Coram, a retired sea captain, in 1742. It is now a children's park with only fragments of the old building left. The **Thomas Coram Foundation** contains items donated by the hospital's distinguished patrons, including paintings by Hogarth and a fair copy of Handel's *Messiah* and other scores. (*Open Mon–Fri 10am–4pm; closed during conferences.*) Furnishings from the Hospital's chapel are now in St Andrew Holborn (*see p.129*). At **Gray's Inn,** which is one of the Inns of Court, the **Gatehouse** dates from 1688, and the **Hall** has been rebuilt using Tudor panelling said to have come from the wood of a Spanish galleon at the time of the Armada. There is also a statue to Sir Francis Bacon, patron of the Inn, who laid out the extensive gardens. Neighbouring streets, notably **Bedford Row** and **Doughty Street,** have fine Queen Anne and Georgian terraces. The latter also has **Dickens's House,** with mementoes of the novelist. (*Open Mon–Sat 10am–5pm; closed Bank hols.*) To the north-east, up

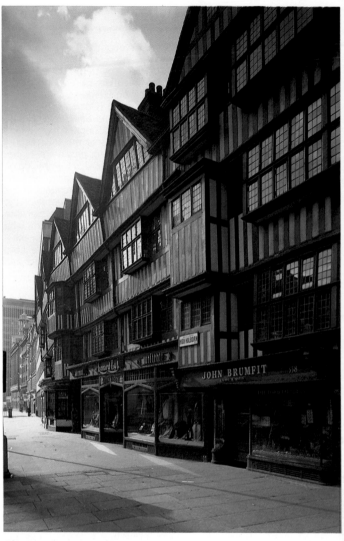

Elizabethan houses, Holborn

Rosebery Avenue, is **Sadler's Wells Theatre** (1931). It was built on the site of an earlier spa, pleasure garden and theatre for Lilian Baylis, creator of the Sadler's Wells Opera and Ballet Company (closely associated with the Old Vic Theatre). This was the forerunner of the present Royal Ballet (Covent Garden) and the English National Opera (Coliseum). The theatre today is used mainly by visiting ballet companies. The original spa well still exists beneath a trap door in the auditorium.

Gray's Inn Road meets High Holborn at **Holborn Circus,** from which Holborn Viaduct leads to the City. On the south side of the Circus is **Staples Inn,** another old enclave of the Law, with its 16th-century **Hall**. It is fronted by a row of timbered houses (1586) which, although heavily restored, recall what much of London was like

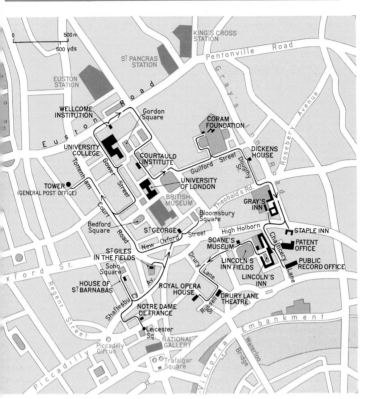

Soho, Bloomsbury and Holborn

before the Great Fire. Opposite is the **Prudential Assurance Building,**
a landmark of the Victorian Gothic Revival (1880, Alfred Waterhouse).
Adjacent Chancery Lane has Sir James Pennethorne's mock-Tudor
Public Record Office. Its **Museum** has a copy of the **Domesday
Book** – the great administrative and geographical survey of Norman
England – Shakespeare's will, letters from English kings and queens,
from Bismarck and Marie Antoinette, and many other treasured docu-
ments. (*Open Mon–Fri, 1–4pm.*) Also in Chancery Lane are the **London
Silver Vaults** where a vast selection of antique and modern silver and
plate is for sale. (*Open Mon–Fri 9am–5.30pm, Sat 9am–12.30pm.*) South
of High Holborn lies **Lincoln's Inn Fields,** one of London's largest
squares. Its most interesting building, on the north side of the square, is
Sir John Soane's Museum, the architect's home, which remains almost
as he left it. His own distinctive façade embellishes the outside of the
original 17th-century house. Within there are models and drawings of
his own work and that of Robert Adam and other architects; drawings
and etchings by the Italian artist and antiquarian Piranesi; paintings by
Hogarth, including the *Rake's Progress* series, Canaletto, Reynolds,
Turner and others; and, at the rear (the Crypt), his collection of
Egyptian, Greek and Roman antiquities. (*Open Tue–Sat 10am–5pm;
closed Bank hols.*) Across the square is the **Old Curiosity Shop**
(1567), named after Dickens's novel of the same name, selling gifts
and curios. The legal connection, however, is still strong. East of the
square, and connected with it, is **Lincoln's Inn,** another of the Inns of

Court, with its **Old Hall** (1492), **Gatehouse** (1518) and **Chapel** (1619) (*chapel and gardens open Mon–Fri noon–2.30pm, hall and library by written application*).

▬▬ COVENT GARDEN ★★

MAP II E5   ✪ Covent Garden

Covent Garden was originally a convent garden, and remained quite rural up to the 17th century, when Inigo Jones, returned from his travels in Italy, was commissioned to create the large Italian-style **Piazza** that has since shaped the area's character and appearance. The 18th-century craze for coffee houses and the proximity of two great theatres attracted such luminaries as Garrick, Goldsmith, Sheridan and Pope, but taverns, gaming houses and brothels gave the place a bad name at that time. Later, it became London's chief vegetable, fruit and flower market. Since this moved to new premises near Vauxhall in the 1970s, the Victorian **Market Hall** in the middle of the cobbled **Piazza** has become an animated arcade, with shops, market stalls, cafés and street entertainers. The whole area around Covent Garden is now one of central London's liveliest neighbourhoods.

On the west side of the **Piazza** is **St Paul's Church**, which Inigo Jones, who built it, called 'the handsomest barn in England'; it was made even more famous as the setting for the opening of Bernard Shaw's play *Pygmalion* and the musical made from it, *My Fair Lady*. Samuel Butler and Thomas Arne, composer of 'Rule, Britannia', are buried there, and it is known as the actors' church. The old **Flower Market Hall**, at the south-east corner, now houses the **London Transport Museum** with a collection of old buses, trams and trains (*open daily 10am–6pm*). The **Theatre Museum**, formerly housed in the Victoria and Albert Museum, is scheduled to move into part of the same building during 1987.

Close by are the **Theatre Royal**, Drury Lane (1819), one of London's largest and most handsome theatres, said to be haunted; and the **Royal Opera House** (1857), with its imposing Corinthian portico. It was built in the amazingly short space of six months, to replace an earlier theatre, destroyed by fire.

▬▬ PLACES TO STOP

Soho:

Soho Brasserie, 23 Old Compton St (*daily 10am–11.30pm*).
Pasticcerie Amalfi, 31 Old Compton St (*daily 10.30am–11pm*); Italian pastries and coffee.
Melati – Malay café, 21 Great Windmill St (*daily noon–11.30pm*).
Cork and Bottle – wine bar, 44 Cranbourn St (*daily to 11pm, Sun to 10.30pm*).
Café Pelican – café and brasserie, 45 St Martin's Lane (*11am–midnight*).
Chuen Cheng Ku, 17 Wardour St (*11am–11.30pm*); dim-sum during day.
Salisbury – pub, 90 St Martin's Lane.

Bloomsbury:

British Museum Coffee Shop, Great Russell St (*Mon–Sat 10.30am–4.30pm, Sun 2.30–5.30pm*).

Pizza Express, 30 Coptic St (*daily 11am–midnight*).
Museum Tavern – pub, Museum St; cream teas served.

Holborn:

Lincoln's Inn Wine Bar, Lincoln's Inn Fields (*Mon–Fri to 10.30pm*).
Corts – wine bar, 84 Chancery Lane (*Mon–Fri to 9pm*).
Princess Louise (Vaux) – pub, 208 High Holborn.
Seven Stars (Courage) – pub, 53 Carey St.
Lamb (Youngs) – pub, 94 Lamb's Conduit St.

Covent Garden:

Les Amis Gourmands – café and delicatessen, 30 James St (*Tue–Sat 9am–7pm, Mon from 10.30am*).
Cranks in the Market – juice and salad bar (*Mon–Sat 10am–8pm*).
Blake's – wine and food bar, 34 Wellington St (*daily 11.30am–10.30pm, Sun to 10pm*).
Neal's Yard Bakery and Tea Room, 6 Neal's Yard (*Mon–Sat 10.30am–8pm, Wed to 3.30pm, Sat to 4pm*).
Café Crêperie, 21 Covent Garden (*daily 10am–midnight*).
Punch & Judy (Courage) – pub, The Market.
Lamb & Flag (Courage) – pub, 33 Rose St; bar food with cheese specialities.
Nag's Head (McMullen) – pub, 10 James St.

SHOPPING

Soho:

Old Compton Street (*Mon–Sat 9.30am–5pm, some close Thu 2pm*) and the neighbouring streets have some of London's best food stores.
Berwick Street Market (*Mon–Sat 9am–5pm*); fruit and vegetables.
Gerrard Street (*daily 10am–8.30pm*); Chinese supermarkets and food shops.
Craftsmen Potters Shop, 7 Marshall St (*Mon–Sat 10am–5.30*); gallery/shop with large selection of pottery, books and tools.

Bloomsbury:

British Museum Shop, Great Russell St (*Mon–Sat 10.30am–4pm, Sun 2.30–5.30pm*); reproduction jewellery, antiquities and works of art.
Westaway and Westaway, 65 Great Russell St (*Mon–Sat 9am–5.30pm*); woollens and tartans.

Holborn:

London Silver Vaults, 53–64 Chancery Lane (*Mon–Fri 9am–5.30pm, Sat to 12.30pm*); underground arcade of shops selling new and antique silver.
Cartoon Gallery, 83 Lamb's Conduit St (*Mon–Fri 10.30am–5.30pm, Sat 1am–2pm*); original cartoons, posters and books.

Covent Garden:

Covent Garden and **Jubilee Markets** (*Mon 9am–5pm antiques, Tue–Sat 9am–5pm crafts*) and the network of surrounding streets, particularly **Neal Street,** are crammed with almost all the best shops for modern-look clothes and accessories and for contemporary home fixtures and furnishings. See the *Time Out Shopping in London* guide for full listings.
Contemporary Applied Arts, 43 Earlham St (*Mon–Fri 10am–5.30pm, Sat 11am–5pm*); ceramics, glass, textiles and other crafts by members of the Crafts Council.
Naturally British, 13 New Row (*Mon–Sat 10.30am–6.15*); gifts and crafts, all British-made.

THE WEST END

This, the largest of London's definable districts or areas, grew up during the 17th and 18th centuries, when residential building sprang up on many of the great estates and the squares centred upon them – Leicester, Hanover, Cavendish, Portman, Berkeley, Grosvenor – so shifting the capital's centre of gravity north and westwards, away from Westminster and the Thames. Most of the great town houses have gone. Commerce and entertainment have succeeded the days of gracious living. But the area's generally excellent street plan, its situation, and its bustle and prosperity have maintained the West End's allure in the eyes of Londoners and visitors alike.

REGENT STREET *
MAP II CD2 E2–3 ↩ Oxford Circus; Piccadilly Circus

This was an important part of John Nash's grand design of 1811, linking Regent's Park with Carlton House, the Prince Regent's former palace on the Mall, and at the same time creating a new north-south thoroughfare for fashionable west London. Nash's own colonnaded section, the **Quadrant,** was modified in 1848, and almost the entire street was rebuilt in the 1920s, creating the major shopping street of today.

Proceeding up the **Quadrant** from **Piccadilly Circus** you arrive at the **Café Royal,** which was founded in 1865 and has been the haunt of royalty and other celebrities. Further round the Quadrant are some famous London stores, including **Austin Reed, Aquascutum** and **Mappin and Webb** (goldsmiths, silversmiths and jewellers). Nearer to Oxford Circus are **Dickins and Jones** and **Liberty's.** The latter presents a Neo-Classical front to Regent Street itself, but the slightly earlier part (1924), in adjoining Great Marlborough Street, is an amazing essay in mock-Tudor style, much of the timbering coming from two old naval men-o'-war. Across the road, belonging to the same decade but in complete contrast, is the black granite and gilt **Palladium House** by American architect Raymond Hood. Next to that, in Argyll Street, is the **London Palladium** (1910), London's principal variety theatre.

West of Regent Street is **Hanover Square** (1720), named after George I, formerly the Elector of Hanover. The Hanover Square Rooms (demolished 1900), on the east side, were London's premier concert hall. J.C. Bach, Haydn, Paganini and Liszt all performed here in their time. **St George's Church** (1724, John James) just to the south, has seen many famous weddings – including those of Lady Hamilton,

Snowdon Aviary at the Zoo

Shelley, Disraeli and George Eliot. The two cast-iron dogs in the porch are a notable feature.

North of Oxford Circus, at the meeting of Upper Regent Street and Portland Place, is **Broadcasting House,** the BBC's administrative and sound broadcasting headquarters since 1932. Its shape, which is something like the prow of a ship, was dictated by the restricted site. A large north wing was added in the 1960s. The sculpture over the main entrance, by Eric Gill, was inspired by Shakespeare's *The Tempest* and represents Prospero sending his messenger Ariel to encompass the world. Next to Broadcasting House is **All Souls Church** (1824), a surviving part of Nash's original Regent Street, with a most unusual circular portico and conical spire. The building's strategic siting in Nash's scheme has been lost by the subsequent scale of the surroundings. A bust of the architect stands by the entrance. On Margaret Street, off Upper Regent Street, is **All Saints Church** (1859), the most remarkable Gothic Revival church in London, built by William Butterfield. The exterior is of polychrome brick, and the same material is used in the interior, together with frescoes, mosaics, stained glass, gilding, alabaster and marble, to give an effect of great richness.

▬▬ OXFORD STREET

MAPS I DE5–6; II D1–4   ⊖ Marble Arch, Bond Street, Oxford Circus, Tottenham Court Road

Oxford Street was for a long time known as Tyburn Way, which led to the notorious place of public executions at its western end (now **Marble Arch**). Although it was once the start of the road to Oxford, the name comes from the Earl of Oxford, who began its 18th-century development. By the end of the 19th century Oxford Street and Regent Street between them formed London's principal shopping area.

It begins, in the east, at St Giles Circus, at the junction with Charing Cross and Tottenham Court Roads, but the main part of the street is between **Oxford Circus** and **Marble Arch**. Its largest department store is **Selfridges,** built in 1909 by American businessman Gordon Selfridge in massive Greek-Revival style (Daniel Burnham), with a clock and figure (*The Queen of Time*) over the main entrance. It is famous for its Christmas window displays. Two of the other leading stores are **D.H. Evans** and **John Lewis** and there are many others, selling clothes, shoes, books, records and souvenirs. Stratford Place, on the north side, is a Georgian enclave, with **Stratford House** (1771), now the premises of the Oriental Club, facing down into Oxford Street.

The area immediately to the north of Oxford Street includes **St Peter's Church** (1721), Vere Street, with windows by Burne-Jones; the **Wigmore** (formerly Bechstein) **Hall** concert room (1890, T.E. Collcutt) with splendid Art Nouveau relief decoration in the apse behind the platform; Cavendish Square, with the **Convent of the Holy Child** and Epstein's sculpture *Madonna and Child* (1953); and Portman Square, with the **Courtauld Institute of Art** (1775, Robert Adam). St Christopher's Place, a narrow pedestrian street leading from Oxford Street to Wigmore Street, has charming boutiques and restaurants.

▬▬ MARYLEBONE ★★

MAP I BC5–6 D6   ⊖ Baker Street, Marylebone   ⇌ Marylebone

The name 'Marylebone' is a contraction of 'St Mary's-by-the-bourne' (stream). The area is bisected by busy Baker Street, but it is still a relatively sequestered district, with squares and streets consisting of many Georgian and early 19th-century terraces. Indeed, **Marylebone High Street** has an almost village-like atmosphere.

The star attraction of the district is the **Wallace Collection** in Hertford House, Manchester Square. Several members of the Hertford family added to this major collection of fine art, furnishings, arms and armour, including Sir Richard Wallace, whose widow bequeathed it to the nation in 1900. As well as Sèvres porcelain, Venetian glass, 17th- and 18th-century French furniture and clocks, Renaissance gold and silver work, and arms and armour from many places and periods, there is an impressive picture gallery, with works by Holbein, Titian, Canaletto, Rubens, Rembrandt, Frans Hals (*The Laughing Cavalier*), Velasquez, Poussin, Fragonard, Watteau, Reynolds, Gainsborough and Lawrence. (*Open Mon–Sat 10am–5pm, Sun 2–5pm; closed 1 Jan, Good Fri, May Day, 24–26 Dec.*)

Just south of Regent's Park, on the Marylebone Road, is **Madame Tussaud's**. The redoubtable lady began her waxworks in Paris at the time of the French Revolution, modelling the heads of victims of the guillotine. She opened her first London exhibition in 1835. In 1884 her grandsons moved her much-enlarged exhibition to the present building, where it remains the world's most famous waxwork show. In the Grand Hall is Madame Tussaud's self-portrait in wax, executed just before she died, and a parade of British monarchs, world statesmen, military leaders, writers and artists. Other sections of the exhibition are: the Conservatory, devoted mainly to film and television stars;

London's Underground

Farringdon Street was the terminus for London's first Underground line, which began at Paddington Station. This Metropolitan Railway used ordinary steam trains. These ran on lines constructed in shallow trenches and then simply roofed over – the so-called 'cut and cover' method of construction. Nevertheless, at the time it opened, the Metropolitan provided a revolutionary kind of urban transport. On its first day, in 1863, the line carried 30,000 passengers. With the addition of the District Line, the Metropolitan was to develop into the Inner Circle, and other lines were built by different companies. In 1890 the first 'tube' was introduced by the City and South London Railway (later the Northern line). This was made by boring through the earth underground; and necessitated lifts to take passengers down to the deeper levels. Electrification further transformed the system, which has continued to develop throughout the present century. In 1933 the whole group of underground railways were united with the bus companies to form the London Passenger Transport Board. As the lines extended further into the rural areas surrounding London during the inter-war years, so the suburbs developed; and for the period of World War II many stations provided shelter against the bombing raids – beds were ranged in rows along the platforms. 20th-century improvements to passengers' comfort and convenience have included sprung upholstered seats, escalators, automatic doors and turnstiles; while recent additions to the service are the Victoria and Jubilee lines and the Piccadilly Line extension, which gives travellers the opportunity of going directly from central London to Heathrow Airport.

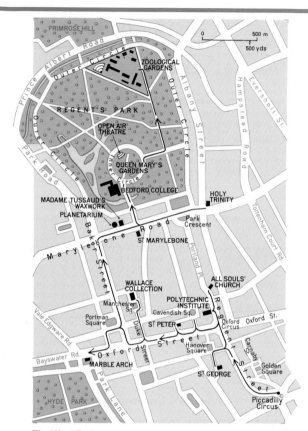

The West End

Superstars, from the worlds of sport and popular entertainment; and the Tableaux, depicting famous historical scenes or scenes inspired by paintings, including the death of Nelson aboard 'HMS Victory' during the Battle of Trafalgar. There is also the ever-popular **Chamber of Horrors,** presenting murderers, infamous scenes of crime, instruments of torture and execution. *(Open daily Apr–Sep, 10am–6pm; Oct–Mar, 10am–5.30pm; closed 25 Dec only.)* Visitors to the adjoining **Planetarium** can see images of stars, sun, moon and planets vividly projected on to a multi-dimensional screen. The **Astronomer's Gallery** contains wax tableaux, paintings and models, tracing the history of astronomy. *(Open daily 11am–4.30pm; closed 25 Dec only.)*

In neighbouring **Baker Street** the offices of the Abbey National Building Society are on the site of what was supposed to be the home **(No. 221B)** of the most famous sleuth of all, Sir Arthur Conan Doyle's Sherlock Holmes. The present occupiers still receive hundreds of letters from around the world, asking for the great detective's help!

▬ *REGENT'S PARK* ★★

MAPS I A3–6 B5–6; II AB1   ⊖ Camden Town, Baker Street, Great Portland Street, Regent's Park

Like most of London's other royal parks, Regent's Park was originally a hunting preserve. Its transformation dates from

Madame TUSSAUD

At the core of the collection at Madame Tussaud's are a remarkable series of wax portraits made from life – or death – during the period of the French Revolution and the Napoleonic Wars. Madame Tussaud, who was born in Strasbourg in 1761, had actually lived among the celebrated men of the French Revolution, and based their portraits on direct observation. She had studied wax modelling under her uncle and in 1780 went to the French court as art tutor and companion to the sister of King Louis XVI. After the outbreak of the Revolution, she was forced to take death masks from guillotined heads: it was her business one day to model the horrible countenance of the assassinated Marat, whom she detested, and on another to imitate the features of his beautiful assassin, Charlotte Corday, whom she admired and loved. At one time she was herself in prison, in danger of the all-devouring guillotine, having there as her associates, Madame Beauharnais and her child, the grandmother and mother of the Emperor Napoleon III. Escaping from France, she led for many years a life of struggle and difficulty, supporting herself and her family by the exercise of her art. Once she lost her whole stock by shipwreck on a voyage to Ireland. Meeting adversity with a stout heart, always industrious, frugal, and considerate, the ingenious little woman was eventually able to set up her models in London, where she enjoyed forty years of constant prosperity, and where she died in her 90th year. Many Victorians were familiar with her neat little figure, seated by the stairs, hard to distinguish in its calm primness from the counterfeits of humanity which it was the business of her life to fabricate.

1811, when John Nash, with backing from the Prince Regent, drew up plans to turn it into a luxurious residential estate, or garden surburb. These plans were never fully realized but the magnificent group of terraces around much of the Park's perimeter endows it with a special distinction.

The grandest terraces are **Chester** (1825) and **Cumberland** (1826), on the east side of the Park, which are adorned with Corinthian columns, broad pediments and connecting archways, and rich stuccoed mouldings that create an almost wedding cake effect. The other main terraces, presenting a variety of styles within an overall scheme, are: **Hanover, Clarence, Cornwall, Nottingham, York,** and **Sussex Place.** The scheme continues on a more modest but equally effective scale south into **Park Square** and **Park Crescent**, where it is bisected by the Marylebone Road. On the Park's west side is a much more recent but interesting addition to the general environment – the **Islamic Cultural Centre** and **Mosque** (1977, Sir Frederick Gibberd) with copper dome and minaret.

The Inner Circle Road within the park was a part of Nash's original plan, and the buildings of **Bedford College** are here, now a centre for European studies of Rockford College (Illinois). The road encloses **Queen Mary's Garden,** with fountains, pond, rose garden and restaurant; and the **Open Air Theatre,** which first opened in 1933 for summer seasons, mostly of plays by Shakespeare. The curiously shaped boating lake is also a surviving part of Nash's scheme.

The **Zoological Gardens** in the Park's north-east corner, occupy land originally intended for more terraces. The Zoological Society was founded in 1826, and the first Gardens, laid out by Decimus Burton, were opened two years later. The number and variety of animals rapidly increased during the 19th century, and the world's first reptile house, aquarium and insect house were erected. During the 20th century, most of the old buildings and cages have been replaced by imaginative new structures, to the advantage of both the animals and visitors. Today's zoological population comprises over 1,000 species of mammal, bird, reptile, fish and insect. The Zoological Society itself is a world centre of scientific study and research. (*Open daily Mar–Oct, 9am–6pm; Nov–Feb, 10am–6pm; Sun and Bank hols 10am–7pm; closed 25 Dec only.*)

St John's Wood Chapel (1813) stands by the west side of the Park, facing Park Road. Beyond it is Lord's Cricket Ground, headquarters of Marylebone Cricket Club (MCC), which became the sport's first governing body as long ago as 1788. The **Cricket Memorial Gallery** has the famous Ashes trophy – an urn containing the ashes of a set of bails ceremoniously burnt in 1883 – and other cricketing memorabilia. (*Open match days 10.30am–5pm, or by prior appointment.*) North of the Park, in Regent's Park Road, is **Cecil Sharp House**, headquarters of the English Folk Song and Dance Society, with the **Vaughan Williams Memorial Library.** (*Open Mon–Fri 9.30am–5.30pm.*)

LITTLE VENICE AND THE REGENT'S CANAL ★

MAPS I A3–4 BCD2–3; Inner London A2–3   ⊖ Warwick Avenue

Little Venice is the comparatively recent name (possibly first coined by the poet Robert Browning) for the area to the south-west of Regent's Park that encompasses a stretch of the **Regent's Canal.** Despite busy Edgware Road and an elevated section of motorway, it remains a secluded and picturesque spot, the canal banks shaded by trees and lined with Regency and Victorian town houses.

The **Regent's Canal** joins up with Paddington Basin, close to I.K. Brunel's majestic iron and glass **Paddington Station** of 1854. The canal was constructed between 1812 and 1820, with locks, bridges and tunnels, to link the Grand Union Canal, coming down from the industrial Midlands, with London's docks. The enterprise was barely completed when the rapid growth of the railway began to take away its business. Happily, it has been preserved, both as a memorial to early industrial London and as a unique and relatively little-known part of the London scene. Converted barges and water buses operate between April and October from **Little Venice,** round the north side of **Regent's Park** and the **Zoo,** as far as **Camden Lock.** The full length of the canal, with its towpath accessible at many points, extends from **Brentford** in west London to **Limehouse Basin** in the east.

PLACES TO STOP

Regent Street:
Austin Reed – Reed's in-store café, 103 Regent St (*Mon–Sat 9.30am–5pm, Thu to 7pm*).
Liberty – in-store café, Regent St (*Mon–Sat 9.30am–6pm, Thu to 7pm*).
St George's Hotel – lounge, Langham Place.
The George – pub, 55 Great Portland St.

Oxford Street:

Café Crêperie, 56 South Molton St (*Mon–Sat 10am–8.30pm*).

Chicago Pizza Pie Factory, 17 Hanover Square (*daily noon–11.30pm, Sun to 10.30pm*).

Justin de Blank – café, 54 Duke St (*Mon–Fri 8.30am–3.30pm, 4.30–9pm, Sat 9am–3.30pm*).

Paling's – wine bar, 25 Hanover Square (*Mon–Sat to 11pm, closed Sat lunchtime*).

Baker Street/Marylebone:

Portman Hotel – Portman Corner, Portman Square (*daily 11am–midnight, tea 3.30–5.30pm*).

Bonne Bouche Pâtisserie, 2 Thayer St (*Mon–Sat 8.30am–7pm, Sun 9am–6pm*).

Reuben's – Kosher food, 20a Baker St (*Mon–Fri noon–3pm, 5–10pm, closed Fri eve, Sun noon–10pm*).

Maison Sagne – café and pâtisserie, 105 Marylebone High St (*Mon–Sat 9am–5pm, Sat to 12.30pm*).

Hungry's – café, 37a Crawford St (*Mon–Sat 8am–3pm*).

Seashell – fish and chips, 51 Lisson Grove (*Tue–Sat noon–2pm, 5.15–10.30pm*).

▬ SHOPPING

Regent Street/Oxford Street (*most shops Mon–Sat 9.30am–6pm, Thu to 7.30pm*).

Most of London's principal department stores are on these two streets (*see p.41*), while **South Molton Street** has some of the most fashionable boutiques. Just around the corner in Davies Street is ***Gray's Antique Market*** (*Tue–Sat 10am–6pm*). North of Oxford Street, Gees Place leads to **St Christopher's Place** with shops specializing in fashion, antiques and gifts, a fascinating corner away from all the bustle.

Marylebone:

Church Street Antiques Market (*Mon–Sat 8am–4.30pm*); includes the covered stalls in **Alfie's,** No. 13–25 (*Tue–Sat 10am–6pm*).

Ninjin Food Shop, 244 Great Portland St (*Tue–Fri 10.30am–7pm, Sat & Sun 9.30am–6.30pm*); Japanese specialities.

Itinerary 9

HYDE PARK, KENSINGTON
AND CHELSEA

The two royal parks, Hyde Park and Kensington Gardens,
combine to form the largest open space in central London.
Yet the distinction between Park and Garden is well made, the
generally open character of Hyde Park and the more intimately
landscaped appearance of much of Kensington Gardens being
attractively separated by the stretches of water known as the
Long Water and the Serpentine. Kensington itself, a large
district situated on rising ground above the old Thames flood
plain, attracted the aristocracy from the 17th century on, and
the names of their dwellings – Campden House, Holland
House, Gore House – are preserved in local place names.
William III's move to Kensington Palace enhanced its reputation, and Kensington's prestige was maintained by its prosperous urban growth in the 19th century, with the construction
of some great public buildings and institutions. Chelsea, by
contrast, has strong artistic and bohemian associations.

━━━ *HYDE PARK AND KENSINGTON GARDENS* ★★

MAP III A3–5 BC1–6 D1–3   ⊖ Knightsbridge, Hyde Park Corner, Marble
Arch, Lancaster Gate, Queensway, Notting Hill Gate

Bordered by Park Lane, Knightsbridge and Bayswater Road, and
to the west by Kensington Gardens, **Hyde Park** was first opened to
the public in 1637, when it was still on the outskirts of the capital.
For a long time to come it had a very stormy and dramatic history.
It was fortified during the Civil War and continued to serve as a
military camp and arsenal until into the 19th century. It was also,
in the 18th century, a notorious duelling ground and haunt of
footpads and highwaymen, before it became London's most
fashionable carriage and riding venue. Its greatest moment of
glory was in 1851, when it was chosen as the site of the Great
Exhibition (housed in Joseph Paxton's Crystal Palace). In 1961
Hyde Park lost some of its land to the widening of Park Lane, but
it remains the capital's most accessible and popular open space.

   Rotten Row, the main equestrian way along the Park's south
side, was the site of the Crystal Palace. The name is a corruption of
Route du Roi (King's Way), and William III, who used the route on his
way to and from Kensington Palace, had lamps hung from the trees to
try to deter highwaymen after dark — the first stretch of English

The Albert Memorial and Royal Albert Hall

roadway to be lit at night. North of Rotten Row is the **Serpentine,** now a boating lake and swimming pool. It was created in 1730 by damming the Westbourne River, which flowed south and east towards the Thames. In 1814, as a part of the peace celebrations following Napoleon's exile to Elba, model sailing ships re-enacted the Battle of Trafalgar to the sounds of cannon and the national anthem. Two restaurants mark its extremities. Just north again, across the bridge, is the old Greek-Doric style Magazine (1805) and the Bird Sanctuary, marked by Epstein's sculpture *Rima.* **Speaker's Corner,** which is in the park's north-eastern corner, has been famous since the 1870s for its open-air orators. **Marble Arch**, which is now isolated by the traffic junction named after it, was designed by Nash in 1827, in the style of a Roman triumphal arch, as the entrance to Buckingham Palace. It was moved to its present site in 1851. At the south-eastern corner of the Park is the bronze **Achilles Statue,** facing towards Apsley House, a tribute to the Duke of Wellington, modelled on the nude Roman figure of a horse-tamer and the source of some embarrassment at its unveiling in 1822.

The transition from Hyde Park to the generally more intimate character of Kensington Gardens is set by the Italianate **Fountain Gardens** and **Queen Anne's Alcove** (Wren) on the north side, near Lancaster Gate. A little way down the **Long Water** is the statue to J.M. Barrie's Peter Pan (1912), and the Elfin Oak with its carved and painted figures. A grander tone is struck by G.F. Watts's *Physical Energy* (1904), which looks down **Lancaster Walk,** a splendid avenue of trees, leading to Kensington Road and Sir George Gilbert Scott's highly ornamental **Albert Memorial** of 1872 to Queen Victoria's husband Prince Albert. Amidst all the elaborate stonework there are symbolic representations of the continents of Europe, America, Africa and Asia,

---

The Crystal Palace

The Great Exhibition, the first of the 'universal exhibitions', or 'world's fairs', held in Hyde Park in 1851, was the brainchild of Albert, the Prince Consort, and its intention was to display the arts and industries of Great Britain, the British Empire and the world. There were nearly 15,000 exhibitors, divided about equally between British and foreign contributors, and over six million visitors, an average of more than 40,000 each day. The exhibition, which was opened on 1 May by Queen Victoria, was accommodated on a site just to the south of the Serpentine, in an immense structure of iron and glass – the Crystal Palace. The building was 1,851ft (555m) long by 408ft (122m) wide, with an additional width of 48ft (14m) for half that length; the highest portion was a centre transept 108ft (32m) high. It was designed by Sir Joseph Paxton, gardener to the Duke of Devonshire, and was an extraordinary example of the application of technology to building, since all the parts – glass, iron and wood – were prefabricated, and the building grew at incredible speed, although everything was moved by man and horse. After it had opened *The Times* wrote, 'Above the visitors rose a glittering arch far more lofty and spacious than the vaults of even our noblest cathedrals. On either side the vista seemed almost boundless.' After the exhibition the Crystal Palace was dismantled and re-erected in Sydenham in South London. It burnt down in 1936, perhaps because of a cigarette left by an absent-minded postmistress, but its name is preserved in the sports centre on the site.

and celebrations of various arts and sciences. A few steps back towards the bridge which divides the Serpentine from the Long Water is the **Serpentine Gallery,** a venue for frequent art exhibitions.

KENSINGTON PALACE *

MAP III C1   ⊖ Notting Hill Gate, Queensway, High Street Kensington

The western end of Kensington Gardens is largely occupied by **Kensington Palace** and its environs. A large Jacobean house already stood on the site when William III, who found Whitehall Palace too close to the Thames for his poor health, bought the property and commissioned Wren and Hawksmoor to reconstruct it as his London home. The Palace was in, and then out, of favour with the Hanoverian monarchs. Queen Victoria was born there, and though she and her court moved to Buckingham Palace, Kensington Palace retains several royal apartments. (*Open Mon–Sat 9am–5pm, Sun 1–5pm; closed Good Fri, May Day Bank hol, 24–26 Dec, 1 Jan.*)

The **King's Staircase,** with murals by William Kent, is the grandest part of the interior. The **Gallery** includes paintings by Rubens and Van Dyck, and there are 17th- and 18th-century furnishings, personal mementoes of Queen Victoria and a collection of court dresses. The **Broad Walk, Sunken Gardens, Orangery** and nearby **Round Pond** (though it is not strictly circular) were all conceived as part of the Palace grounds.

HOLLAND PARK

MAP Inner London C1   ⊖ Holland Park, High Street Kensington, Olympia

Like many of the parks all around London, **Holland Park** has its origins in the gardens surrounding one of the capital's old noble mansions. **Holland House,** a splendid Jacobean building of 1606, was an important social and political centre around 1800, and in the 1890s was famous for its masked balls and garden parties, but was largely destroyed by bombs in World War II. The formal gardens have now been well restored, and make a most attractive summer setting for open-air plays and concerts.

At the south end of Holland Park is the highly original structure of the **Commonwealth Institute** (1962), which displays exhibits from 40 Commonwealth countries and is the venue for frequent film, theatre and dance shows. (*Open Mon–Sat 10am–5.30pm, Sun 2–5pm.*) **Leighton House** (1865), a little further west in Holland Park Road, was the home of Lord Leighton, a fashionable Victorian artist. Part of the interior is most fancifully decorated in the style of an Islamic courtyard, with mosaics and a fountain, and there are many paintings from Lord Leighton's collection. (*Open Mon–Sat 11am–5pm, closed Bank hols.*)

KENSINGTON HIGH STREET AND KENSINGTON ROAD

MAPS Inner London C1–2; III D1–3   ⊖ High Street Kensington, Knightsbridge

The High Street is one of London's busiest shopping streets, and there are several large modern hotels just to the south, while Kensington Church Street is famous for its antique shops. At the corner with Church Street the High Street becomes Kensington

Road, continuing west to Knightsbridge and Hyde Park Corner. Kensington, the 'Royal Borough', was largely developed in the 19th century, but behind the High Street the grand Victorian terraces give way to the older and more intimate character of Kensington Square – one of the best-preserved pockets of Queen Anne and Georgian London, with many notable past residents to its credit.

Kensington Palace Gardens by the Royal Garden Hotel, known as 'Millionaire's Row', is a private road lined with opulent mansions, many of them now embassies. Further east, opposite the Albert Memorial, stands one of Kensington's – and London's – most celebrated buildings, the **Royal Albert Hall,** named after Queen Victoria's consort. Opened in 1870, the massive circular edifice is similar in size and plan to the Roman Coliseum and is largely the work of Francis Fowke, an army engineer. The brick and stone structure is surmounted by an iron and glass domed roof, around the base of which runs a decorative frieze, *The Triumph of Art and Letters.* Inside there is seating for 8,000, and a 150-ton organ, the world's largest when installed. Many great composers have appeared there, including Wagner and Bruckner, and it has long been the home of the famous summer season of Promenade Concerts.

Victorian confidence and idealism are further expressed in many of the neighbouring institutions. In the immediate vicinity of the Hall are the buildings of the **Royal College of Organists,** in exuberant Italianate style, the **Royal College of Music** and, just a little to the south, the handsome Italianate tower of the original **Imperial Institute** (succeeded by the **Imperial College of Science and Technology**). In sharp contrast to these is the **Royal College of Art** (1961), where exhibitions are sometimes held. Beyond the Royal Albert Hall is the splendid building of the **Royal Geographical Society** (1874, Norman Shaw), originally a private residence and the first house in London to have a passenger lift installed. A little further on, the road changes its name again, to **Knightsbridge,** and on the left are the **Horse Guards Barracks,** accommodated in a tower block 270ft (82m) high (1966, Sir Basil Spence).

▬▬ *KNIGHTSBRIDGE, BELGRAVIA AND SOUTH KENSINGTON* ★

MAP III D4–6 E2–6   ⊖ Knightsbridge, Hyde Park Corner, South Kensington

Knightsbridge is believed to have taken its name from an old bridge over the River Westbourne, where two knights once met in legendary combat. Some of London's most exclusive town houses and apartments are situated in and around such charming period streets and squares as **Brompton Square** and **Beauchamp Place**. A little way down **Brompton Road** stands the terracotta emporium of **Harrods** (1905), one of the world's largest and most famous department stores, employing a staff of

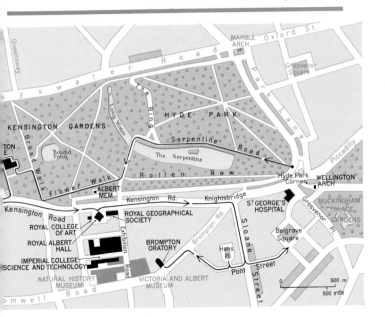

Hyde Park, Kensington and Chelsea

5,000. Interior decoration includes Art Nouveau tiling (in the main food hall) and Art Deco motifs.

Belgravia, east of Sloane Street, is a district that had long been neglected in favour of Kensington further to the west, but since the early 19th century it has stood shoulder to shoulder with Knightsbridge as one of the capital's most exclusive areas. Its heart is **Belgrave Square** (1825–40), which was created by property developer Thomas Cubitt and mostly planned and built on a suitably grand scale by George Bavesi, a pupil of Sir John Soane. It has been the address of many famous people, but is now occupied almost entirely by embassies, consulates and institutions. A recent addition is a statue to South American patriot Simon Bolivar. Just behind it is elegant **Wilton Crescent.** A little to the south is **Eaton Square** (1826–53), also conceived by Cubitt, though more of a spacious rectangle divided by the King's Road than a true square. In keeping with its lofty scale and appearance, it has been the home of three prime ministers, Russell, Baldwin and Chamberlain. **St Peter's Church** (1824), in the Classical Revival style, harmonizes well.

Pont Street, whose Dutch-style houses have elaborate terracotta decoration, leads back, by way of **Beauchamp Place,** a narrow street lined with fashionable shops and restaurants, to Brompton Road, at whose western end stands the **Brompton Oratory** (1884). Named after the Oratory of St Philip Neri, Rome, it was London's main Roman Catholic church until the building of Westminster Cathedral. It is in Italianate Baroque style, with statues of saints from Siena Cathedral.

Beyond are the South Kensington museums, on Cromwell and Exhibition Roads, the largest group of museums in London. On the east side of Exhibition Road is the **Victoria and Albert,** founded in the wake of the Great Exhibition of 1851, although the present building, topped with a tower in the form of an imperial crown, was not completed until 1909. It is devoted to the fine and applied arts of almost all places and periods and includes many European and Oriental treasures. A short distance to the west along Cromwell Road is the remarkable building of the **Natural History Museum** (1873, Alfred Waterhouse), in bright and colourful Neo-Romanesque style, decorated inside and out with the carved images of animals and plants. Between these two, back in Exhibition Road itself, are the **Science Museum** (1913), and the **Geological Museum** (1935). Its lively atmosphere and the nature of its exhibits make the Science Museum especially attractive for families with children. (*Open Mon–Sat 10am– 6pm, Sun 2.30–6pm.*) *For full details of the Victoria and Albert, Natural History and Science Museums, see pp.196–209.* Further west still, at the corner of Cromwell Road and Queen's Gate is **Baden Powell House,** with a memorial exhibition to the founder of the Scout Association (*open daily 9am–6pm*).

▬▬ CHELSEA ★

MAP Inner London D2   ⊖ Sloane Square

The place name Chelsea may come from a very old Anglo-Saxon word meaning 'Chalk Wharf', since there are traces of riverside chalk in the prevailing London clay. The two men who really put Chelsea on the map were Sir Thomas More, who built a large country house there in 1520, and Henry VIII, who bequeathed his even grander mansion to his sixth wife Catherine Parr. The porcelain works of 1745 (which only functioned for about 50 years) gave the name and reputation of Chelsea an even wider circulation. Neat 18th-century streets and squares, where many celebrated writers and artists have lived, as well as antique shops and fashion boutiques, give today's Chelsea its charm and its chic, in contrast to the more august character of neighbouring Knightsbridge and Belgravia.

With mainly Queen Anne, Georgian and Regency houses facing the Thames, trim little public gardens, and house boats moored along the river bank, **Cheyne Walk** is one of London's most charming stretches of riverside.

The most impressive dwelling, at its west end, is **Lindsey House** (1675), one-time home of engineer I.K. Brunel and of the artist Whistler. **Crosby Hall,** the 15th-century mansion of a wool merchant, has period panelling, windows and timber roof. (*Open daily 10am– noon, 2–5pm; closed Tue pm and Sat.*) Standing a short way back from the river is **Chelsea Old Church** (All Saints), which has Norman origins and contains monuments to Sir Thomas More and others as well as the only chained books in a London church. **Thomas Carlyle's House,** Cheyne Row, a Queen Anne house, is preserved largely as the writer and historian knew it. (*Open Wed–Sun 11am–5pm, Sun, Bank hol Mon 2–5pm.*) Nos. 19–26 Cheyne Walk occupy the site of Henry VIII's former manor house.

East of **Albert Bridge** (1871–3, R.M. Ordish), the most picturesque of the Thames bridges, begins **Chelsea Embankment,** a part of Sir Joseph Bazalgette's 19th-century reconstruction of London's riverside. Across the road from the river, by Swan Walk, is the **Chelsea Physic Garden,** established as a herbal and botanical garden by The Society of Apothecaries in 1676. It has long been noted for its splendid Cedars of Lebanon, the first to be planted successfully in England. Cotton seed produced in the Garden was taken to what were then the American colonies, and the great Swedish botanist Linnaeus pursued some of his studies in the Garden. (*Open mid-Apr–mid-Oct, Sun, Wed, and Bank hols 2–5pm; also week of Chelsea Flower Show noon–5pm.*)

Hans SLOANE (1660–1753)

The physician and naturalist Hans Sloane was born at Killyleagh, County Down, and studied natural history and medicine there until 1679, when he went to London. He was elected a Fellow of the Royal Society in 1684 and the following year went to Jamaica, where he collected a herbarium of some 800 species. After his return he became physician to Christ's Hospital (1694–1724), and among numerous other positions, he succeeded Sir Isaac Newton as President of the Royal Society in 1727 (the same year he was appointed Royal Physician). On his retirement he purchased an estate in Chelsea, including a garden (now the Chelsea Physic Garden) which he later bequeathed to the Society of Apothecaries. Following his death in 1753, his museum and library of 50,000 volumes and 3,560 manuscripts were offered to the nation and formed the basis of the British Museum. His survival to the age of 93 exemplified his favourite maxim – that sobriety, temperance and moderation are the best preservatives that nature has granted to mankind. Though noted for his hospitality, there were three things Sir Hans Sloane never had at his table – salmon, champagne and burgundy.

THE ROYAL HOSPITAL *

MAP Inner London D2–3   ⊖ Sloane Square

A little further along Chelsea Embankment, and standing well back in its own extensive grounds, is the **Royal Hospital,** founded as a home for veteran soldiers by Charles II in 1682, who was inspired by the similar institution of the Hotel des Invalides in Paris, which he had known during his years of exile. The main plan of the building, by Sir Christopher Wren, is based on that of Les Invalides, with a few later additions by Robert Adam and Sir John Soane. The residents (420 campaign veterans, known as Chelsea Pensioners), wear 18th-century uniforms, with dark blue coats for winter and scarlet coats for summer, and with special tricorne hats for the Oak Apple Parade on 29 May, in honour of the founder's birthday.

The **Chapel, Great Hall** and adjoining **Museum** (*open Mon–Sat 10am–noon and 2–4pm, Sun 2–4pm*) are mainly dedicated to the Hospital's history. In the south court is a bronze statue of Charles II in Roman costume by Grinling Gibbons. Just to the west, on Royal Hospital Road, is the **National Army Museum,** which traces British Army history over a period of 500 years. (*Open Mon–Sat 10am–5.30pm, Sun 2–5.30pm; closed Bank hols.*) **Ranelagh Gardens,** directly to the east of the Royal Hospital and now incorporated into the hospital grounds, is the site for the annual Chelsea Flower Show in May.

On the far side of the Royal Hospital runs the **King's Road,** the path once taken by Charles II to Nell Gwynne's house in Fulham, now lined with stylish antique shops, boutiques, restaurants and pubs. In **Sloane Square** is the **Royal Court Theatre,** noted for its adventurous productions, and the architecturally much-praised **Peter Jones** department store (1936). **Holy Trinity Church** (1888), which is just in Sloane Street, is rich in Pre-Raphaelite decoration, with stained glass windows by Burne-Jones.

Street Markets

Although Portobello Road was the site of a market in the 19th century, it is only since World War II that it has become London's principal market for antiques, with a quite bewildering array from old English silver, glass and china to fairground horses, jukeboxes and second-hand clothes. But it is only one of many street markets in London, where you can still buy practically everything needed for everyday life (and much else besides) if you know where to look. Markets in London have a long and flourishing tradition, dating back to Roman times when Londinium was established, at the lowest crossing point on the River Thames, as a trading post and port. Numerous London street names indicate the former sites of specialist trading; Bread Street, Ironmonger Lane, Wood Street and Leather Lane, tell clearly what used to be sold there – medieval traders all dealing in one product would group together in guilds in order to protect themselves from excessive trading regulations. The product which took up most space was the hay – in enormous quantities – needed to feed London's horses, which, until the end of the last century, pulled virtually every kind of transport used in the capital. This was sold not only at Haymarket, but at Whitechapel and Smithfield too. And streets like Cheapside would have been trading centres early in London's history, for the Anglo-Saxon word 'ceap' meant 'market'.

Although many of the markets have changed their location and what they sell, the street trading tradition is still very strong. Some date from only the last ten years or less (Hampstead Community, Jubilee and Swiss Cottage markets, for instance); some have vanished leaving streets of shops instead (Oxford Street); many sell everything, as at Brick Lane, others tend to specialize: Bermondsey, and Camden Passage as well as Portobello for antiques, Columbia Road for plants. Some are open six days a week (Chapel Street and North End Road), others take place once or twice a week (Brick Lane). (*See p.42 for details.*)

Markets have always reflected the character of the surrounding inhabitants, and while Petticoat Lane is a traditionally Jewish area connected with the rag trade (clothes), many of the other East London markets now have a distinctively Asian flavour; and South London's Brixton market offers an exotic range of Caribbean fruit, vegetables, fish and other food unknown elsewhere in London, whilst resounding to the beat of reggae records which are also for sale.

▬ BAYSWATER AND PADDINGTON

MAPS I CDE1–3; Inner London B1   ⊖ Paddington, Bayswater, Queensway, Notting Hill Gate, Ladbroke Grove

North of Kensington Gardens lie the districts of Bayswater and Paddington. Residential development started around Marble Arch at the beginning of the 19th century, but in the early part of Queen Victoria's reign there were still fields between the turnpike road to the west (now Bayswater Road) and the canal and, later, railway.

The whole area is still mainly residential, with many hotels and lodging houses around **Paddington Station**. This majestic iron and glass construction (1854, I.K. Brunel) was the terminus of the Great Western Railway and is still the main London station for destinations in the west of England. **Queensway** and **Westbourne Grove** are lively streets with restaurants and cafés open late into the night. Further west are **Notting Hill Gate,** once the site of the Kensington Gravel Pits, and Ladbroke Grove. One of London's most colourful festivals, the annual West Indian Carnival, is held here over the August Bank Holiday weekend.

Just behind Notting Hill Gate is the beginning of **Portobello Road,** famous for its antiques market, which on Saturdays stretches along the road for more than a mile and spills over into neighbouring side-streets. A little beyond the north end of Portobello Road, beside the canal, lies **Kensal Green Cemetery,** founded in 1830, with many splendid Victorian funerary monuments, including the tombs of the Brunels, of Thackeray, Trollope and Wilkie Collins and of the great Victorian chef Alexis Soyer, buried beside his wife in the monument he himself designed, inscribed only, in huge letters, 'TO HER'.

PLACES TO STOP

Kensington High Street:

Muffin Man – tea shop, 12 Wright's Lane (*Mon–Sat 8.15am–5.45pm*).
Pâtisserie Parisienne, 2a Phillimore Gardens (*Mon–Sat 8.30am–7.30pm, Sun 10am–6pm*).
Scarsdale Arms (Watneys) – pub, 23 Edwardes Square.
Windsor Castle (Charringtons) – pub, 114 Campden Hill Rd.

Knightsbridge:

Sheraton Park Tower – restaurant (*daily 6.30am–midnight, tea 3–5.30pm*).
Hyde Park Hotel – Park Room (*Mon–Sat breakfast 7.30–10.30am, tea 3.45–6pm, Sun breakfast 8–11am, tea 4–6pm*).
Harvey Nichols – Harvey at the Top, in-store restaurant (*Mon–Sat 9.30am–5.30pm, Wed to 6.30pm*).
Grenadier (Watneys) – pub, 18 Wilton Row; traditional English food.
Nag's Head – pub, (Benskins and Burton), 53 Kinnerton St.

Sloane Street:

Bendicks – pâtisserie, No. 195 (*Mon–Fri 9.30am–5pm*).
L'Express – café, No. 16 (*Mon–Sat 9.30am–5.30pm, Sun 11am–5.30pm*).
Hyatt Carlton Tower – Chinoiserie, 2 Cadogan Place (*8am–1am, tea 3–5.30pm*).
General Trading Company – Justin de Blank's, No. 144 (*Mon–Sat 9am–5.15pm, Sat to 1.30pm*).

Brompton Road:

Richoux – pâtisserie, No. 86 (*daily 9am–7pm, Wed to 8pm, Sun from 10am*).
Harrods – Dress and Upper Circle Restaurants; Health Juice Bar; New England Ice Cream Parlour; Georgian Restaurant and Terrace for tea (*Mon–Sat 9.30am–5.30pm, Wed to 6.30pm*).
Le Métro – wine and coffee bar, 28 Basil St (*Mon–Fri to 10.15 pm*).

South Kensington:

Victoria and Albert Museum – Restaurant and café, Cromwell Rd (*Mon–Thu, Sat 10am–5pm, Sun 2.30–5.30pm*).
La Brasserie, 272 Brompton Rd (*breakfast daily 8am–noon, Sun from 10am*).
Daquise – café-restaurant, 20 Thurloe St (*daily noon–10.45pm*).

Maison Verlon – café and bakery, 12 Bute St (*Mon–Sat 9am–8pm, Sun 10.30am–6pm*).
Corks – wine bar, 3 Harrington Rd (*Mon–Fri to 10.30pm*).
Anglesea Arms – pub, 15 Selwood Terrace.

Chelsea:

Blushes – wine bar, 52 King's Rd (*daily to midnight*).
Charco's – wine bar, 1 Bray Place (*Mon–Sat to 11pm*).
Draycott's – wine bar, 114 Draycott Ave (*Mon–Fri to 10.30pm, Sat–Sun lunchtime*).
Le Bouzy Rouge – wine bar, 221 King's Rd (*daily to 11pm, closed Sun–Mon lunchtime*).
Parsons – café-restaurant, 311 Fulham Rd (*daily noon–midnight*).
Ferret & Firkin (Bruce's) – pub, 114 Lots Rd.
Henry J. Bean's – bar/grill, 195 King's Rd.
Cross Keys (Courage) – pub, Lawrence St; bar food.
White Horse (Vintage) – pub, 1 Parsons Green; breakfast Sat–Sun and famous bar meals.
King's Head & Eight Bells (Whitbread) – pub, 50 Cheyne Walk; gourmet pies and salads, hot meals and pub food.
Admiral Codrington (Bass) – pub, 17 Mossop St; charcoal grills.
Forests Bakers, 401 King's Rd (*Mon–Sat 7am–5.30pm*); café bakery.

Bayswater and Paddington:

Victoria (Charringtons) – pub, 10a Strathearn Place.
Gyngleboy – wine bar, 27 Spring St (*Mon–Fri to 9.30pm*).
Maison Pechon - pâtisserie, 127 Queensway (*Mon–Sat 8am–7pm, Sun 9am–6pm*).
Maison Bouquillon – pâtisserie, 45 Moscow Rd (*daily 8.30am–5.30pm*).
L'Etoile – pâtisserie, 73 Westbourne Grove (*daily 9am–11pm*).

Holland Park:

Julie's Champagne Bar, 137 Portland Rd (*Mon–Sat 11am–11pm, Sun noon–10.30pm*); also teas.

Ladbroke Grove:

Frog & Firkin (Bruce's) – pub, 41 Tavistock Crescent.
Narrow Boat (Fullers) – pub, 346 Ladbroke Grove.

▬ SHOPPING

Kensington High Street (*Thu to 7.30pm*):
Kensington Market, No. 49; modern and revival fashion shops.
Hyper Hyper, No. 26; fashion by young designers.
Many antique shops in Kensington Church Street.

Knightsbridge (*Wed to 7pm*):
Bradley's, No. 85; lingerie.

Sloane Street (*Wed to 7pm, some shops close early on Sat*):
Kenzo, No. 17; Japanese designer fashions.
Issey Miyake, No. 21; Japanese designer fashions.
Joseph Tricot, No. 18, and **Joseph Bis,** No. 166; fashion.
Cobra and Bellamy, No. 149 (*Mon–Sat 10.30am–6pm, Sat to 4pm*): 20th-century jewellery.
General Trading Company, No. 144; gifts and household goods.

Brompton Road:
Scotch House, No. 2 (*Mon–Sat from 9am, Mon–Wed to 5.30pm, Thu to 6.30pm, Fri–Sat to 7pm*); Scottish woollens and tartans.

Harrods (*Mon–Sat 9am–6pm, Wed 9.30am–7pm*); world-famous department store with over 200 departments.

Beauchamp Place – off Brompton Rd, many boutiques for fashion, gifts and antiques:

Janet Reger, No. 2 (*Mon–Fri 10am–6pm, Sat to 5pm*); lingerie.
Break of Day, No. 10 (*Mon–Sat 10am–6pm, Sun 11am–5pm*); gifts.
Fouquet of Knightsbridge, No. 58 (*Mon–Sat 9.30am–6.30pm, Wed to 7pm, Sat to 6pm*); Parisian confectioner.

South Kensington:

Victoria and Albert Museum Craft Shop, Cromwell Rd (*Mon–Thu, Sat 10am–5pm, Sun 2.30–5.30pm*).
Plantation, 270 Brompton Rd (*Mon–Sat 10am–6pm, Wed to 7pm*); Issey Miyake fashions.
Conran Shop, 77 Fulham Rd (*Mon–Fri 9.30am–6pm, Tue from 10am*); household goods and furnishings.

Fulham Road (*Mon–Sat 10am–6pm*):

Comme des Garçons, No. 113 (*Wed to 7pm*); Japanese new-wave fashions.
Butler and Wilson, No. 189; fashion jewellery.

King's Road (*Mon–Sat 10am–6pm*):

Antiquarius, No. 135; antique market.
Givans Irish Linen Store, No. 207 (*Mon–Fri only 9.30am–5pm*): Irish household linens.
Pasta Factory, No. 261 (*to 8pm, Mon from noon*).
Rococo, No. 321 (*to 6.30pm*); fashionable chocolate shop.

Notting Hill Gate:

Gourmets des Gascognes, Hillgate St (*Mon–Sat 9.30am–9.30pm, Sat to 9pm*); delicatessen.

Portobello Road:

Antiques Market (*Fri 5am–3pm, Sat 8am–5pm*).
Portobello Green Arcade (*Mon–Sat 10am–6pm*); shops and workshops selling clothes, accessories, jewellery and crafts.
Graham & Green, 4 & 7 Elgin Crescent, off Portobello Rd (*Mon–Fri 10am–6pm, Sat 9.30am–6pm*); home furnishings, pottery, rugs (traditional and modern).

LONDON'S RIVER

Though small by world standards, the Thames (Roman 'Tamesis') broadens into an estuary through London, and at one time was much wider at certain points than it is today. This gives rise to the strong tides that flow in and out twice every 24 hours, with big variations between high and low water marks. The Thames has been central to London's history, allowing it to prosper as a major seaport until well into this century, when ships became too big for most of its docks and handling facilities. Several of its local tributaries, notably the Fleet (no longer visible), have also played a big part in the city's history and development. From Roman times until the 18th century, London was served by a single bridge over the Thames. Longest standing was the 12th-century London Bridge, cluttered with tall houses and a chapel, and constantly menaced by fire and flood. It survived, nevertheless, until the early 19th century (the buildings having already been removed). Today, 31 bridges – road, rail and pedestrian – span the river from Hampton Court to Tower Bridge. *(Regular riverboat services – Easter to September – operate from Westminster and Charing Cross piers, to points downstream to Greenwich and upstream to Hampton Court).*

FROM CHARING CROSS TO THE TOWER *

MAPS IV AB5–6; V C1–3 D1–6

The Pier at Charing Cross (Embankment) is right by **Hungerford Bridge** (1864), a rail and pedestrian bridge, featured in several of Monet's Impressionist paintings of London river scenes. The next bridge downstream is Sir Giles Gilbert Scott's **Waterloo Bridge,** begun just before World War II and finished just after it, replacing the earlier bridge that was sinking on its piles. It is London's biggest, spanning the Thames at the broadest point of its curve round the Embankment, and affording splendid views of the **Embankment** itself with **Somerset House,** and of **St Paul's** and the **City.** The three ships moored along the Embankment below are two World War I naval sloops, **'Wellington'** and **'Chrysanthemum'** (headquarters of naval organizations), and the World War II frigate **'President'** (the floating Livery Hall of the Honourable Company of Master Mariners).

Blackfriars Bridge (1869) is an interesting essay in the Victorian Gothic Revival style, with the massive Victorian cast-iron stanchions of the old railway bridge between it and today's railway bridge serving Blackfriars and Holborn Viaduct stations. The City river bank between

The Thames from above Tower Bridge

the Blackfriars bridges and **Southwark Bridge** (1919) was once lined with warehouses, redolent of spices, coffee and tea. One of them has survived, as the **'Samuel Pepys'** riverside pub, which also overlooks the small Queenhithe inlet, London's principal dock in the Middle Ages. The twin towers remaining from **Cannon Street Station** (1866) still rise proudly above the river before **London Bridge** is reached. The replacement for the medieval bridge was taken down and re-erected at Lake Havasu City, Arizona, USA, while the present bridge, London's newest, was constructed in its place between 1967 and 1972.

What was once the **Pool of London,** the heart of the capital's maritime trade, is now distinguished by the presence of **HMS Belfast,** a World War II cruiser that saw action during the D-Day landings of 1944. Moored by Symon's Wharf, across the river from Tower Bridge, she is a floating extension of the Imperial War Museum (*open daily Apr–Oct, 11am–5.50pm; Nov–Mar, 11am–4.30pm; closed 1 Jan, Good Fri, May Day, 24–26 Dec*). **Tower Bridge** (1894) is one of London's most celebrated landmarks. It is a double bascule draw-bridge, designed to allow shipping into the old Pool of London. The twin Gothic Revival towers house the bridge machinery and the lifts which originally conveyed pedestrians to a high-level footbridge, since the main bridge was often raised several times a day. Now the raising of the bridge is a rare occasion. The towers and power house contain a museum (*open daily Apr–Oct, 10am–6.30pm; Nov–Mar, 10am–4.45pm; closed 1 Jan, Good Fri, 24–26 Dec*).

▬▬ *FROM TOWER BRIDGE TO THE THAMES BARRIER* ★★
MAP Outer London

Tower Bridge is the last bridge before the sea. Beyond it the Thames broadens considerably, and at one time both banks were lined for many miles with ocean-going docks. These are now almost all closed and their sites are undergoing various redevelopment schemes. Old **St Katharine's Dock,** just to the east of Tower Bridge, has taken on a new lease of life as a marina and museum of old river and coastal craft (*open daily 10am–5pm or dusk; closed 1 Jan, 25 Dec*). Some of the fine old warehouses built by Thomas Telford have also been restored and converted into shops, restaurants and pubs, making the whole area a charming pleasure centre. A little further downstream, keeping to the north bank, is the 16th-century **'Prospect of Whitby'** at Wapping, London's best-known riverside pub, frequented by Pepys, Dickens and other celebrities of past times. At **Execution Dock** nearby, pirates were hanged until the beginning of the 19th century.

The river makes a great U-turn round the curiously named **Isle of Dogs** (which is not really an island but may take its name from some royal kennels once kept there), passing Deptford, where many famous sailing ships were built, and **Greenwich,** and on to the **Thames Barrier** at Woolwich. This, the river's greatest engineering achievement, was completed in 1982. It is designed to protect London from flooding, caused by the growing risk of exceptionally high tides, occasioned partly by the fact that the whole of south-east England is gradually sinking at the rate of about 1ft (30cm) per century. The Barrier spans 500 yds (460m) from bank to bank, with four main steel gates, each weighing 3,000 tons, and six smaller ones. When opened – lowered into the water – ships are able to pass over them.

▬▬ *FROM CHARING CROSS TO TEDDINGTON LOCK* ★
MAP Outer London

Returning to Charing Cross Pier, the river journey upstream (after passing beneath Hungerford Bridge) begins with the stretch of the Embankment to **Westminster Bridge** (1862). This bridge replaces its 1750 predecessor, which was only the second of London's stone bridges to be built, and inspired Wordsworth's famous sonnet. On the other side of it is the riverside frontage of the **Houses of Parliament.** The river proceeds past **Millbank** and **Lambeth, Pimlico** and **Battersea, Chelsea** and **Wandsworth;** the most attractive of the bridges along that stretch being the **Albert Suspension Bridge** (1873, R.M. Ordish), which links **Cheyne Walk** and **Chelsea Embankment** with **Battersea Park.** It is a structure of Victorian fancy rather than pomp. **Putney Bridge** (1884) is the start of the famous Oxford and Cambridge Boat Race, the south bank of the river being lined with the boat houses of local rowing and sailing clubs. **Hammersmith Bridge** (1887), by Sir Joseph Bazalgette, is another Victorian suspension bridge of exuberant appearance, replacing an earlier one of similar construction.

From this point on, the riverside is noticeably more peaceful and rural. The river itself gradually narrows as it passes **Chiswick, Barnes, Kew Gardens** and **Syon Park** to **Richmond.** Richmond footbridge (1890) forms part of an interesting lock, where sluice gates control the tidal flow. Beyond the Twickenham road bridge and adjacent railway bridge is old **Richmond Bridge** (1774), which levied a toll until well into the 19th century and, although subsequently widened, retains its country-town character. The stretch of river as seen from the heights of **Richmond Hill** inspired several artists, notably Turner and Reynolds. Further up river, past the pastures of **Petersham Meadows** and the landmarks of **Marble Hill House, Ham House** and **Strawberry Hill,** is **Teddington Lock,** which marks the tidal limit. From that point on, one can follow the river upstream past **Hampton Court** to **Windsor** and the quiet towns of the Thames Valley.

--- **PLACES TO STOP**

Riverside pubs upstream from Greenwich to Twickenham (all offer hot or cold food, ranging from bar snacks to gourmet restaurant meals):

Yacht, Crane St, Greenwich (south bank).
Trafalgar, Park Row, Greenwich (south bank).
Grapes, 76 Narrow St, Limehouse (north bank): seafood specialities.
Prospect of Whitby, Wapping Wall, Wapping (north bank).
Mayflower, 117 Rotherhithe St, Rotherhithe (south bank).
Angel, Bermondsey Wall East, Bermondsey (south bank).
Dickens Inn, St Katharine's Way, St Katharine's Dock (north bank).
Market Porter, 9 Stoney St, Southwark (south bank).
Anchor, 1 Bankside, Southwark (south bank).
Samuel Pepys, Brooks Wharf, Upper Thames St, City (north bank).
Founders Arms, 52 Hopton St, Bankside, Southwark (south bank).
St Stephen's Tavern, 10 Bridge St, Westminster (north bank).
King's Head and Eight Bells, 50 Cheyne Walk, Chelsea (north bank).
Dove, 19 Upper Mall, Hammersmith (north bank).
Black Lion, 2 South Black Lion Lane, Hammersmith (north bank).
Bull's Head, 373 Lonsdale Rd, Barnes (south bank). Modern jazz.
Ship, 10 Thames Bank, Riverside, Mortlake (south bank).
City Barge, Strand-on-the-Green, Chiswick (north bank).
Bull's Head, 15 Strand-on-the-Green, Chiswick (north bank).
London Apprentice, 62 Church St, Isleworth (north bank).
White Swan, Old Palace Lane, Richmond-upon-Thames (south bank).
White Swan, Riverside, Twickenham (north bank).
Eel Pie, 9 Church St, Twickenham (north bank).

LONDON'S PRINCIPAL MUSEUMS AND GALLERIES

London's museums, which were largely created during the 19th century, are unparalleled for the breadth and richness of their collections, and their range includes antiquities, European paintings, sculpture, new decorative arts, Oriental, African and Oceanic art, as well as imaginatively displayed historical and scientific collections. The principal collections are described in the following sections, while other museums and galleries are treated more briefly within the various itineraries: Bethnal Green Museum of Childhood (*p.134*), Courtauld Institute Galleries (*p.147*), Dulwich College Picture Gallery (*p.214*), Geffrye Museum (*p.134*), Geological Museum (*p.166*), Horniman Museum (*p.215*), Imperial War Museum (*p.139*), Jewish Museum (*p.147*), London Transport Museum (*p.150*), Museum of Garden History (*p.140*), Museum of Mankind (*p.101*), Musical Museum (*p.214*), National Army Museum (*p.167*), National Maritime Museum (*p.226*), National Portrait Gallery (*p.86*), National Postal Museum (*p.130*), Percival David Foundation of Chinese Art (*p.147*), Public Record Office (*p.149*), Queen's Gallery (*p.98*), Sir John Soane's Museum (*p.149*), Wallace Collection (*p.155*).

THE BRITISH MUSEUM ★★★

Great Russell Street, WC2   ☎636 1555

II C4   ⊖ Russell Square, Goodge Street, Tottenham Court Road

The various departments, many of which have holdings numbered in the millions, cover Egyptian Antiquities (the largest collection outside Egypt), Greek and Roman Antiquities (including the Parthenon sculptures), Medieval and later Antiquities, Oriental Antiquities (including the most representative collection of Islamic pottery anywhere in the world), Prehistoric and Romano-British Antiquities, Coins and Medals, Prints and Drawings, Western Asiatic Antiquities and the British Library. The Museum's remarkable Ethnography Department, known as the Museum of Mankind, is separate and is located in Burlington Gardens near Piccadilly (*see p.101*).

Caryatid in the British Museum

━━ *HISTORY*

The British Museum was founded by Sir Hans Sloane, the great collector and physician, whose immense private collection – some 80,000 objects – was offered to the nation at the time of his death in 1753. Shortly afterwards the great Cotton and Harley libraries were added to the institution, which opened in 1759 in Montague House, the old 17th-century mansion which stood on the site of the present Museum. The collections increased rapidly – George II transferred the old Royal Library in 1756; the Rosetta Stone and other Egyptian antiquities were added in 1802; and the so-called Townley Classical Collection and Elgin Marbles entered into the Museum in the early 19th century. In 1823 George IV presented his father's library, and Parliament voted funds to house it in the new East Wing, which was built by the architect Robert Smirke and completed in 1827. The present building gradually arose over the next thirty years under the supervision of Smirke and his successor, his younger brother Sydney Smirke. The Duveen Gallery, designed to house Elgin's sculptures, was opened in 1938 only to be bombed in 1940; it was rebuilt and finally completed in 1962.

━━ *VISIT*

Mon–Sat 10am–5pm, Sun 2.30–6pm; closed 1 Jan, Good Fri, May Day Bank hol, 24–26 Dec.
Admission free.
Disabled access (wheelchairs available).
Free films Tue–Fri.
Free lectures (see notice boards) Tue–Sat.
Taped commentaries to some of the rooms for hire at Information Desk (at Main Entrance, from Great Russell Street).
Museum shop; coffee shop.

The richness of the vast collections of the British Museum and its enormous size – the site itself covers over 11½ acres (4.5ha) – makes it impossible to see everything in one day. For the tourist whose time is limited, visits to some of the rooms in each of the departments are recommended, particularly:

Egyptian Antiquities
Rosetta Stone (Room 25)
Two-coloured granite torso of Rameses II (Room 25)
Mummies (Rooms 60–61)

Greek and Roman Antiquities
Harpy Tomb (Room 5)
Bassae Frieze (Room 6)
Elgin Marbles (Duveen Gallery, Room 8)

Western Asiatic Antiquities
Colossal human-headed winged bulls from Khorsabad (Room 16)
Relief sculptures of Ashurbanipal's royal lion hunts (Room 17)

Prehistoric and Romano-British Antiquities
Witham Shield (Room 39)
Mildenhall silver platters (Room 40)

Medieval and Later Antiquities
Early medieval ivories (Room 41)
Sutton Hoo finds (Room 41)
Lycurgus Cup (Room 41)
Royal Cup, and medieval tiles (Rooms 42–43)

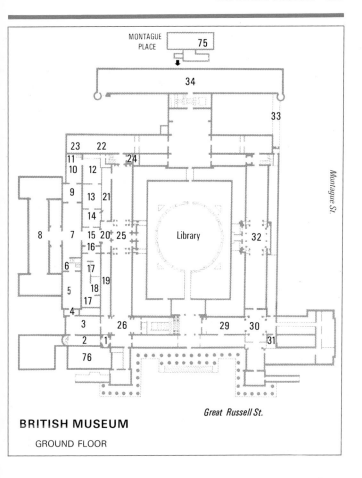

BRITISH MUSEUM

GROUND FLOOR

Oriental Antiquities

Sculptures from Orissa (Room 34)
Bimaran gold relic casket (Room 34)
Bronze seated figure of Siva (Room 34)
Stone standing figure of Garuda (Room 34)

Library Galleries

Lindisfarne Gospels (Room 30)

The following itineraries are arranged according to the Departments of the Museum – all of which begin at the Main Entrance (Great Russell Street), with the exception of Oriental Antiquities and Prints and Drawings, which may be entered from the North Entrance (Montague Place).

Egyptian Antiquities

(Ground floor: Room 25; First floor: Rooms 60–66)
The Egyptian Sculpture Gallery (Room 25) is located immediately to the left of the Main Entrance, and just inside the Gallery is the **Rosetta Stone,** a black basalt slab which is inscribed in ancient Greek and in two forms of ancient Egyptian script. After it was brought to England in 1802, it provided a key to the deciphering of hieroglyphic script unread

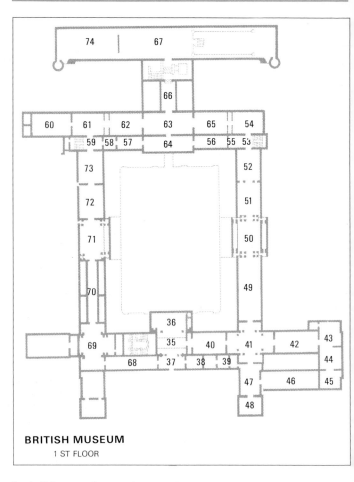

BRITISH MUSEUM
1 ST FLOOR

for 1,400 years. Among the many impressive sculptures, note the two **red granite lions** (18th Dynasty, 1400 BC) from Gebel Barkal in the Sudan; the painted limestone **tomb figure of Nenkheftka,** a 5th Dynasty nobleman (c.2400 BC); and the imposing torso, made of two colours of granite, of **Rameses II** (c.1270 BC) from Thebes. Among the architectural fragments is the **painted false door** of the tomb of the nobleman Ptahshepses (c.2520–2435 BC), who lived under at least eight pharaohs; and the stela of the official Tjetji (c.2100 BC), which gives information on a period of civil war.

Continue this tour on the first floor (take the western stairs at the rear of the Egyptian Gallery past the spectacular Roman mosaics) to Rooms 60–61 for the **mummies** and mummy cases; note the superbly wrapped mummy from Thebes (21st Dynasty, c.1050 BC) and its painted, human-form wooden coffin. Room 62 includes wall paintings from private and royal tombs, and various editions of the *Book of the Dead* on papyrus, ranging in dates from the 18th Dynasty (c.1340 BC) to the 2nd century AD. Small sculptures, pottery, jewellery (note the pair of gold and lapis lazuli bracelets inscribed for Nemareth, son of King Sheshong I of the 22nd Dynasty, c.940 BC) and other funerary objects are found in Rooms 63–65; while Room 66, the Coptic Corridor, includes Roman portraits in which ancient Egyptian, Classical and Christian elements appear together.

Greek and Roman Antiquities
(Ground floor: Rooms 1–16; Lower Ground floor: Rooms 77–85; First floor: Rooms 68–73)
The small collection of marble vessels and **figurines of women** with folded arms in the Cycladic Room (Room 1) are representative of the culture that flourished in the Cycladic Islands from c.3200–2000 BC. Material from Minoan Crete is included in Room 2 – note the gold ornament, the **Aegina Treasure** (c.1600 BC) showing the so-called Master of the Animals, holding a goose in each hand; while Archaic Greek art in Room 3 includes fine geometric-decorated pottery and stone sculpture fragments from the archaic Temple of Artemis. **Kouroi statues** are located in Rooms 4–5; the important stone reliefs from the **Harpy Tomb** from Xanthos in Lycia are located in Room 5, as are Athenian vases, terracotta figures from Boeotia, bronzes, and a splendid **cup with Aphrodite riding a goose** (c.460 BC).

A staircase leads to Room 6 for the remarkable marble **frieze from the Temple of Apollo at Bassae** (c.400 BC); on the other side is Room 7 with the impressive reconstructed façade of the **Nereid Monument** (c.400BC). The Duveen Gallery (Room 8) houses the **sculptures of the Parthenon** brought to England by Lord Elgin, including a section of the great frieze, traditionally interpreted as the Panathenaic procession, now thought to show the presentation of heroes of the battle of Marathon (490 BC) to the Olympian Gods. Also here are several beautiful sculptures from the outside of the Parthenon, various sculpted metopes (square panels) and other sculptural fragments.

The Room of the **Caryatid** (Room 9) features one of the six female figures used as pillars – known as Caryatids – from the 'Porch of the Maidens' of the Erechtheion (finished in 409 BC). Also shown are **friezes from the Temple of Athena Nike** and marble grave-reliefs. Among the smaller objects note the rare early 4th-century BC Greek panel-painting of a seated goddess from excavations at Saqqara in Egypt.

Next, in Room 10, is the **Tomb of Payava** from Xanthos, decorated with scenes from Payava's career. Among the showcase materials note the Siris bronzes, decorated shoulder straps from a breastplate (c.390–360 BC) showing Greeks fighting Amazons, as well as fine vases. Room 12 features the **Mausoleum at Halicarnassus frieze.** In the ancient world, the Tomb of Mausolos (died 353 BC) was numbered among the Seven Wonders of the World because of its architectural daring and rich sculptural decoration; this section of the frieze shows the battle of Greeks and Amazons. From another of the Seven Wonders, the Temple of Artemis at Ephesus, comes a splendid sculptured column-drum.

Take the staircase in the corner down to the Room of Greek and Roman Architecture and of Latin and Greek Inscriptions. Note especially the Athenian votive sculpture; sculptures from a later Temple of Artemis at Ephesus; Roman sarcophagi and portrait busts, and Charles Townley's great 18th-century collection of Classical art in Room 84.

Return upstairs to Room 13, note the marble statue of a seated Goddess (330 BC); the head of Asclepius from Melos (300 BC); and the relief of the Apotheosis of Homer with Zeus (signed by Archelaos of Priene, 150–120 BC). The Roman Rooms (14–15) include the famous **Portland Vase,** a jar of blue and white glass with scenes illustrating the story of Peleus and his immortal bride Thetis. Roman pottery and glass as well as gold and silver vessels, including part of the **Chaourse Treasure,** are also shown here. Wall-paintings excavated from Pompeii are found in Room 14, while Roman portraits are located in Room 15.

The Upper Galleries (take the west staircase) feature terracotta sculptures and bronzes, a special room showing Greek and Roman daily life (Room 69) and an exhibition, The Image of Augustus (Room 70), featuring the use of portraits of the emperor as instruments of propaganda. The Etruscan collection in Room 71 contains pottery, metalwork, paintings, and important terracotta sarcophagi. Greek vases from the Museum's collection, one of the largest and most comprehensive in the world, are temporarily shown in Gallery 72.

Western Asiatic Antiquities
(Lower Ground floor: Rooms 88–90; Ground floor: Rooms 17–26; First floor: Rooms 51–59)

The collections cover antiquities of the Sumerians, Babylonians and Assyrians, the ancient Persians, the Urartians and Hittites, other peoples of Syria and ancient Palestine, and all the states of the Arabian peninsula, especially North and South Yemen.

Left of the Main Entrance (just before the entrance to the Egyptian Sculpture Gallery) is Room 26, the Assyrian Transept, which includes colossal **human-headed winged lions and bulls** from the palace of Ashurnasirpal II (883–859 BC) at Nimrud; and the bronze gates of Shalmaneser III (858–824 BC) from Balawat, which show Assyrian victories, processions of tribute-bearers and other scenes of Assyrian life. Room 19 (left of the Egyptian Gallery) features the very beautiful **sculptures from the palace of Ashurnasirpal** at Nimrud, including panels from the royal throne room, showing hunting and military scenes as well as the king and his courtiers. In the centre of the gallery is the **Black Obelisk of Shalmaneser** (c.826 BC), with carvings of the king receiving tribute from various foreign rulers. Sculptures in Room 20 show the conquests of King Tiglath-pileser III (745–727 BC) in Babylonia and Syria; followed by Room 21 with intricately carved reliefs from the Palace of Sennacherib at Nineveh.

Just off the Classical courtyard is Room 16 with the colossal **human-headed winged bulls** from a citadel gate at Khorsabad; and in Room 17 are the sculpted panels showing the **Capture of Lachish** by the Assyrian King Sennacherib in 701 BC; and the very beautiful series of **Ashurbanipal's royal lion hunts** (c.645 BC) from Nineveh.

From Room 17 take the stairs down to Room 89 for reliefs concerning the wars of Ashurbanipal (668–627 BC) as well as remarkable small bronzes. Adjacent (Room 90) are sculptures from the Ishtar Temple at Nineveh showing a royal procession.

The upper galleries (take the western staircase) include bronze and sculpture collections from North and South Yemen (Room 59), and the fascinating ivory room, with ivories principally from Nimrud (9th–7th centuries BC). Syrian and Phoenician antiquities from the 2nd millenium BC to the Roman period are covered in Room 57 and feature bronzework, jewellery, sculptures and tombstones.

Room 56 (beyond the sixth Egyptian Room, Room 64) is devoted to the early history of writing, and Room 55 features an exhibition on the beginnings of agriculture and urbanisation in Western Asia (7000–3000 BC). Across the Hittite Landing (Room 53) to the left is the Babylonian Room (54) which includes objects discovered in the Royal Cemetery at Ur (c.2500 BC). Note the **Standard of Ur** with various mosaic scenes, including war and peace; and the superb **goat and tree,** an object that probably supported a small table, also from Ur. In Room 53 are sculptures from Carchemish (10th–8th centuries BC); while Room 52 to the right contains antiquities from Turkey, Hittite jewellery from Carchemish, the Urartian bronzes from Toprak Kale (8th–7th centuries BC), and the **Oxus Treasure** and other Persian antiquities from the 3rd millennium BC to the 7th century AD.

Prehistoric and Romano-British Antiquities
(First floor: Rooms 35–40)
The items featured here include a small carving in reindeer antler of a mammoth from France, dating from c.10,500 BC; and the splendid gold-alloy torc (neck-ring) from the first century BC, found in Norfolk. The **Witham Shield** (c.200–100 BC) was found in the River Witham, Lincolnshire, and is one of the best surviving examples of early Celtic fine metalwork from Britain. Note also the mosaic roundel showing **Bacchus on a tiger** (1st or 2nd century AD), which was found in Leadenhall Street, London. Room 40 presents objects that date from the period when Britain was a province of the Roman Empire, including the spectacular **silver tableware** from Mildenhall, Suffolk (4th century AD). Also located here are sections from a 4th-century frieze from a Roman villa at Lullingstone, Kent, as well as the Hinton St Mary mosaic pavement.

Medieval and Later Antiquities
(Rooms 41–48)
Room 41 features early medieval art, and among the most important of the superb objects found there is the **Lycurgus Cup,** a late Roman cage-cup (c.AD 400) carved from a single block of pea-green glass, which turns red in transmitted light and shows the legendary Thracian King Lycurgus caught by a vengeful vine. Early Christian and Byzantine ivories, including the marvellous diptych leaf with the archangel from Constantinople (6th century) are included here; also the 8th-century Northumbrian whale-bone box known as the Franks Casket with runic inscriptions, lovely representations of Germanic folklore and scenes from Roman history and the Bible. The fascinating **Sutton Hoo finds** from the Anglo-Saxon royal ship-burial in Suffolk (7th century) are also located in Room 41.

A spectacular collection of **medieval ivories** and Limoges enamels is located in Room 42: note especially the walrus ivory Scandinavian **Lewis chessmen** (12th century), which were discovered on the Isle of Lewis. Also here is the celebrated Royal Gold Cup of the Kings of France and England, made of gold with pointille (punched work) and enamel, and showing scenes from the life of St Agnes. Note also the fragments from the frescoes at St Stephen's Chapel (Palace of Westminster). A very fine German limewood relief carving of the *Adoration of the Magi* (1505–10) by Tilman Riemenschneider is also located here. At the end of the Medieval Gallery is the impressive collection of medieval tiles and pottery in Room 43, including the Canynges pavement from Bristol (15th century).

The popular collection of **clocks and watches** dating from the Middle Ages to the beginning of this century is found in Room 44; note especially the 'nef' or ship clock made by Hans Schlottheim c.1580 for Emperor Rudolph II in Prague. Figures move to a musical accompaniment, the hours are struck on bells in the crow's nest, and the gun on the bow fires. The Waddesdon Bequest Room (Room 45) features goldsmiths' work and enamels, and leads to the Renaissance Corridor (Room 46) with objects from the Renaissance to the 18th century, featuring British objects of historical and personal association such as a signet ring which belonged to Mary Queen of Scots and the silver seal-dies of Sir Walter Raleigh. Room 47 contains a fine jewellery collection as well as pottery, porcelain (note the **Pegasus Vase,** which Josiah Wedgwood considered the finest he had made) and glass.

Among the objects in the Modern gallery (Room 48) is a selection of silver, tableware, glassware and studio pottery from the Bauhaus and Art Deco periods.

Oriental Antiquities
(Ground floor: Rooms 34, 75; First floor: Room 74)
From the North Entrance on Montague Place go directly upstairs to the large Oriental Gallery (Room 34), which contains collections from South and South-East Asia, the Islamic lands of the Near East, Central Asia and the Far East. The visitor is advised to follow the display in a clockwise direction in the west wing of the gallery, since the exhibits are arranged by cultural province. The collections from the Indian sub-continent are considered to be the most comprehensive in the West and include a rich series of **Buddhist sculptures from Gandhara,** (1st–6th centuries AD). The unique **Bimaran gold relic casket** (2nd–3rd century), is set with rubies and represents the Buddha and gods in attendance. Note also the seated sandstone figure of Ganesa (10th century AD) from Western India. The **stone sculptures,** Buddhist and Hindu, from Eastern India and Orissa make up the finest collection outside India (8th–12th centuries). They include the Trivkvanama, and Incarnation of Vishnu (10th century). The group of stone and bronze images from South India, including the standing **stone figure of Garuda** (c. AD 700) and the bronze **seated figure of Siva Vishapaharana** (c.AD 950), is outstanding in the collection.

The Islamic collections occupy the west end of the gallery and include pottery, glass, jade, metalwork and ivories from the 8th to the 19th centuries.

Chinese porcelains and stoneware and Korean pottery are next, followed by very fine **Chinese bronze ritual vessels** and weapons of the Shang and Western Zhou dynasties (1300–700 BC); note the famous container formed by two addorsed rams (12th–11th century BC). Large pottery tomb figures, including glazed earthenware tomb figures of camels, from the Tang dynasty (AD 618–906) are located in the centre of the room.

Oriental Gallery III (Room 75), to the left of the North Entrance, contains a remarkable collection of **Islamic pottery,** with very fine examples of lustreware from Spain. Oriental Gallery II (Room 74), on the First Floor, is devoted primarily to temporary exhibitions of paintings and prints, mainly from Persia, India, China and Japan.

Prints and Drawings
(First floor: Room 67)
Adjacent to Gallery 74 is the gallery of the Department of Prints and Drawings where temporary exhibitions (changed usually three times a year) are on display from the Museum's great collection of European prints and drawings. Among the highlights of the Department's holdings are groups of drawings by Michelangelo, Raphael, Dürer, Rubens, Rembrandt, Claude Lorraine and Watteau.

The British Library
Permanent display galleries, Ground floor: Rooms 29–33)
A selection of treasures from the British Library is always on display in the three popular galleries (Rooms 29, 30, 31), which are found to the right of the main hall. Among the most famous items on display are two of the four surviving copies of the ***Magna Carta*** (1215); the **Lindisfarne Gospels** (c.698), one of the greatest masterpieces of English book painting, written and illuminated by Eadfrith, Bishop of Lindisfarne; ***Shakespeare's First Folio*** (1623) and the ***Gutenberg Bible*** (c.1453), the first book to be printed using movable metal type. On the floor above, Room 33, is a changing selection of exhibitions from the Map Room.

At present a new building (adjacent to St Pancras Station) is under construction to house the Reference Division of the British Library; however, the Main Reading Room is still in use but admission is by reader's pass only (application may be made to the Reader Admissions Office just off the main hall of the Museum). The domed Reading Room itself may be shown to visitors on the hour, every hour from 11am to 4pm.

THE NATIONAL GALLERY ★★★

Trafalgar Square, WC2 ☎839 3321; recorded information ☎839 3526
MAP IV B4   ⊖ Charing Cross, Leicester Square   ⇌ Charing Cross

The National Gallery is one of the greatest collections of European paintings in the world and is certainly one of the museums not to be missed in London. Over 2,000 works represent all schools of painting from the 15th to the 19th century; and because of their exceptional quality, frequent rotations of works take place. Some important 18th- and 19th-century British paintings are in the National Gallery, although the Tate Gallery, which formed part of the National Gallery until 1954, is dedicated to the British school and the modern collection.

HISTORY

The London National Gallery was founded in 1824, relatively late compared to national collections in other European cities, and was based not upon a royal collection but upon private collections and donations; beginning with the purchase of 38 paintings from the collection of Sir John Julius Angerstein, a Russian emigré banker, who had lived in London at 100 Pall Mall for some years before his death. The Gallery opened in his house in May 1824. Fairly rapid acquisitions led to the building of new premises in Trafalgar Square under the direction of William Wilkins, which were completed in 1838; many additions have been made since, including those by E. M. Barry (1870s), Sir John Taylor (1880s), and the PSA North Extension (1975). A new wing is to be built by the American architect Robert Venturi.

VISIT

Mon–Sat 10am–6pm, Sun 2–6pm; closed 1 Jan, Good Fri, May Day Bank hol, 24–25 Dec.
Admission free.
Disabled access (Orange Street entrance) a limited number of wheelchairs are available).
Lectures Tue–Fri 1pm, Sat noon.
Films Mon 1pm.
Guided tours Mon–Sat.
Museum shop and restaurant.
The visitor can follow a roughly chronological tour of the collections beginning with Room 1, or select specific schools of painting in the following rooms:

Early Italian *(Rooms 1–6, 10–13)*
The Battle of San Romano (Uccello)
Venus and Mars (Botticelli)

Italian 16th-century *(Rooms 7–9, 14, 30)*
The Entombment (Michelangelo)
Bacchus and Ariadne (Titian)

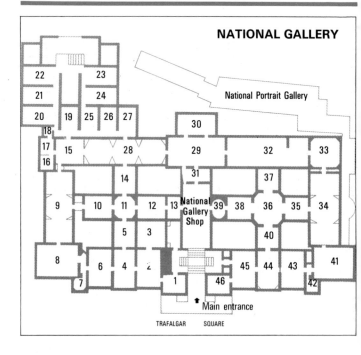

NATIONAL GALLERY

Dutch *(Rooms 15–19, 26–28)*
Woman Bathing in a Stream (Rembrandt)
A Young Woman Standing at a Virginal (Vermeer)

Flemish *(Rooms 20–22)*
The Judgement of Paris (Rubens)
Equestrian Portrait of Charles I (Van Dyck)

Early Northern *(Rooms 23–25)*
The Ambassadors (Holbein)
Portrait of the Artist's Father (Dürer)
The Arnolfini Marriage (Jan Van Eyck)

Italian after 1600 *(Rooms 29–34)*
The Supper at Emmaus (Caravaggio)

French before 1800 *(Rooms 32–33)*
Adoration of the Golden Calf (Poussin)
Enchanted Castle (Claude Lorraine)

British *(Rooms 35–39)*
Mr and Mrs Andrews (Gainsborough)
The Haywain (Constable)
Rain, Steam and Speed (Turner)

Spanish *(Rooms 41–42)*
The Agony in the Garden of Gethsemane (El Greco)
The Toilet of Venus (Velasquez)

French after 1800 *(Rooms 40, 43–46)*
Bathers (Cézanne)
Cornfield with Cypresses (Van Gogh)

Early Italian Painting

(Rooms 1–6, 10–13)
Among the most celebrated and one of the oldest paintings in the collection in Room 1, though not in fact Italian, is the **Wilton Diptych** (probably French School, 1395), which shows the presentation of a banner by King Richard II to the Virgin Mary. Painted on both sides, it is hinged and can be shut like a book. Also located in the Italian Primitive galleries (Rooms 1 and 3) is Duccio's *Annunciation* (1311). Paolo Uccello's extraordinary **Battle of San Romano** (c.1450) is in Room 2; as well as his *Saint George and the Dragon* (c.1460). Also here is Pisanello's remarkable *The Vision of Saint Eustace*. Among many major 15th-century Italian works, Room 4 contains Antonio Pollaiuolo's *Martyrdom of St Sebastian* (c.1475), Piero della Francesca's *The Baptism of Christ*, and Fra Filippo Lippi's *The Annunciation,* which was originally bought by the Medici family. Room 5 features the work of Sandro Botticelli, including the fine *Head of a Young Man* (c.1480–90) and the marvellous **Venus and Mars** (c.1485).

Leonardo da Vinci and 16th-century Italian Painting

(Rooms 7–10, 14, 30)
Leonardo da Vinci's grey chalk cartoon of **The Virgin and Child with St Anne and St John the Baptist** (c.1490) is shown in Room 7; and his second version (1483) of the famous *Virgin of the Rocks* (the other is in the Louvre) is located in Room 8. Here too are Michelangelo's **The Entombment** (1503); Raphael's *Ansidei Retable* (c.1505), showing the Madonna and Child between St John the Baptist and St Thomas, and his beautiful *Portrait of Pope Julius II* (1511–12).

Venetian painting in Room 9 features Titian's **Bacchus and Ariadne** (early 1520s). Also here is the remarkable late work *The Death of Ariadne* (c.1559). Tintoretto is represented by several fine works, including *The Origin of the Milky Way* (late 1570s) and *St George and the Dragon* (1560s), which shows the rescue of the princess in the foreground. The room is dominated by Veronese's impressive *Family of Darius before Alexander the Great* (c.1570s). Giovanni Bellini's splendid *Portrait of the Doge Leonardo Loredan* (c.1501), painted when both the artist and the sitter were over 70 years old, is in Room 10.

Northern Italian painting is included in Room 14, featuring an excellent collection of works by Lorenzo Lotto, including *A Lady as Lucretia* (c.1530). Room 30 contains the very beautiful *Portrait of a Man* (known as the tailor) by Giovanni Battista Moroni (c.1570).

Dutch 17th-century Painting

(Rooms 15–19, 26–28)
The first room (15) features Frans Hals's *Young Man holding a Skull* (1626–8), while Rooms 16–19 display smaller works, including Jacob Van Ruisdael's *Two Watermills* (c.1650); and Jan Steen's *Woman Playing the Harpsichord* (1659). Major Dutch landscape painting, still lifes and work by Rembrandt are located in Rooms 26–27. Among the works by Rembrandt, note especially: **Woman Bathing in a Stream** (1654), *Belshazzar's Feast* (mid-1630s), his wife *Saskia Dressed as Flora* (1635), and two **Self-Portraits** (at age 34 and 63). Jan Vermeer is represented in Room 28 by two lovely interiors: *Woman Seated Playing a Virginal* (c.1670) and **A Young Woman Standing at a Virginal** (c.1670); here too is Pieter de Hooch's *Courtyard of a House in Delft* (1658).

Flemish Painting

(Rooms 20–22)
Among the many fine works in the collection by Rubens, note especially his *Drunken Silenus Supported by Satyrs* (c.1620) in Room 20, as well

---

Thomas GAINSBOROUGH (1717–1788)

The son of a cloth-merchant, Gainsborough showed a talent for drawing at an early age and in 1740 went to London, where he studied at various artists' studios. He began painting landscapes as well as some portraits and received his first important landscape commission from the Duke of Bedford in 1755. A few years later he moved to Bath, where he entered into fashionable society and turned to painting life-size, full-length portraits.

In 1768 Gainsborough became a founder member of the Royal Academy, and he moved to London in 1774. There he achieved further success as a portraitist and was patronized by George III and Queen Charlotte. Throughout Gainsborough's career his work always revealed a love of landscape painting, which he combined with portraiture. Experiments with techniques of transparency painting, mixed media drawing and printmaking as well as new subjects, including historical scenes and seascapes, characterize his later work.

---

as two versions of **The Judgement of Paris.** Anthony Van Dyck, Rubens's student and official painter to the English Royal Family, is represented by several works, including a fine **Equestrian Portrait of Charles I** (1638) in Room 21.

Early Northern Painting

(Rooms 23–25)
Lucas Cranach is represented in Room 25 by several paintings, including his *Cupid Complaining to Venus*. One of the Gallery's most famous works, Holbein's **The Ambassadors** (1533) is also located here, along with his lovely full-length *Portrait of Christina of Denmark* (1538). Note also the remarkable *Crowning with Thorns* (c.1500) by Hieronimus Bosch. Room 23 features Dürer's **Portrait of the Artist's Father** (1497) and Hans Baldung Grien's *Trinity and Mystic Pietà* (1512).

Netherlandish painting is found in Room 24, and includes Jan Van Eyck's *Man in a Red Turban* (1433) and the celebrated **Arnolfini Marriage** (1434) – in the mirror one sees in silhouette a portrait of the artist. Here too are Roger Van der Weyden's *Magdalene Reading* and Hans Memlinc's *Donne Triptych* (c.1470s).

Italian Painting after 1600

(Rooms 29, 34)
Room 29 features work by Caravaggio, including his *Boy Bitten by a Lizard* (late 1590s) and **The Supper at Emmaus** (c.1600). Room 34 features numerous works by Canaletto, including two fine versions of the **Grand Canal** (1738, c.1740) and various works by Tiepolo.

French Painting before 1800

(Rooms 32–33)
Nicolas Poussin is represented in the collection by several important works, including the **Adoration of the Golden Calf** (late 1630s) and the *Triumph of Pan* (1636). Claude Lorraine is also featured by works that include *Landscape with Narcissus* (1644), *Seaport with the Embarkation of the Queen of Sheba* (1648) and the late **Enchanted Castle** (1664). Among the smaller paintings, note especially Jean-Antoine Watteau's late work *La Gamme d'Amour*, and Jean-Baptiste Chardin's *The Young Schoolmistress* (c.1740).

Constable: The Haywain

British Painting

(Rooms 35–39)

Several major works by Gainsborough are located here, including his *Portrait of Mrs Siddons* (1785) and the double portrait of **Mr and Mrs Andrews** (1748). William Hogarth is represented by *The Shrimp Girl* and the paintings for his series of engravings **Marriage à la Mode.** John Constable's celebrated **The Haywain** (1821) and *Salisbury Cathedral from the Meadows* (1831–4) are also here, as are important works by J.M.W. Turner, including **Rain, Steam and Speed** (1844), and *The Fighting Téméraire* (c.1839).

John CONSTABLE (1776–1837)

Constable first began to follow his father's profession as a miller, but he was encouraged by the connoisseur Sir George Beaumont and the painter Joseph Farrington to become an artist. After beginning in 1779 at the Royal Academy Schools, Constable soon gave up formal training in favour of the direct study of nature, especially around his home near the River Stour in Suffolk. He worked from the oil sketches or notebooks he made out of doors for a series of landscapes for exhibition at the Royal Academy, and with these works began to achieve a certain degree of recognition. It was in France, however, that Constable was most enthusiastically received; Géricault was in fact responsible for the idea to exhibit *The Haywain* at the 1824 Salon in Paris. This was also the period of Constable's large commissioned work for the Bishop of Salisbury. His famous series of cloud studies date from 1821–2 and were made in Hampstead. Towards the end of his life Constable also started giving lectures at the Royal Academy on the history of landscape painting.

J.M.W. TURNER (1775–1851)

Joseph Mallord William Turner was born in London, where his earliest artistic activity is said to have been the colouring of prints, which were sold in his father's barber's shop. Turner studied with the architectural topographer Thomas Malton and entered the Royal Academy Schools c.1789. Soon afterwards he began a series of annual sketching tours in Britain, which provided material for topographical watercolours intended for exhibition or for engravings. Along with Thomas Girtin and others, from around 1794 to 1797 Turner also made many copies of drawings by artists such as J.R. Cozens for the collector Dr Munro.

By 1802 Turner had been made a full member of the Royal Academy, and his early recognition was accompanied by a determination to succeed as a painter whose works challenged the old masters. This led him to the study of Titian, Poussin and especially Claude. In 1817, after the final defeat of Napoleon, Turner went to the Low Countries, in part to gather material for *The Field of Waterloo* (1818) and also to renew a study of Dutch landscape painting. Two years later Turner made his first visit to Italy, where he was especially impressed by Venice.

Many of Turner's oil sketches (beginning in the late 1820s), were probably intended for later completion as pictures for exhibition. His subjects include atmospheric effects in the countryside or on water, the changing light of the Venetian cityscape and experimental works which were stimulated by the reading of Goethe's colour theories. Turner's late work (of the 1840s) has been valued in recent times for its affinities with 20th-century abstract painting.

Spanish Painting

(Rooms 41, 42)

The fine collection of Spanish paintings includes Zurbaran's beautiful *St Margaret* (1630s) and *St Francis in Meditation* (1630s); El Greco's **Agony in the Garden of Gethsemane** (late 1590s), *Christ Driving the Traders from the Temple* (c.1600) and *The Adoration of the Name of Jesus* (c.1578). Works by Velasquez are especially noteworthy, including the full-length *Portrait of Philip IV*, as well as what is probably the last portrait painted by Velasquez of his patron in c.1656. The famous painting known as *The Rokeby Venus*, or **The Toilet of Venus** (c.1651) is also here. In the adjacent room, note Goya's *Portrait of Doña Isabel de Porcel* (c.1805).

French Painting after 1800

(Rooms 40, 43–46)

Highlights of the National Gallery's fine collection of 19th- and early 20th-century painting include: Jean-Auguste Ingres's *Madame Moitessier* (1856), Eugène Delacroix's *Portrait of Baron Schwiter* (1825), Renoir's *The Umbrellas* (early 1880s), Douanier Rousseau's *Tropical Storm with a Tiger (Surprise!)* (1891), Degas's *Young Spartans* (c.1860) and his *La-La at the Cirque Fernando* (1879). Cézanne is represented by several exceptional works, including a small *Self-portrait* (c.1880) and the great **Bathers** (1898–1905). Manet's painting **Execution of Maximilian** (1867–8) is located here (in cut sections), as is his *Tuileries Gardens* (1862). Note also Monet's famous **Bathers at La Grenouillère** (1869), Seurat's *Bathers at Asnières*, Van Gogh's **Cornfield with Cypresses** (1889–90) and his *Chair and Pipe* (1889). The Gallery's collections end with works by Matisse and Picasso.

THE TATE GALLERY ★★

Millbank, SW1 ☎821 1313, recorded information   ☎821 7128
MAP IV F4   ⊖ Pimlico, Vauxhall   ⮯ Vauxhall

The Tate Gallery collections are divided into two sections: British art from the 16th century to around 1900; and modern art, including works by British artists born after 1860 together with foreign works from the Impressionists onwards. Among the British artists especially well represented at the Tate are William Hogarth, William Blake, George Stubbs, John Constable, J.M.W. Turner and the Pre-Raphaelites. Some of the same artists are also represented in the National Gallery, and the Tate's complete catalogue of works in the British and Modern collection is annotated to account for these. The Print Collection is part of the Modern Collection and contains prints by British and foreign artists – of the Tate's holdings of some 13,000 works, more than half are on paper.

▬ HISTORY

The Tate was founded by Sir Henry Tate (1819–99), whose collection of contemporary British painting formed the basis of the Gallery collections. The present premises were officially opened in 1897 in the building designed by Sydney J. R. Smith, the architect whom Tate had himself chosen, on ground formerly occupied by the Millbank Prison. In addition, Tate financed the Gallery's first extension; Sir Joseph Duveen subsequently funded extensions to house the Turner paintings and drawings (1910), modern foreign art (1926) and sculpture (1937); the Calouste Gulbenkian Foundation contributed to further extensions in 1979. The new Turner Galleries, funded by the Clore Foundation and designed by James Stirling, Michael Wilford Associates, are due to open on 1 April 1987.

▬ VISIT

Mon–Sat 10am–5.50pm, Sun 2–5.50pm; closed 1 Jan, Good Fri, May Day Bank hol, 24–26 Dec.
Admission free (except for major loan exhibitions).
Disabled access, wheelchairs provided, ramp at Atterbury Street entrance; pushchairs available.
Gallery lectures Tue–Fri 1pm; theatre lectures Sat and Sun 3pm; 15-minute 'Painting of the Month' talks Sat and Sun 2.30pm.
Guided tours Mon–Sat.
Gallery shop, coffee shop, and restaurant (reservations ☎834 6754).

British Collections

Generally speaking, the British collections occupy the left-hand side of the building from the Main Entrance, including several galleries at the rear of the building on the lower ground floor. Turn left from the Main Entrance for British painting of the 16th and 17th centuries. Note the *Saltonstall Family Portrait* (c.1637–9) attributed to David Des Granges, and the charming *The Cholmondeley Sisters* (British School, c.1600–10) in Room 2. Here too is Sir Peter Lely's *Two Ladies of the Lake Family* (c.1660). Room 3 in the Rotunda includes numerous works by William Hogarth; note especially **O the Roast Beef of Old England ('Calais Gate')** (1748) and *Heads of Six of Hogarth's servants* (c.1750–5). Rooms 4–5 show the development of the British School in

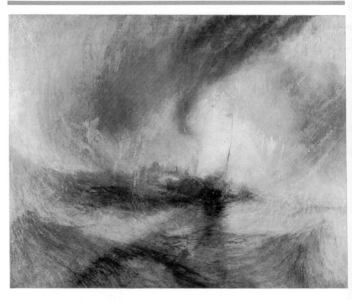

Turner: Snow Storm, Steamboat off a Harbour's Mouth

The second half of the 18th century; note especially George Stubbs's very fine **Mares and Foals in a Landscape** (c.1762–8), and his companion pieces, *Haymakers* and *Reapers*, from 1785. Also here is work by Thomas Gainsborough, including the beautiful **Giovanna Baccelli,** (1782) and a typical landscape, showing *Cadmus and the Dragon* (1765). Richard Wilson's *Meleager and Atalanta* (c.1760–70) is located here, and the German painter Johann Zoffany, who arrived in England in 1761, is represented by *The Bradshaw Family* (1769). Gallery 8 includes John Singleton Copley's *Death of Major Peirson, 6 January 1781* (1783).

William HOGARTH (1697–1764)

The painter, engraver, and satirist William Hogarth was born in London, where he lived and worked all of his life. He was first employed as an apprentice to a silver-plate engraver, and in c.1720 he opened his own business as an engraver. Hogarth also devoted much of his time to painting, especially portraits. However, his first public success came from the satirical engravings he made (1730–2) of *The Harlot's Progress* (after a series of paintings now destroyed), followed in 1735 by the engravings of *A Rake's Progress* (the original paintings are now in the Soane Museum). Another series, this time satirizing upper-class society, *Marriage à la Mode* (the original paintings are in the National Gallery) appeared in 1745. Hogarth published *The Analysis of Beauty* in 1753, a treatise on art in which he related his experiments in form to their expression and meaning. Hogarth, deeply conscious of being English, promoted a pride in English tradition and its culture among his fellow artists, attacking and satirizing Lord Burlington and the Palladians for their enthusiasm for Italian architecture and opera.

George STUBBS (1724–1806)

The painter Stubbs, who was acknowledged during his lifetime as a master of the sporting picture, had little formal training, but was fascinated from an early age by natural history, especially anatomy. In 1766 he published his widely respected *Anatomy of the Horse* with his own text and illustrations. About this same time Stubbs achieved recognition as a hunting and horse painter, and his pictures met with great success – in the 1790s he enjoyed the patronage of the Prince of Wales. Stubbs's interests extended to wild animals, beginning with the zebra (1760–2) and then to the subject of the mortal combat of horses and lions.

Later in his life Stubbs also worked with various printmaking techniques and with enamel painting on large ceramic plaques, which were specially manufactured by Wedgwood. A second major scientific investigation, *A Comparative Anatomical Exposition of the Structure of the Human Body with that of a Tiger and a Common Fowl* was begun towards the end of his life and, although never finished, chalk and pencil studies for the illustrations have survived.

The Turner collection is now in the new Clore Gallery. Among the many fine works here, note Turner's **Snow Storm: Hannibal and His Army Crossing the Alps** (1812) and *The Lake, Petworth, Sunset* (c.1828), as well as the wonderful series of Venetian paintings from 1842.

The popular Pre-Raphaelite collection is represented in Room 15 and includes many famous works: Dante Gabriel Rossetti's *The Beloved* (1865–6) and **Beata Beatrix** (1860–70), William Holman Hunt's *The Awakening Conscience* (1853), and Sir John Everett Millais's **Ophelia** (1881–2).

Among the large-scale Victorian paintings in Room 16, note John William Waterhouse's *The Lady of Shalott* (1888), Sir Edward Burne-Jones's **The Golden Stairs** and Frederic, Lord Leighton's *The Bath of Psyche* (1890). Works by the American artist James McNeil Whistler, who may be considered an important contributor to the development of the British School, are located in Room 17; note especially *Miss Cecily Alexander: Harmony in Grey and Green* (1872) and the well-known **Nocturne in Blue and Gold: Old Battersea Bridge** (c.1872–5).

Among the smaller 19th-century paintings in Room 12, note especially Richard Dadd's very curious *The Fairy-Feller's Master-Stroke* (1855–64) and Augustus Leopold Egg's *Past and Present, No. 1* (1858).

Works by John Constable are located in Room 11 and include a very lovely *Cloud Study* (1822) as well as the large *Valley Farm* (1835), and a full-sized *Sketch for 'Hadleigh Castle'* (c.1828–9).

For Modern British Painting in the Lower Galleries, take the stairs off Room 16 past George Frederick Watts's **Hope,** or those down from Room 10. Included here are drawings by Aubrey Beardsley; Wyndham Lewis's very fine *Portrait of Ezra Pound* (1939); and works by, among others, Augustus John, Edward Burra, Walter Richard Sickert, Ben Nicholson, Henry Moore (principally drawings) and Graham Sutherland. Larger works by many of these artists are located in the Modern Galleries on the main floor.

William BLAKE (1757–1827)

The illustrator and poet Blake first studied drawing and engraving, for a brief time at the Royal Academy Schools. His illustrations, made in the unusual medium of hand-coloured relief etching, first accompanied his own poems, *Songs of Innocence* (1789) and *Songs of Experience* (1794). His dark obsession with prophetic subjects, heavily influenced by the Bible and Milton, preoccupied him throughout his life.

His own poem *Milton* appeared in 1803, and *Jerusalem* in 1809. From 1799 to about 1805 Blake produced 37 paintings in tempera and some 100 watercolours on biblical subjects for his only patron at the time, a minor government official, Thomas Butts. Blake's famous series of watercolours to *The Book of Job* (1805–6), which were engraved in 1823–5, like many of his works, used the text to illustrate his own philosophy.

During his lifetime Blake was thought to be an eccentric, but he achieved some recognition from 1818 onwards, when he became friendly with a group of young artists that included John Linnell (for whom Blake painted a second series of watercolours to *The Book of Job*) and the painter Samuel Palmer. It was not, however, until after Blake's death that a greater appreciation of his work began, first with Alexander Gilchrist's publication of the *Life of William Blake* (1863), and then with the enthusiasm of Dante Gabriel Rossetti and his circle, who started the cult of Blake as poet-painter-philosopher.

Modern Collection

Turn right from the Main Entrance for the Modern Galleries, beginning with Impressionism and Post-Impressionism as well as Aspects of British Painting c.1890–1920. Among the many fine works by French artists in Room 30, note especially Claude Monet's ***Poplars on the Epte*** (1891); a late work by Paul Cézanne, *The Gardener* (1906); Paul Gauguin's *Faa Iheihe* (1898) and Pierre Bonnard's very beautiful *The Bath* (1925). Room 30 also includes several important Fauvist works, including Derain's *Portrait of Matisse* (1905) and Matisse's *Portrait of Derain* of the same year; and Matisse's *Standing Nude* (1907). Walter Richard Sickert's *Ennui* (c.1914) in Room 31 is the British artist's most famous work.

The Tate owns an impressive collection of Cubist works (Room 33), including Georges Braque's *Clarinet and Bottle of Rum on a Mantelpiece* (1911), Juan Gris's *The Sunblind* (1914), Pablo Picasso's ***Still Life*** (1914) and several very fine works by Fernand Léger, including *Still Life with a Beer Mug* (1921–2). Note also Futurist works here: Giacomo Balla, *Abstact Speed – the Car has Passed* (1913) and Umberto Boccioni's sculpture, *Unique Forms of Continuity in Space* (1913). The Vorticists, a group of mostly English artists who aimed at a synthesis of Cubism and Futurism, are represented here by an important collection, including Wyndham Lewis's *Workshop* (c.1914–15); William Roberts's *The Cinema* (1920); and the *Hieratic head of Ezra Pound* by the French sculptor Henri Gaudier-Brzeska (who spent almost all of his short life in England). David Bomberg, who painted in response to the Vorticist group, is represented by several fascinating works, including *The Mud Bath* (1914).

Room 35 features European Abstraction and includes several important British artists, notably the sculptor Dame Barbara Hepworth,

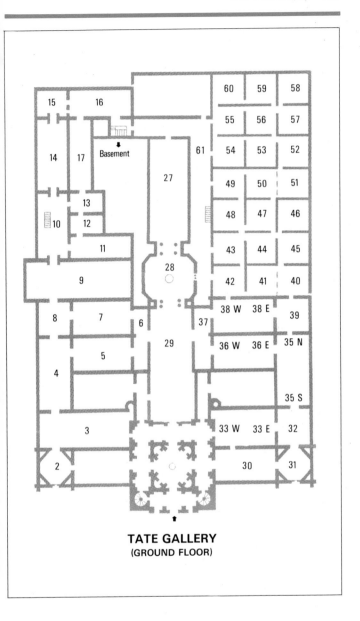

TATE GALLERY
(GROUND FLOOR)

Ben Nicholson and various works by Henry Moore. Here also are works by the Constructivists, including Kasimir Malevich *(Dynamic Suprematism,* c.1916) and Laszlo Moholy-Nagy *(K VII,* 1922), as well as important works by Piet Mondrian, including the early *Tree* (1912–3), and a work from the early 1920s *Composition in Grey, Red, Yellow and Blue.*

The Tate's collection of Surrealist art is especially strong and includes Giorgio de Chirico's *The Uncertainty of the Poet* (1913), Max Ernst's *Celebes* (1921), René Magritte's *The Reckless Sleeper* (1927), and several lovely works by Joan Miró, including a large *Blue Painting* of 1927. Picasso's major work of 1925 **The Three Dancers** is located among the Surrealist works in Room 36; and an important group of works by Alberto Giacometti, including paintings and sculptures, is located in Room 46.

The Post-War collection in the Tate is impressive and includes an extremely good representation of works by Jackson Pollock and Mark Rothko. Among the British artists, note especially Francis Bacon's *Three Studies for Figures at the Base of a Crucifixion* (1944) and his *Three Figures and Portrait* (1975). Art of the last twenty-five years is represented in the Tate by the works of a number of well-known American artists, including Roy Lichtenstein, Andy Warhol, Carl Andre (when his *Equivalent VIII*, 1966, was purchased for the Tate it caused a sensation), Frank Stella, Agnes Martin and Eva Hesse. A number of contemporary British artists are also represented, including Anthony Caro, David Hockney and Richard Long.

THE VICTORIA AND ALBERT MUSEUM ★★★

Cromwell Road, SW7   ☎589 6371
MAP III E3   ⊖ South Kensington

The 'V & A' (as it is known in London) houses some of the finest collections anywhere of decorative and applied arts, especially in the areas of Medieval, Renaissance and British art. Particularly strong are the collections of ceramics, English ivories and alabasters, metalwork, jewellery, silver, musical instruments, furniture and textiles. Moreover, the museum holds exceptional collections of Italian Renaissance and British 16th–19th-century sculpture, including the unique 19th-century Cast Courts.

The V & A's vast and rich collections are divided into Primary Galleries, where major works from the collections are presented chronologically, and Study Collections, which are arranged according to themes and are of particular interest to researchers, students and specialists. The National Art Library is also housed in the V & A and is open to the public for research.

The Henry Cole Wing (Exhibition Road entrance) houses the collection of the Department of Prints, Drawings and Photographs as well as paintings, including some 300 watercolours, drawings and paintings by Constable.

▬▬ HISTORY

The Museum was originally an idea of Prince Albert, the Prince Consort, and began as the Museum of Manufacturers, founded in Marlborough House in 1852. The collections became part of the South Kensington Museum in 1857, under the directorship of Sir Henry Cole. Its name was changed to the Victoria and Albert Museum by Queen Victoria in 1899, when she laid the foundation stone of the Museum's extension. The main façade on Cromwell Road and the colonnaded open cupola are the work of Sir Aston Webb. A number of the rooms were decorated by leading British designers of their day, including Philip Webb and Sir Edward Burne-Jones (the Green Dining Room), E.J. Poynter (the Grill Room) and Frederic, Lord Leighton (frescoes

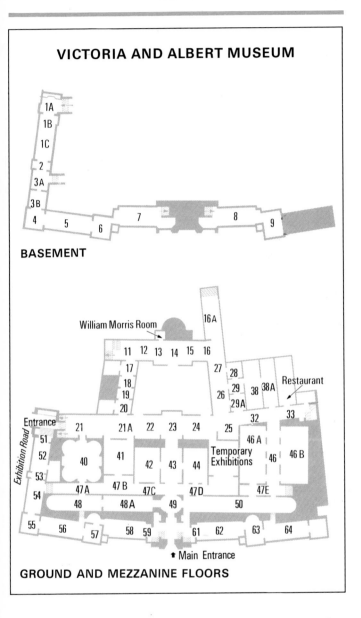

VICTORIA AND ALBERT MUSEUM

BASEMENT

William Morris Room

Restaurant

Entrance

Exhibition Road

Temporary Exhibitions

↑ Main Entrance

GROUND AND MEZZANINE FLOORS

in Rooms 102, 199); and on the exterior, Owen Jones and Godfrey Sykes (ornamental details). In 1979–82 part of the Imperial College of Science (originally constructed in 1867–71 under the supervision of Major General Henry Scott) was converted into the Henry Cole Wing of the V & A.

▬ VISIT

Mon–Thu, Sat 10am–5.50pm, Sun 2.30–5.50pm; closed Fri, 1 Jan, May Day Bank hol, 24–26 Dec.

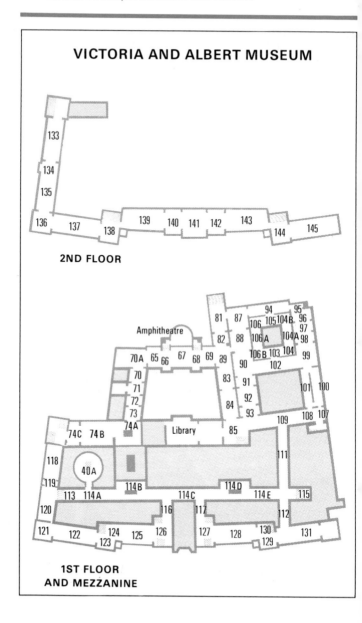

VICTORIA AND ALBERT MUSEUM

133
134
135
136   137   138   139   140   141   142   143   144   145

2ND FLOOR

81   87   94   95
82   88   106 105 104B 96
Amphitheatre   106 A   97
106 B   103 104   98
70A 65 66   67 68 69 89   90   104A   99
70   102
71   83   91   101 100
72   92
73   84   93   109   108 107
74A   85
74C 74 B   Library   111

118   40A
119
113 114A   114B   114C   114D   114E   115
120   116   117   112
121   122   124 125   126   127   128   130   131
123   129

**1ST FLOOR
AND MEZZANINE**

Admission: voluntary contribution.
Disabled access and wheelchairs available.
At the Cromwell Road entrance is the huge Museum shop; the
Museum cafeteria is located at the eastern end of the ground floor; the
Henry Cole Wing also has a shop and restaurant near the Exhibition
Road entrance.

The V & A is currently (1986–7) undergoing major renovation and
the visitor is warned that galleries may be closed for varying lengths of
time on any given day. Masterpieces of the collection, however, are

normally on view even if the gallery in which they are usually located is closed. Because of the great size of the building, covering 13 acres (5ha) of ground and containing 7 miles (11km) of galleries, the following guide is organized according to general subjects, so that the visitor may choose different routes through the museum to see, for example, sculpture on one visit and ceramics on another. If the visitor has only one day, the following are not to be missed:

The Medieval Treasury *(Room 43)*
Lorsch Book Cover
Eltenberg Reliquary

Tapestry Court *(Room 38)*
Guerre de Troie
Devonshire Hunting Tapestries

Raphael Cartoons Gallery *(Room 48)*
Tapestry Cartoons (Raphael)
Neptune and Triton (Bernini)

Italian Renaissance *(Rooms 11–21)*
Marble relief of Ascension (Donatello)
Virgin and Child roundel (Donatello)

Indo-Persian Miniatures *(Room 41)*

Far Eastern Collections *(Rooms 44, 47)*
Bodhisattva Maitreya (Gandhara)
Ardabil Persian carpet
Chinese and Korean ceramics

The Toshiba Gallery of Japanese Art *(Room 45)*

Constable Collection *(6th floor, Henry Cole Wing)*

The study collections of applied arts on the first floor are of extremely fine quality and of great interest, but because of the richness of each department, the visitor is advised to select only one or two of the collections for special study. However, for the visitor with very limited time, there are a few collections that do stand out and merit a special visit:

Elizabethan Silver *(Rooms 65–69)*

Jewellery Collection *(Rooms 91–93)*
Armada Jewel (c.1588)
Canning Jewel (16th century)

Musical Instruments *(Room 40a, above the Costume Court)*

Ironwork *(Rooms 113–114)*

Most of the following subject-matter itineraries begin at the Main Entrance on Cromwell Road; thus for several of them, the visitor should return to this starting point for each route, rather than moving from room to room.

Medieval and Renaissance Art

(Rooms 43, 11–29, 38)
From the Cromwell Road entrance make your way past the shops directly to Gallery 43 in the centre of the ground floor for the **Medieval Treasury.** The works here are all noted for their superb quality, and the new installation is designed as an introduction to the history of decorative arts in Europe. Note especially the unique Byzantine ivory statuette of the Virgin and Child (late 11th–12th century); the **Lorsch Book Cover,** a 9th-century Carolingian ivory relief of the Virgin and Child enthroned with saints; the Symmachi Diptych (late 4th century), which represents a priestess of Bacchus making an offering before the altar of Jupiter; the Gloucester Candlestick (c.1105), made in gilt

bronze cast in three pieces by the lost-wax process and showing a wild dance of men and monsters; and the famous **Eltenberg Reliquary** (c.1180), made by Rhenish goldsmiths in the form of a Byzantine church cupola; the oak foundation is mounted with champlevé enamel and copper gilt and decorated with ivory panels showing scenes from the life of Christ and the Apostles.

Other works of special interest in the Medieval Treasury include: the marble statue of a prophet by Giovanni Pisano from the façade of Siena Cathedral; the stained glass window (c.1400), from Winchester College chapel; the **Syon Cope,** one of the finest examples of English 14th-century embroidery; the Soissons ivory diptych (School of Paris, 13th century), which shows scenes of the Passion as a kind of mystery play in front of a Gothic façade; and the Ramsey Abbey Censer (mid-14th century).

At the foot of the stairs leading to the art library (Room 24) is an early 15th-century Spanish retable attributed to Marzal de Sas, showing St George and the Dragon. One of the masterpiece collections of the V & A is located in Room 38, the medieval tapestries, including the **Guerre de Troie,** two tapestries begun in 1472 in Bruges, and the four tapestries known as the **Devonshire Hunting Tapestries,** made between 1425 and 1450, probably at Tournai. The style and design of the hunting scenes seem to be inspired by French 15th-century miniatures.

Late Gothic and early Renaissance art is represented in Rooms 26–29, featuring especially the **Burghley Nef,** a salt-cellar in the form of a ship, made in Paris in 1528 by Pierre Le Flamand. Note also the Limoges Louis XII triptych, made in France c.1500 with painted enamel panels. The master German wood sculptor Veit Stoss, (late 15th–early 16th century) is represented in Room 26 by a boxwood statuette of the Virgin and Child.

The V & A's world-famous collection of Italian Renaissance art, principally sculpture, is arranged in Rooms 11–21 around the garden. Note especially Donatello's **marble relief of the Ascension** (c.1430), which shows St Peter receiving the keys from Christ, and his **bronze roundel of the Virgin and Child,** (1456). Terracotta sculptures by the

---

William MORRIS (1834–1896)

Morris was born into a wealthy family and was educated at Marl-borough and Exeter College, Oxford, where he met his life-long friend Edward Burne-Jones, with whom he studied illuminated manu-scripts and literature. Morris began as an architect (he worked for a short time in the office of G.E. Street), but first earned a reputation as a poet: his first book, *The Defence of Guenevere* (1858) was dedicated to the leader of the Pre-Raphaelites, Dante Gabriel Rossetti, who interested him in painting. In 1863, with his friends, Morris founded an establishment for the manufacture of wall-papers, tiles and other household objects; and painted furniture and stained glass made by the firm was shown at the International Exhibition of 1862. Morris involved himself in politics and in the 1880s edited and financed the paper *The Commonweal* for his own Socialist League. In later years he devoted much of his energy to his Kelmscott Press: from 1881–6 the Press published in special typo-graphy some fifty works, including translations of medieval French romances, Shelley, Keats, Rossetti, Herrick, parts of Shakespeare, Coleridge, Swinburne, Chaucer and some of his own poems.

della Robbia family and studio are found in several of the rooms, notably the large panel dedicated to René d'Anjou (1450) by Luca della Robbia and the twelve terracotta sculptures representing the *Months* by Luca della Robbia and his students, made to decorate a panel in the Medici Palace in Florence. Also located here is a fine collection of Majolica pottery, including the Cafaggiolo dish (c.1510), made near Florence. The excellent collection of bronzes includes this *Shouting Horseman* (c.1505–10) by the Paduan sculptor, Andrea Briosco, called Riccio.

Before continuing around the garden, visit the three rooms at the rear which were specially designed for the Museum: the **William Morris Green Dining Room,** the tiled Gamble Room and E.J. Poynter's Grill Room.

Continue around the Italian Renaissance Galleries to see some 16th-century majolicas (some are attributed to Nicola Pellipario), examples of Northern Italian Renaissance art, and in Room 21, the extraordinary **wax model of a slave by Michelangelo** (c.1516). There is thought to be a close connection between this and his unfinished figure, *A Young Slave,* designed for Pope Julius II's tomb in Florence. Also here is Giambologna's *Samson Slaying a Philistine* (c.1562).

British and Continental Sculpture and Cast Collections
(Rooms 50, 46a/b, 48)
Return to the Main Entrance to begin a tour of the V & A's remarkable European sculpture and cast collections. Beginning in Room 50, among the fine examples of British 16th–19th century sculpture note Louis-François Roubiliac's statue of *Handel,* 1738. Of special interest in the adjacent room is the fine collection of Italian architectural sculpture, including the whole of the **Chancel Chapel** from the 15th-century church of Santa Chiara in Florence; and the Monument of Marchese Spinetta Malaspina from Verona, c.1435.

The Architectural Courts (Cast Courts, Room 46a/b) were originally opened at the V & A in 1873 and are today a wonderful and unique example of a 19th-century phenomenon. The collection is divided into casts of northern European and Spanish sculpture, including the façade of the Cathedral at Santiago de Compostela and Trajan's Column in the West Court, and casts of Italian monuments in the East.

Before going to the western part of the ground floor go upstairs (above the Sculpture Room 50) for the very fine and extensive study collection of English ivories and alabasters, small Continental sculptures and bronzes.

Lorenzo Bernini's **Neptune and Triton,** the only large-scale group by the Italian artist in any museum outside Italy, is located in the Raphael Cartoons Gallery on the other side of the main entrance (Room 48).

At the Exhibition Road entrance and continuing into Room 51 is a group of Neo-Classical sculptures and works by Auguste Rodin.

Raphael Cartoons Gallery
(Room 48)
Located at the western end of the ground floor, Room 48 contains Raphael's seven magnificent **Cartoons** (on loan to the V & A from the Queen). Made in 1515 for Pope Leo X as designs for tapestries for the Sistine Chapel in the Vatican, these full-size compositions are painted in sized colours on paper; note the *Miracle of the Draught of Fishes.*

Dress Collection
(Room 40)
Near Room 48 is the popular but crowded gallery devoted to costumes, illustrating the evolution of western fashion from 1600 to c.1950.

Eastern Arts
(Rooms 47, 41, 42, 44)
Beginning at the Main Entrance, behind the shops and to the left are Rooms 47a/b/c, 41 and 42, which cover Islamic, South-East Asian, Tibetan and Indian art. What looks like a corridor behind the shops is actually a marvellous gallery (Room 47a/b/c) containing early Islamic and South-East Asian objects, and important smaller Indian sculpture, including the grey schist **figure of the Bodhisattva Maitreya,** from Gandhara. Note also the potstone sculpture of Durga as Maheshasura-mardini, mortally wounding a buffalo demon, which was originally one of many sculptures that covered the outside of a temple in Mysore (south India) (early 13th century). The graceful Indian sandstone torso of a Bodhisattva, (probably 9th century) was originally part of an upright slab or stele. Near the entrance to Room 41 are South Indian bronzes, including the dancing figure of Shiva Nataraja (11th century) shown with his foot on a demon.

Room 41 features a superb collection of Indo-Persian miniatures, including *The Celebrations at the birth of Prince Murad,* a page from the *Akbarnama* painted on cloth, c.1590, and *The Giant in the Well,* a page from the *Hamzanama,* (c.1570). Also in Room 41 is Shah Jahan's Cup, an extraordinary carving of opalescent jade (1607). *Tipu's Tiger* is an unusual, carved and painted late 18th-century sculpture which contains a pipe organ and was originally made for the amusement of Tipu Sultan, ruler of Mysore.

The Art of Islam is presented in Room 42 and among the fine carpets note the **Ardabil Persian Carpet** (1539–40). Here also is the small 13th-century Syrian beaker known as The Luck of Edenhall with its 14th-century European leather case.

Located in Rooms 44 and 47d (to the right of the central gallery, Room 48, on the ground floor) are the collections of Chinese and Japanese art, including important examples of 15th–17th-century furniture and silk screen panels. Among the Chinese sculptures, note the 13th-century painted wood sculpture of Bodhisattva Guanyin and the earthenware tomb figure of a horse from the T'ang dynasty (8th century). The Chinese bronze collection includes a fine tripod ritual vessel from the Shang dynasty (12th century). Among the ceramics collection are **Korean porcelains,** including a 17th-century jar decorated with a copper-red dragon. The Japanese collections include important examples of painted stoneware and a collection of Japanese armour in medieval style **(Oyoroi)** made in the mid-19th century.

European Decorative Arts 1700–1800
(Rooms 1–7)
From the Cromwell Road entrance, take the steps in front of the shop down to the lower ground floor for European decorative arts and some smaller sculptures, including Jean-Antoine Houdon's marble bust of Armand-Thomas Hue, 4th Marquis de Miromesnil; also note the lovely terracotta *Cupid and Psyche* (c.1800) by Claude Michel, called 'Clodion', and François Boucher's painting of his patron **Madame de Pompadour** (1758). Especially fine examples of French furniture include an oak wardrobe, veneered with ebony and marquetry of engraved pewter and brass, made in c.1700; a work-table (c.1785) veneered with tulipwood and decorated with marquetry ormolu and a Sèvres porcelain plaque. The French porcelain includes a Sèvres vase (c.1700), depicting Jupiter and Callisto (after Boucher) and the group, *L'Heure du Berger* (Vincennes c.1749–52), also based upon an engraving after Boucher.

Several especially fine German objects are also located here, including a marquetry writing cabinet (1716); a bureau-cabinet made for Augustus III of Saxony (Dresden, 1750) and a table fountain (c.1775) with Meissen figures.

English Renaissance and Baroque Art
(Mezzanine floor, Rooms 52–58)
From the Main Entrance in front of the shops take the stairs up to the Mezzanine for the English Renaissance and Baroque Galleries and for examples from the V & A's unrivalled collection of English furniture. Included is the famous, gigantic Elizabethan oak bed, known as the **Great Bed of Ware** (c.1590). Other objects of special notice include the Vyvyan Salt, (1592–3), a large salt-cellar decorated with panels and medallions of verre eglomisé (glass decorated on the back with colours and foils); the silver Churchill bottle (1702–14), which bears the mark of Pierre Platel, one of the most notable goldsmiths of his time; and the overmantel mirror (c.1753) from the Norfolk House Music Room in London.

English 18th–19th-century Decorative Arts
(Rooms 118–131)
To continue this tour of English Decorative Arts, go upstairs to the Mezzanine above the first floor. Among the fine examples of English furniture, note especially the Kimbolton Cabinet (1771) designed by Robert Adam for the Duchess of Manchester; and the Gothic Revival bookcase designed by A.W.N. Pugin, which was shown at the Great Exhibition of 1851. Very fine porcelain, including an 1874 Worcester 'Moorish' vase, and silver such as the Newdigate Centrepiece (1743–4), are also shown here.

British Art and Design
(Room 74)
A separate primary collection is located at the far western end of the first floor overlooking Exhibition Road. Fine examples of English Art Nouveau and 1930s furniture are displayed as well as ceramics by English potters, including Bernard Leach and Lucie Rie.

Applied Arts Study Collections
Musical Instruments *(Room 40a)*
English and European Silver *(Rooms 65–70a, 82–84)*
Enamels *(Room 89)*
Jewellery *(Rooms 91–93)*
Armour, bronzes, arms *(Rooms 88, 90)*
Stained glass *(Rooms 116, 111)*
Embroidery, fans, tapestries, textiles, carpets *(Rooms 109, 107, 94–102)*
Ironwork *(Rooms 113–114)*
Ceramics *(Second Floor, Rooms 127, 133–145)*

The Toshiba Gallery of Japanese Art
(Room 45)
Opened in December 1986, this gallery contains fine examples of Japanese objects from different periods, including Buddhist art, lacquer-work, woodblock prints, costume and contempory crafts.

Henry Cole Wing
Enter from the Exhibition Road entrance through Rooms 151 and 155, where souvenirs of Sir Henry Cole, founding father of the Museum, are available. The collections of this wing are presented on quite a different scale from the galleries of the main building. Here intimate spaces, diffused lighting and many works on paper invite leisurely study. English painting from 1700 to 1900 is located on Level 2, (Rooms

217–221) and among several landscapes by Turner is his **East Cowes Castle, Isle of Wight.** Photography and Watercolours are located on Level 3 with changing and permanent exhibitions. A fine collection of miniature portraits is located on Level 4: Hans Holbein's **Portrait of Anne of Cleves,** Isaac Oliver's unfinished *Portrait of Queen Elizabeth* and Nicholas Hilliard's **Young Man in a Garden** are outstanding. Also located in Rooms 403 and 421 is the Ionides Collection of European painting including a small collection of works from the Renaissance to the 19th century, featuring Le Nain, Ingres and Degas. The highlight of the Henry Cole Wing is the collection of Constable paintings, including *Salisbury Cathedral* and a full-scale study of **The Haywain** as well as drawings, watercolours and pastels.

Boilerhouse Project

Located on the Lower Ground Floor at the Exhibition Road entrance, the Boilerhouse Project takes its name from its site in the Museum's old boilerhouse yard and was established by the Conran Foundation to become Britain's first centre for exhibitions about the history, theory and practice of design in consumer products.

The Theatre Museum, formerly housed on the first floor of the V & A, is due to open in Covent Garden in part of the London Transport Museum, May 1987 (*see p.150*).

NATURAL HISTORY MUSEUM ★★

Cromwell Road, SW7 ☎589 6323
MAP III E2–3 ⊖ South Kensington

The Natural History Museum is the home of national collections of living and fossil plants, animals and rocks, minerals and meteorites. Only a fraction of the Museum's more than 50 million specimens are exhibited, the remainder providing raw material for scientific research. There are more than twenty public galleries and several informal, special exhibitions concerning modern natural history. If the visitor is pressed for time, visit two of these: **Origin of Species,** located on the upper level of the West Wing, and in the Central Hall, **Dinosaurs and their Living Relatives.** The Museum also owns a large collection of botanical and natural history drawings, which may be seen by appointment.

▬ HISTORY

The Natural History Museum was formed in 1753 as part of the British Museum, which included the important natural history collections of Sir Hans Sloane (1660–1753). The Natural History Department was split off in 1860, and a new museum was built (1873–81) for its collections on the site of the International Exhibition at South Kensington. Sir Alfred Waterhouse designed the present premises in a Neo-Romanesque style. The building, which opened to the public in 1881, includes in its ornamentation hundreds of different kinds of animals: the terracotta mouldings of the western half of the Museum represent living organisms, while those in the eastern half depict extinct specimens. In 1963 the Natural History Museum became completely independent of the British Museum.

▬ VISIT

Open Mon–Sat 10am–6pm, Sun 2.30–6pm; closed 1 Jan, Good Fri, May Day, 24–26 Dec.

Admission free.
Taped commentary guide available for hire.
Free public lectures or film shows in Lecture Theatre Tue, Thu, Sat 3pm.
Facilities for disabled (toilets on ground floor).
Bookshop, gift shop, souvenir shop (left of main entrance); cafeteria (rear first floor) and snack bar (North Hall, ground floor).
Children's Centre and Information desk also located behind stairs on the ground floor.
Continuing north is a ramp that connects this part of the Natural History Museum with the Science Museum.

Ground Floor

Central Hall: special exhibition, **Dinosaurs and their Living Relatives,** displaying the remains of dinosaurs found in rocks all over the world, including Britain, dating from between 140 and 65 million years ago. The exhibition shows birds and crocodiles as their closest living relatives. Other fossil reptiles, including remains of plesiosaurs and ichthyosaurs, which were relatively common in Britain, are represented in the Museum, which has some of the finest specimens in the world.

Following Waterhouse's architectural, ornamental division – living organisms are to the left and fossils to the right of the Central Hall (note the floral ceiling decoration) – the galleries devoted to insects and their relatives are at the left. These traditional galleries, which are

---

Charles Robert DARWIN (1809–1882)

A naturalist who developed the theory of natural selection, Darwin was born in Shrewsbury in 1809. His grandfather was Dr Erasmus Darwin (who originated a crude theory of evolution), his father was Dr Robert W. Darwin and his mother was the daugher of Josiah Wedgwood, the celebrated potter. Darwin studied first at Edinburgh University (1825–7) and in 1828 he entered Christ's College, Cambridge, where his interests in botany and zoology were encouraged by the botanist Professor Henslow, who later recommended him as naturalist to the expedition on HMS Beagle. The voyage, which was to carry out a scientific survey of South American waters, lasted from December 1831 to October 1836. It was during this long expedition that Darwin obtained specimens, and studied the fauna, flora and geological conditions of tropical, subtropical and temperate climates that would later form the basis for his theory of biological evolution.

Darwin returned to England in 1836 and began to publish (1839) his researches into the geology and natural history of the various countries he had visited on HMS Beagle; *Zoology of the Voyage of the Beagle* appeared from 1840–43; *The Structure of Distribution of Coral Reefs* in 1842; *Geological Observations on Volcanic Islands* in 1842 and *Geological Observations on South America* in 1846. After the voyage of the Beagle, the problem of the origin of species preoccupied Darwin for the rest of his life. In 1859 he published *The Origin of Species by Means of Natural Selection*, a work that was first received throughout Europe with great interest but also with violent opposition. Darwin continued his research and publication on evolutionary biology until he died in 1882. He was buried with unusual honours in Westminster Abbey.

located around the central area, are extremely well lit and handsomely installed. They include Spiders, Marine Invertebrates, Insects and Birds (the latter two have special exhibits devoted to British species).

West Hall, Central Gallery: the special exhibition, **Human Biology – an Exhibition of Ourselves** offers numerous displays that involve the visitor's participation, including computerized quizzes. Among the many objects is part of the skull of the earliest known Briton, about 250,000 years old, reconstructed from three bones found at Swanscome near London.

West Wing, rear: the **Whale Hall,** one of the most popular exhibitions in the Museum. The centre is occupied by a model of one of the largest living whales, the **blue whale.** Remains of fossil whales up to 50 million years old, found in southern Britain and other parts of the world, are also displayed. Other galleries are devoted to **fossils** – of plants, invertebrates, sea reptiles, fish and mammals. Several special exhibitions are incorporated in this area, including Introducing Ecology, Wildlife in Danger and Classification. The **Elephant Gallery** at the far eastern end of the ground floor is another of the most popular exhibits in the museum.

First Floor

To the left of the grand staircase is the **Mammals Gallery** which leads to the special West Wing exhibition **Origin of Species.** This informative and lively exhibition offers the visitor opportunities to operate exhibits, which range from computerized quizzes relating to the principles of evolution to producing sounds of insects by touch-panels. Interspersed among the various exhibits are short audio-visual programmes. At the far end of the gallery is a room devoted to African mammals.

The East Wing on the upper level is devoted to **minerals, rocks, and gemstones,** with a fascinating exhibit of **meteorites** at the far end of the gallery.

Second Floor

British Natural History: extremely well-designed and compact exhibits are presented according to habitat – urban and wasteland, woodland, heath, etc.

SCIENCE MUSEUM ★★

Exhibition Road, SW7 ☎589 3456
MAP III E3   ⊖ South Kensington

The Museum is dedicated to the history of, and present-day developments in science, industry and technology. British contributions to science, medicine (the **Wellcome Museum of the History of Medicine** is located on the third and fourth floors), and especially the Industrial Revolution, make the historical collections of the Museum quite exceptional. Special emphasis is given to motive power and engines, agricultural and industrial machinery, optics and astronomy, aeronautics, space science and technology, and medicine. On the lower ground floor is a **Children's Gallery,** which contains working demonstrations illustrating fundamental principles of mechanical and physical phenomena, and on the ground floor is **Launch Pad,** a permanent exhibition of experiments and demonstrations which visitors can operate themselves.

▬ HISTORY

The Science Museum opened in 1857, following the new interest in science and technology stimulated by the Great Exhibition of 1851. Originally based upon the scientific and educational collections of the South Kensington (now the Victoria and Albert) Museum, the Science Museum moved to its present site in 1864, and construction of the present buildings took place in stages from 1913. The East Block (1914–38) was designed by Sir Richard Allison and was the first public building in London to use reinforced concrete.

▬ VISIT

Open Mon–Sat 10am–6pm, Sun 2.30–6pm; closed 1 Jan, Good Fri, May Day Bank hol, 25–26 Dec.
Admission free.
Disabled access and lavatories (ground floor).
Lectures and films in the Lecture Theatre: times displayed near the Museum shop.
Public demonstrations of working exhibits take place daily.
The Launch Pad exhibition of experiments and demonstrations is located on the ground floor to the right of the Museum entrance, where tickets are available. Although admission is free, you must come early to obtain a ticket.
Museum shop situated close to Information Office (ground floor); tea bar situated on third floor through Aeronautics Gallery.

Ground Floor

The East Hall is dedicated to motive power and features 18th- and 19th-century engines, including Thomas Newcomen's **first pumping machine** (1712), the Boulton & Watt rotative engine (1788), the original Parsons high-speed dynamo (1884), the **first steam locomotive engine** built by Richard Trevithick (1803) and a handsome

---

James WATT (1736–1819)

Watt was perhaps the greatest engineer of the Industrial Revolution. He is known as the improver and almost inventor of the steam engine. Born in Greenock, Scotland, Watt first went to Glasgow in 1754, then to London to learn mathematical instrument making, and in 1757 he taught this trade at Glasgow University. He was then employed as a surveyor for the canal projected to unite the Forth and the Clyde, later working on other canals (including the Caledonian), and on improving the harbours of Ayr, Glasgow, and Greenock. During the winter of 1763–4 Watt began investigations which led to his improvement of Thomas Newcomen's steam engine, including an air pump, a steam-jacket for the cylinder and double-acting and rotative engines. After an unsuccessful partnership with John Roebuck, in 1774 Watt joined Matthew Boulton, and the commercial manufacture of Watt's new engine commenced at Soho Ironworks. The installation of Boulton & Watt engines in Cornish mines and at the Albion Flour Mills was important to the developing mechanization of production methods which became a major force in the Industrial Revolution. During his lifetime Watt obtained patents for a series of inventions concerning sun and planet motion, the expansion principle, the smokeless furnace, a letter-copying press and even a machine for copying sculpture.

marine triple-expansion steam engine, originally designed as a trawler type (in use from 1790–1950). On the Mezzanine is a reconstruction of James Watt's workshop. Through the central section (Information Office and Museum shop), the Space Science and Technology Gallery features the **Apollo 10 capsule.** At the rear of the ground floor are excellent displays of rail transport, covering the historical development of locomotives, including **Puffing Billy,** the oldest surviving locomotive (1813), and Robert Stephenson's **Rocket** (1829); and all forms of road transport, including the **oldest known motor car** in running condition (Benz, 1888), as well as excellent collections of bicycles and fire fighting appliances.

First Floor

Located at the western end is an impressive collection of **astronomical instruments** and **models,** where their precision is matched by the highest standards of craftsmanship and materials. Thomas Wright's **Orrery** (a working model of the solar system), made in 1733, was used for the education of the royal children and features a large, flamboyant sculptural telescope. In the time-measurement collection is the **Wells Cathedral clock** (nearly 600 years old, and in working order) with moving figures, astronomical dials and ringing bells. Next is the agricultural collection, which includes relics such as Bell's reaper, the first agricultural tractor and even the earliest lawnmower, as well as modern equipment, including a tractor and combine harvester, which can be set in motion by the visitor. The importance of England's role in the Industrial Revolution is highlighted with the extensive display of the history of the textile industry, including a model of Falcon's loom (1728), the first machine controlled by punch cards, and **Arkwright's original spinning machine** (1769). A fine set of early mass-production machinery (1805) used for the Royal Navy in Portsmouth dockyard is shown, as is recent computerized machinery, including a paint-spraying robot, which is occasionally programmed to draw pictures on an easel. There are also excellent exhibits devoted to iron (note Philip James de Loutherbourgh's painting, *Coalbrookdale by*

Isambard Kingdom BRUNEL (1806–1859)

England's greatest railway engineer first studied in England and France and then served under the master-craftsman Louis Breguet in the making of watches and scientific instruments. At the age of 18, he assisted in his father's great engineering project, the Thames Tunnel. In 1831 Brunel himself won a competition to design the Clifton Suspension Bridge at Bristol, which was begun in 1835, but not actually completed until 1864. Brunel was appointed Engineer to the Great Western Railway in 1833 and was responsible for the design and construction of all the tunnels, bridges (including the world's largest brick-built span located at Maidenhead over the Thames, 1838, and the Saltash bridge over the Tamar River, 1859), viaducts and arches on that line. Brunel worked on the designs and modifications for both the Bristol and Sunderland docks, and was also actively interested in steam navigation. His 'Great Western' steamship made its first Atlantic crossing in 15 days in 1838 (the same year the first section of the Great Western Railway opened). It was followed by the 'Great Britain' (1843) and a third ship, the 'Great Eastern' (1858), which met with disaster the year of Brunel's death (1859).

Night, 1801); and to the history of glass, including a 10th-century Islamic distillation apparatus as well as examples of its most sophisticated use in vacuum vessels and **fibre optics.**

Second Floor

The upper floors are mostly devoted to subjects which require some special knowledge, although exhibits in all areas are accessible to visitors of all ages. Not far away from the **history of newspapers** and the fine collection of presses on the second floor are the **chemistry collections** (including Graham's diffusion apparatus, Dalton's atom models and Faraday's chemical cabinet) and a section on nuclear physics. Working demonstrations show the properties of the atomic nucleus. Also on the second floor are several galleries devoted to navigation, marine engineering, the history of docks and the evolution of sailing ships from ancient times.

Third Floor

The **Photography** and **Cinematography Galleries** feature an important collection of cameras from 1835 to the present, in addition to exhibits on the origins of cinema. **Light** and **Sound** are featured next in exhibits which range from the history of telescopes and microscopes to demonstrations of the principles of optics and the effects of polarized light; note especially **King George III's collection of scientific instruments,** amassed for the education of his children, including a large compound microscope finished in silver and decorated in the Neo-Classical style, made for the Prince of Wales in the 1780s. The popular **Aeronautics Gallery** is located beyond the escalators and contains some 24 actual aircraft, including a Vickers Vimy (1919), the first aircraft to make a direct non-stop flight across the Atlantic, a Spitfire and a Gloster E28/29, the first British jet-propelled aircraft.

Wellcome Museum

Do not miss the third and fourth floors, which house the **Wellcome Museum of the History of Medicine.** Excellent life-size dioramas in the lower galleries (third floor) include a reconstructed 1905 pharmacy as well as a genuine **operating theatre** (1980) for open-heart surgery. The upper galleries (fourth floor) interweave art and science through the exhibition of a large number of objects of high artistic quality, illustrating tribal medicine in China and India, prehistoric disease, and medical artefacts from Ancient Egypt, Greece and Rome.

Children's Gallery

(Lower ground floor)
Simple demonstrations of scientific principles can be operated by children. Adjacent is a particularly entertaining gallery devoted to the history of domestic appliances.

THE MUSEUM OF LONDON ★★

London Wall, London EC2 ☎600 3699
MAP V A3   ✆   Barbican (Cl. Sun), St Paul's, Moorgate ≼ Moorgate

The main purpose of the Museum is to display aspects of London's development from prehistoric to modern times, including the life of its people, their customs, work and celebrations. The collections include a wide range of materials from fine and decorative arts and crafts, a comprehensive costume collection, everyday objects and printed ephemera, to shopfronts, vehicles and archeological finds. Galleries are arranged chronologically with objects set in social context, sometimes accompanied by music. The visitor should not expect, however, a traditional 'museum' installation, rather each area appears like a wonderfully constructed and elaborate set for theatre or film. Children especially will enjoy the exhibits, as will amateur collectors of everyday objects.

HISTORY

The Museum of London was formed by the amalgamation of the **Guildhall Museum,** administered by the Corporation of London since 1826, and the **London Museum,** a national museum dating from 1911. The two museums occupied separate buildings until the present premises, designed by Powell, Moya and Partners, were opened to the public in 1976. As part of the Barbican complex (*see p.133*), the London Museum is designed around a central courtyard, which is well suited to the display of objects.

VISIT

Open Tue–Sat 10am–6pm, Sun 2–6pm; closed Mon, 1 Jan, 24–26 Dec.
Admission free.
Lectures, films, and workshops at times displayed.
Disabled access by Museum lift from car park or by wheelchair on high walk to Main Entrance; tape guides for blind visitors.
Museum shop (at Main Entrance) and restaurant (at lower level).
Roman Fort Gate (adjacent to Museum) open monthly on 1st Tue 10.30am–noon and 3rd Fri 2.30–4.30pm.

Ground Floor

To the right of the Main Entrance is the first gallery, which is devoted to the **Thames in Prehistory;** in many ways this provides an introduction to one of the continuing themes of the whole museum, the significance of the Thames to the social, economic and geographical development of the city. Next is the gallery devoted to Roman London, which presents a side of London's history that is less familiar to many visitors, in an extremely evocative way. In exhibits such as the domestic interior showing the **Buddersbury pavement** (3rd century AD), or the small case of hairdressing paraphernalia, for instance, the sense of the everyday life of Roman Londoners is conveyed. Of special interest is the reconstructed section of the Blackfriars barge (built sometime after AD 88), which carried ragstone from Maidstone in Kent to London. Note also the **sculptures** from the **Temple of Mithras,** including a handsome head of Mithras and the circular relief showing him slaying the bull of evil. Next, in the dimly lit Saxon and Medieval London galleries, there are wonderful examples of **pottery** (the Museum's pottery collection is strong in all areas) and interior furnishings, such as the panel from a chest (c.1400) showing part of a story from the *Canterbury Tales*. Note the limestone slab, carved in the early 11th-century Anglo-Saxon 'Ringerike' style, which comes from a Danish burial at St Paul's. Tudor and Early Stuart London comes next and includes very fine examples of **armour** (note the cannon and suit of armour made by the Greenwich Armouries, c.1630–40) as well as smaller objects of exquisite materials: especially the **Parr Pot,** which is made of white striped Venetian-style glass with silver-gilt mounts and the coat-of-arms of Sir William Parr (uncle and chamberlain to Queen Catherine Parr) on the lid, and the **Cheapside Hoard,** a collection of jewellery dating from c.1600. Dirck Stoop's painting *Entry of Charles II*

Samuel PEPYS (1633–1703)

The celebrated diarist Pepys studied in Huntingdon and at Magdalene College, Cambridge. During his lifetime he had an accomplished career as an official in naval affairs, but it is with his *Diary*, which commenced on 1 January 1660, that his fame is associated. The *Diary*, which was written in a personal code, is a unique work in the literature of the world, for not only is it a history of manners and events of his day, but it also presents a remarkable psychological study of its author. Pepys enjoyed a prosperous life and held several high offices, becoming twice Master of Trinity House (1676, 1685), Master of the Clothworkers Company (1677) and President of the Royal Society (1684–6). His diary was first published in two volumes (covering the years 1660–69) in 1825 and in eight volumes (including a later period) in 1893–6. Pepys's library was bequeathed to Magdalene College, where it remains intact today.

---

into the City on 22nd April 1661 shows the customary procession of the monarch through the city on the day before his coronation. At the end of this gallery is an audio-visual programme on the **Great Fire of London** in 1666, which is especially popular with children, and a Dutch-school painting, *The Fire of London,* dated that same year.

Lower Ground Floor

A ramp leads down into the Late Stuart London gallery, which features a special display devoted to Samuel Pepys, including an inlaid backgammon board (c.1680) given to the diarist by James II. The pinewood-panelled interior of the gallery is particularly fine and includes a painted ceiling, showing the personification of Summer, and furniture with oriental motifs (c.1670s) that reflect both the taste of a Stuart merchant and also the influence of the East India Company's trade. A lovely virginal made in Old Jewry (the old Jewish quarter of the City) by James White in 1656 is still in working order. Just outside the room is Jacob Knyff's painting *The River at Chiswick* showing Tudor houses. At that time Chiswick was a popular summer retreat for Londoners.

The Georgian and early 19th-century galleries include some of the larger exhibits, with **shopfronts**, vehicles, even the interior walls of a Georgian prison. In the 19th-century section the **Great Exhibition of 1851** is featured, with a **model of the Crystal Palace** as well as prints and souvenirs. In the wing showing theatrical and pub interiors is Walter H. Lambert's large group-portrait of Edwardian musical hall personalities, *Popularity* (1901–3).

The 20th-century galleries cover changing aspects of life for Londoners, including Women at Work. They also reflect modern taste, especially of the late twenties and thirties. Note the **Selfridge's lift** of 1928, made by Edgar Brandt and the Birmingham Guild of Metalworkers, which features Art Deco style decorative bronze panels with flying storks and the signs of the Zodiac.

The last exhibition area is devoted to Ceremonial London and features the **18th-century coach,** drawn by six horses, which is used in the annual ceremonial procession of the Lord Mayor in November (a special exit from the Museum was designed for this purpose). Made in 1757, the coach is elaborately carved and decorated with panel paintings by the Florentine artist Cipriani.

OUTER LONDON

Apart from the dense urban concentration of the City, Westminster and some parts of the West End, London has a looser, more open structure than most other great cities. This is partly explained by the fact that, while the city itself extended outwards, the many neighbouring towns and villages also grew, until they added to and were absorbed into the expanding city. Consequently, London has much to offer that is often overlooked by the main tourist itineraries. Other parts of the London area of outstanding interest – some requiring a day's excursion, some surprisingly close to the centre – are listed here alphabetically (*see map pp. 20–21*).

CHISWICK ★

⊖ Gunnersbury, Chiswick Park, Turnham Green ⇝ Gunnersbury, Chiswick

Situated on a bend of the river west of Hammersmith, **Chiswick** remained almost a village until a little over a century ago, when a shipyard and other local industries, together with the railway, brought a sharp population rise. The last 35 years have seen the enormous growth of Heathrow international airport, a few miles west, with the consequent building of an arterial road and a huge volume of traffic passing to and from central London. Luckily the proximity of all this has not entirely destroyed Chiswick's riverside charm and seclusion.

The **Mall**, by the river itself – marked at that point by the small island of **Chiswick Eyot** – is a very pleasant spot, with some splendid Georgian and other period town houses. At its western end is the parish church of **St Nicholas,** a fine building, which, though dating back to the 15th century, was largely built by J.L. Pearson a hundred years ago, and which adds to the village-like atmosphere. Among those commemorated in its churchyard is the artist William Hogarth. The house that was for many years his 'country retreat' – now, alas, a little too close for comfort to the main road – is now a museum dedicated to his work and other mementoes of his life. (*Open Apr–Sep, Mon, Wed–Sat 11am–6pm, Sun 2–6pm; Oct–Mar, Mon, Wed–Sat 11am–4pm, Sun 2–4pm.*)

Chiswick House was built by Lord Burlington in 1729 as a country villa, where he entertained the likes of Handel, Swift and Pope. It is modelled very closely on Palladio's famous Villa Capra or Rotonda near Vicenza, and is therefore a prime example of the Classical Palladian style. Burlington employed William Kent both to decorate the interior

Great Pagoda at Kew Gardens

with beautiful plasterwork and to lay out the grounds, now a public park, which contain such items of note as Roman statues of Julius Caesar, Pompey and Cicero, brought back from Hadrian's Villa at Tivoli, and a gate designed by Inigo Jones. (*Open Mar–Oct, Tue–Sun 9.30am–6.30pm; Oct–Mar, Wed–Sun 9.30am–4pm*.)

Other local places of interest are the **Musical Museum** in Brentford High Street, which presents a unique collection of mechanical pianos, organs, phonographs and musical boxes (*open Apr–Oct, Sat & Sun 2–5pm*); and **Kew Bridge Engines Trust,** Kew Bridge Road, which houses early beam engines and traction engines, in working order, and many excellent models of early industrial hardware. (*Open Sat & Sun, Bank hol Mons 11am–5pm.*)

▬▬ DULWICH ★

➤ North Dulwich, East Dulwich, West Dulwich

While much of south London is a vast suburban sprawl, **Dulwich** has to a large degree retained its strong local character. Its once extensive woods and fields were for centuries the hunting ground of kings. The village grew up around a small spa (Dulwich Wells), and many fine old houses remain on or close to the road actually named **Dulwich Village**. There is also the only toll-gate still operating in the London area.

The most prominent group of buildings are the Victorian – partly Gothic Revival, partly Italianate – premises of **Dulwich College** (a boy's public school), dating from 1870, designed by Charles Barry (son of the architect of the Houses of Parliament). The College itself was founded in 1619 by Edward Alleyn, a colourful character who made a small fortune as an actor and impresario (and acquaintance of Shakespeare) at the Globe Theatre and nearby pleasure grounds. Alleyn also bequeathed to his 'College of God's Gift' a number of paintings, which form the nucleus of **Dulwich Picture Gallery**. Sir John Soane built the present gallery in 1814, which is still administered by the College, and is the oldest public art gallery in England. It has canvasses by Rembrandt, Van Dyck, Rubens, Poussin, Canaletto, Gainsborough and Reynolds. Soane also added a mausoleum, with touches of the Neo-Egyptian style then popular for such buildings, for three later benefactors of the Gallery. (*Open Tue–Sat 10am–1pm, 2–5pm, Sun 2–5pm; closed 25–26 Dec, Good Fri.*)

Across College Road from the Gallery is **Dulwich Park,** occupying land originally owned by Alleyn, once a duelling ground, now one of south London's most attractive open spaces, with sculptures by Barbara Hepworth. Beyond the Park and the College, going south, in Seeley Drive, is **Kingswood House,** a large mansion in fanciful Victorian-Gothic Revival style, one-time home of several rich or eminent people, including the creator of 'Bovril' beef extract. It is now a library and local community centre.

Further south still, at the end of College Road, is **Crystal Palace Park,** named after Joseph Paxton's showcase for the Great Exhibition of 1851, which was moved there soon after, and remained one of the sights of London until it burnt down in 1936. Large models of prehistoric animals grouped around a lake are now a rather touching memorial to the days when the Palace attracted huge crowds to the Park. It has, however, enjoyed a renaissance with the creation of the **National Sports Centre,** the venue of international athletics and many other big sporting events.

Not far away, on London Road, Forest Hill, is the **Horniman Museum,** a striking building of 1898 (C.H. Townsend) in Art Nouveau style. It houses a collection of tribal masks, musical instruments and other devices and artefacts gathered by its founder, F.J. Horniman, during his travels as a tea merchant. (*Open Mon–Sat 10.30am– 5.45pm, Sun 2–5.45pm; closed 24–26 Dec.*)

EALING *

⊖ Ealing Broadway, Ealing Common, North Ealing, South Ealing
⇝ Ealing Broadway, West Ealing

Up to the beginning of the 19th century, **Ealing** was still a rural retreat for the landed gentry. By the end of the century, it prided itself as the 'Queen of the Suburbs' on account of its good housing, public amenities and transort – qualities that still apply to this large residential west London district.

For the visitor it has two places of special interest. The first is **Pitshanger Manor,** Walpole Park. In 1800 Sir John Soane bought and converted an existing manor house for his growing collection of antiquities, before moving to his house in Lincoln's Inn Fields (*see p.149*). The surrounding grounds have long been a public park; while the Manor, until recently used as local government offices, has been restored to something of its former glory and re-opened to the public as a library.

Ealing's second claim to fame is **Gunnersbury Park.** Though its history, as a large estate, goes back centuries, it took its present form early in the last century, with the building of two large Regency-style houses. In 1835 the entire property was acquired by the Rothschild family. They added other interesting features to the Park, including an orangery, stables and a Gothic folly, and remained in possession until 1917. Today, the larger of the two houses, **Gunnersbury House,** is a museum of local history with sections on archeology, transport and costume. (*Open Mar–Oct, Mon–Fri 1–5pm, Sat, Sun, Bank hols 2–6pm [Nov–Feb, 4pm].*)

EPPING FOREST *

⊖ Loughton, Theydon Bois, Epping   ⇝ Chingford

The 6,000 acres (2,400ha) of **Epping Forest** go a long way to compensate north-east London for its general lack of open spaces compared with other parts of the capital, although most of the Forest lies outside the Greater London area. It is, for all its size, only a remnant of a once huge forest that covered most of eastern England from the Thames to as far north as Lincoln-shire and the Wash. By the beginning of the 19th century, the once great primeval forest was in danger of disappearing alto-gether. After a series of legal battles, the surviving acres were handed over to the Corporation and people of London in 1878, together with the herds of deer, once reserved for the sport of kings and queens.

The earliest works of man still visible are the remains of two Iron Age settlements, at **Loughton Camp** and **Ambersbury Banks,** con-sisting of some quite considerable earthworks. Moving on to Roman times, Epping Forest was probably the scene of Queen Boudicca's last battle against the Legions, after which she is said to have committed suicide, with her daughters, by eating poisonous berries. The actual place of her death and burial, however, remains a mystery.

Epping Forest

Waltham Abbey, now separated from the main part of the Forest, was founded in the 11th century and enlarged by King Harold just before his defeat and death at the Battle of Hastings in 1066. He is buried there. Most of the Abbey was demolished at the time of Henry VIII's dissolution of the monasteries, but part of the old Norman nave serves as a parish church. Nearby, in Sun Street, is the **Epping Forest District Museum,** housed in Queen Elizabeth's Hunting Lodge. It includes a Tudor herb garden and oak panelled room. (*Open Mon, Fri–Sun 2–5pm, Tue 12–5pm.*)

Not far from the small part of the Forest that does penetrate into London, in Forest Road, Walthamstow, is the **William Morris Gallery,** in the house where the leading light of the Arts and Crafts movement lived and worked for many years. It exhibits many examples of his work – wallpaper and textiles, ceramics, furniture, stained glass, embroidery, tapestry, book design – together with work by some of his colleagues. (*Open Tue–Sat 10am–1pm, 2–5pm; first Sun each month 10am–12, 2–5pm; closed 1 Jan, Good Fri 25–26 Dec*).

GREENWICH

See pp. 225–6

HAMPSTEAD AND HIGHGATE ★★

⊖ Highgate, Chalk Farm, Belsize Park, Hampstead, Swiss Cottage, Finchley Road   ⇌ Hampstead Heath

Hampstead, with its Heath rising to the highest point for miles around, was for a long time also the wildest spot in the vicinity of London, where wolves lurked among its dark woods until well into the Middle Ages. Its history goes back much further than that, to prehistoric times, but the Hampstead we know today dates largely from its time as a popular 18th-century spa. Its handsome Georgian houses, and its aspect facing southward on the slope of the hill, established it as one of London's most attractive and sought-after residential districts – the home of many rich and famous people, and a vital part of the capital's social scene. Neighbouring **Highgate,** on the eastern side of the hill, though now traversed by one of the busiest roadways into central London, has retained a little more of its own village atmosphere than bustling Hampstead.

Hampstead Heath (with **Parliament Hill**) was long a place of refuge for Londoners at such times of crisis as the Black Death, the Great Plague and the Fire of 1666. It remains Hampstead's biggest attraction, commanding magnificent views right across the capital to the Surrey Hills (North Downs). Thousands flock to its celebrated Bank Holiday fairs. There are several well-known pubs in the vicinity, including **Jack Straw's Castle,** named after a leader of the Peasants' Revolt of 1381, and the **Spaniards Inn** and **Toll House,** associated with the famous highwayman Dick Turpin. Its crowning glory is **Kenwood House,** with beautiful interior decoration, largely the work of Robert Adam. The collection of paintings (the Iveagh Bequest) includes works by Rembrandt, Frans Hals, Vermeer, Gainsborough and Romney. Summer open-air concerts are given in the grounds. (*Open daily Apr–Sep 10am–7pm; Oct, Feb–Mar 10am–5pm; Nov–Jan 10am–4pm.*)

The library, Kenwood House

Hampstead also has other attractions. **Church Walk** is a lovely, tree-lined enclave of Georgian houses, with **St John's** parish church of the same period, where the artist John Constable is buried. Nearby are **Fenton House** of 1693, a museum of keyboard instruments and porcelain (*open Apr–Oct, Mon–Wed, Sat 11am–6pm, Sun 2–6pm*) and **Romney's House** (1797), with distinctive exterior weatherboarding. Right at the foot of the Heath is **Keats House,** originally two semi-detached Regency houses, where the poet wrote some of his finest verses including the 'Ode to a Nightingale'. The house contains mementoes of himself and his circle of friends. (*Open Mon–Sat 10am–1pm, 2–6pm, Sun 2–5pm.*)

Near Finchley Road is the newly opened **Freud Museum,** at 20 Maresfield Gardens, preserving the consulting room and library of the founder of psycho-analysis in the house where he took refuge during the last year of his life (*open daily except Mon 1–5pm*).

Highgate has **Waterlow Park,** with **Lauderdale House,** originally a Tudor residence and at one time the house of Charles II's mistress Nell Gwynne. It is now a museum of local history and a community centre. Next to it, by Swain's Lane, is the district's greatest claim to fame – **Highgate Cemetery** – planned in the early 19th century with Neo-Egyptian catacombs as its set piece, and the burial place of such famous men and women as Michael Faraday, Christina Rossetti and John Galsworthy. The original part of the cemetery was for many years in a bad state of neglect (though with a powerful Gothic atmosphere), but it is now being restored and maintained by a local society. The newer, less romantic part contains the celebrated monument to Karl Marx, with a massive bust of his head. George Eliot, Herbert Spencer, and Sir Ralph Richardson are buried there.

Neighbouring **Muswell Hill** boasts **Alexandra Palace,** built in 1875 as North London's rival to the Crystal Palace. The world's first television transmission was made from here in 1936. It is now an exhibition hall.

▬▬ *HAMPTON COURT* ★★★

See pp. 229–31

▬▬ *HARROW* ★

⊖ ⇌ Harrow-on-the-Hill

Harrow-on-the-Hill rises like an island of gracious period houses and venerable buildings above the surrounding expanse of 'Metroland', the capital's largest area of suburban growth between the two world wars, stimulated by London Transport's Metropolitan Line. The place name is derived from a Saxon word 'hergae', meaning a shrine or temple. The history of the Hill and its once thickly wooded slopes is indeed very ancient, and Harrow Manor is recorded in the *Domesday Book*. From the Middle Ages until the 17th century, the town on the hill – still miles out in the country – was the focal point of important markets, fairs and tournaments (a field in the neighbourhood is still called High Capers). In the Civil War, the township raised a regiment to fight with Cromwell and Parliament.

The biggest event in the town's history was the founding, in 1572, of **Harrow School** – the great rival to Eton as England's premier public school. The school premises have been much enlarged during the past two centuries, but the original classroom still exists, its panelled walls inscribed with the names of such celebrated former pupils as the poet **Lord Byron** and prime ministers **Sir Robert Peel** and **Sir Winston Churchill.** (*Guided tours in term time by arrangement ☎422 2196, ext. 225.*)

Associated with Harrow School is the church of **St Mary,** founded in 1087, with a rich history from the time of **Thomas à Becket** to that of Byron. The spire, north-west London's clearest landmark, was added in 1450. Inside there are many fine monuments, brasses, a 13th-century marble font, 17th-century carved pulpit, and a series of stained glass windows commemorating the town's history from the 9th century to 1872, the year of the school's tercentenary. Another local feature is the old town well, plunging 700ft (213m) down into the Hill.

▬▬ *KEW GARDENS* ★★

➲ Kew Gardens   ≽ Kew Bridge

The **Royal Botanic Gardens** at Kew, originally in the grounds of a royal palace, grew in size and importance from the 17th century on. In 1772 they were landscaped by Lancelot 'Capability' Brown (who also worked on **Syon Park** across the river); and in 1841, the 300-acre (120ha) Gardens, with over 20,000 species of plants, were given to the nation as both a park and a scientific institution. (*Open daily 10am–4pm, summer 10am–8pm.*)

Of special interest are: the two large conservatories, the **Palm House** (1844), the finest iron and glass structure of its day, and the **Temperate House** (1860), both designed by Decimus Burton and engineer Richard Turner; the **Orchid House;** the **General Museum,** facing the Palm House across the Pond; the **Marianne North Gallery,** with a collection of over 800 botanical paintings by the artist; and, close by, the 225ft (69m) high flagstaff, made from the trunk of a Douglas fir, and presented by the government of British Columbia. There is, in addition, a great wealth of trees, shrubs and flowers growing in different parts of the grounds, many of exceptional botanical interest.

The Gardens are endowed with many other buildings and monuments. **Kew Palace,** also known as the **Dutch House,** down by the river, is a Jacobean mansion, with one of the few surviving examples of a 17th-century herb garden. The Hanoverian monarchs added the **Orangery,** the **Queen's Cottage,** a large summerhouse set in its own area of woodland, several Greek-style temples, and other fanciful structures. A distinctly oriental note was first struck by Sir William Chambers's **Great Pagoda** of 1761, a monument to his travels in China. There are also two stone **Chinese Guardian Lions** by the pond and an elaborate **Japanese Gate,** commemorating an exhibition of 1910.

Kew Green, by the main entrance to the Gardens, is graced by Georgian and Regency houses and by **St Anne's Church** (1710–70) where Thomas Gainsborough is buried.

▬▬ *RICHMOND* ★★

➲ Richmond   ≽ Richmond

Richmond-on-Thames owes its name to Henry VII, who built a palace there, naming it Rychemond after his estates in Yorkshire. The town prospered, thanks to his palace, to its strategic position in relation to other royal homes, at Kew, Hampton Court and Windsor, and to its own attractive site, rising steeply above a bend of the river. The coming of the railway brought fresh prosperity by way of residential development. Together with its neighbouring Park, Richmond is also one of London's most popular recreational areas.

The **Green,** a Tudor jousting ground, retains many fine Georgian houses, notably those in **Maids of Honour Row.** The **Richmond Theatre** (1899) recalls the Green's theatrical past, marked by such figures as David Garrick, Edmund Kean and Sarah Siddons. Nearby are reminders of the **Palace** (mostly destroyed during the Civil War), including the **Gateway,** with Henry VII's coat-of-arms, the **Wardrobe** building, and the handsomely converted **Trumpeter's House** (once the home of Austrian statesman Metternich). By the river is **Asgill House** (1760), home of a former Lord Mayor of London. Of the town's four bridges, the two most attractive are the old bridge of 1774, and, a little way downstream, the Victorian footbridge which forms a part of Richmond Lock (*see p.175*). The parish church of **St Mary Magdalene** is mainly Tudor, with some fine brasses and monuments, including one to Edmund Kean.

Richmond Hill, lined along its crest with handsome 18th- and 19th-century terraces, commands a splendid view of the river and **Petersham Meadows,** immortalized in paint by both Turner and Sir Joshua Reynolds, who lived in neighbouring **Wick House.** Behind it lies the gently rolling landscape of **Richmond Park,** by far the largest of the royal parks (2,470 acres, 1,000ha) noted for its deer and other wildlife and for its ancient and majestic groves of oak trees. Two of its special features are the **Isabella Plantation,** with an almost tropical profusion of greenery and flowers, and **Sawyer's Hill,** near Richmond Gate, with views of St Paul's and the City way over to the east, and of Windsor Castle to the north-west. Two notable buildings in the Park are **White Lodge** (1727), now a part of the Royal Ballet School (*open Aug, 2–6pm daily*); and **Thatched House Lodge** (1670), a royal residence. A third, **Pembroke Lodge,** with gardens, is a cafeteria restaurant.

Down by the river, and a walk upstream from Richmond, is **Ham House** (1610), with Jacobean furnishings, including paintings and tapestries, and gardens laid out in the same period style. (*Open Apr–Sep, Tue–Sun 2–6pm; Oct–Mar, Tue–Sun noon–4pm.*)

▬ *TWICKENHAM AND ISLEWORTH* ★
≋ St Margarets, Twickenham, Isleworth, Strawberry Hill

For sportsmen, **Twickenham** means the international rugby football ground, but this large west London suburb, with adjoining **Isleworth,** across the Thames from Richmond, also has a history, with some places of notable interest and architectural merit.

Twickenham's most noteworthy buildings are all close to the river. **Marble Hill House** is a splendid early 18th-century Palladian-style villa. Standing well back from Richmond Road, in its own park and with the river beyond, it was built by Henrietta Howard, mistress of George II, and frequented by her friend the poet Alexander Pope, the district's most distinguished resident. The interior has been restored as closely as possible to the original. (*Open daily except Fri; Feb–Oct 10am–5pm; Nov–Jan 10am–4pm; closed 24–25 Dec.*) Next to it, upstream in a riverside garden, is the **Orleans House Gallery,** the remaining wing of a large 18th-century mansion, once the home of the exiled French Duke of Orleans, later Louis-Philippe. The Gallery has changing exhibitions. (*Open Tue–Sat 1–5.30pm, Sun and Bank hols 2–5.30pm; Oct–Mar closes 4.30pm*.) Between these two buildings is **Montpelier Row,** a fine group of early Georgian terraced houses. Also near the river and the colourfully named **Eel Pie Island** is the parish church of **St Mary the Virgin,** mainly 18th century, but with a medieval tower. It has a handsome interior, with a memorial to Pope, who is buried there.

Further upstream is **Strawberry Hill House,** built in 1776 by Horace Walpole, man of letters and son of the prime minister. It is one of the earliest and most remarkable essays in the Gothic Revival style, with a sense of fantasy looking forward to the even more exotic and extravagant Royal Pavilion at Brighton. Though the building is now part of a teachers' training college, there are conducted tours, for which advance application should be made.

On the borders of Twickenham and Isleworth is **Kneller Hall,** built in the early 18th century by the court artist Sir Godfrey Kneller, but largely rebuilt in the middle of the last century in Neo-Jacobean style. It is now the home of the Royal Military School of Music.

▬ SYON PARK AND OSTERLEY PARK ★★

⊖ Osterley   ⇝ Syon Lane, Osterley

On the fringes of Isleworth itself are two more major attractions, both adding to west and south-west London's abundance of open spaces, and both featuring the work of Robert Adam at its finest.

Syon Park, facing Kew Gardens across the Thames, was laid out by the great 18th-century landscape architect Lancelot 'Capability' Brown. Today it boasts a large conservatory, a rose garden, and an extensive garden centre. The house dates from the 16th century and has a dramatic and sometimes lurid past, as on the occasion when Henry VIII's coffin, resting there on its way from Westminster to Windsor Castle, burst open in the night. The magnificence of the building, however, dates from the 18th century, when it was renovated by Robert Adam (1761–8). The west front, castellated but otherwise unadorned, gives no hint of the splendours within. These include the **Red Drawing Room,** with crimson silk walls, displaying portraits of royalty by Van Dyck and others; the **State Dining Room,** classically styled with niches, half domes, mirrors, friezes and copies of antique statuary; and the **Long Gallery,** 136ft (41m) long and only 14ft (4m) wide, most cunningly designed by Adam to compensate for these proportions. (*Open Good Fri–Sep, Sun–Thu noon–5pm; Oct, Sun only noon–5pm*.)

Osterley Park, the name of the house as well as the surrounding parklands, was originally built for Sir Thomas Gresham, financier to Elizabeth I. It was altered to some extent by Sir William Chambers at the behest of Francis and Robert Childs, of another famous banking family, then extensively restyled by Adam (1763–7). The most notable external feature is Adam's Greek-Ionic double entrance portico. The majestic **Entrance Hall** has a double apse, with marble floor and ceiling decorated with floral scrolls. The **Drawing Room** is rich in gilding and other ornamentation, with French Neo-Classical sofas and chairs. The **Library** has furniture and fittings by John Linnell, one of the leading 18th-century cabinet makers. The **Tapestry Room,** with more Adam motifs, has very fine Gobelin tapestries and chairs in matching style. (*Open Apr–Sep, Tue–Sun 2–6pm; Oct–Mar, Tue–Sun noon–4pm; closed 1 Jan, Good Fri, May Day, 24–26 Dec*.)

WIMBLEDON

⊖ ⇌ Wimbledon

This south London district has a long history, centred around the High Street at the top of Wimbledon Hill, although little of historical interest remains. Its great fame comes from its international tennis championships; while its attraction for many Londoners is the Common, one of the capital's largest open spaces.

The **All England Lawn Tennis and Croquet Club,** to give its official title, was founded in 1896 and moved to its present site, on Church Road, in 1922. Its annual tennis championships (the world's premier competition, held over a two-week period in June–July) have grown in fame and called for continual enlargements and ground improvements. The associated **Lawn Tennis Museum** records many aspects of the game from its earliest days. (*Open Tue–Sat 11am–5pm, Sun 2–5pm; closed Mons and Bank hols; open only to spectators during championship fortnight.*)

Wimbledon Common has 1,000 acres (400ha) of mainly open heathland, as well as a golf course, and London's best-preserved **Windmill** (1817), restored to working order and with a small museum of agricultural relics attached. (*Open Apr–Oct, Sat & Sun 2–5pm.*) It was near here, on neighbouring **Putney Heath,** that Cromwell raised some of his regiments during the Civil War. **Putney** itself, an attractive riverside residential district with many Victorian and Edwardian town houses, was famous for the Putney Debates, policy meetings of Cromwell's Parliamentary army.

WINDSOR AND ETON

(See pp.233–6)

PLACES TO STOP

Chiswick:

Carwardine's – café and coffee shop, 286 Chiswick High Rd (*Mon–Sat 9am–5.30pm*).

Dulwich:

Crown & Greyhound (Taylor Walker) – pub, 73 Dulwich Village

Hampstead and Highgate:

Burgh House Buttery, New End Square (*daily 11am–5.30pm*).
Louis's Pâtisserie, 32 Heath St (*daily 9.30am–6pm*).
Pinot's – wine bar, 34 Rosslyn Hill (*Mon–Sat to midnight, Sun to 10.30pm*).
Marine Ices, 8 Haverstock Hill (*Mon–Sat 10am–6.30pm, Sun 11am–6pm*).
Flask (Ind Coope) – pub, 77 Highgate West Hill.
Spaniards (Vintage) – pub, Spaniards Rd.
Holly Bush (Taylor Walker) – pub, Holly Mount.
Freemasons Arms (Charringtons) – pub, Downshire Hill.
Jack Straw's Castle (Charringtons) – pub, North End Way.
Bull & Bush (Ind Coope) – pub, North End Way.

Kew:

Maids of Honour – teashop, 288 Kew Rd.

Richmond:

Orange Tree (Youngs) – theatre pub, 45 Kew Rd.
White Swan (Courage) – pub, Old Palace Lane.
Angel & Crown (Fullers) – pub, 5 Church Court.

Twickenham and Isleworth:

White Swan (Watneys) – pub, Riverside, Twickenham; snacks and hot meals.
Eel Pie (Badger) – pub, 9 Church St, Twickenham.
London Apprentice (Watneys) – pub, 62 Church St, Isleworth; restaurant and bar food.

Wimbledon and Putney:

Green Man (Youngs) – pub, Wildcroft Rd, Putney Heath; bar food, barbecues in fine weather.
Rose & Crown (Youngs) – pub, 55 High St, Wimbledon.
Mr Fish – fish and chips, 393 Upper Richmond Rd; (*Mon–Sat noon–2.30pm, 6.30–11pm, Sun 1–2.30pm, 6.30–9.30pm, closed Mon lunchtime*).

SHOPPING

Hampstead:

Ackerman's – confectioner, 9 Goldhurst Terrace; hand-made chocolates.
That New Shop – Perrins Court (*Mon–Sat 9.30am–6pm*); gifts.

GREENWICH AND BLACKHEATH

Four miles downstream from Tower Bridge and rising above a broad bend of the River Thames, **Greenwich** is the perfect setting for some of London's finest sights and places of interest. The 15th-century Greenwich Palace was a favourite with Tudor royalty, especially with Henry VIII, who was born there. After the Restoration, Charles II put in hand work on the great series of buildings for which Greenwich is famous. By the 18th century Greenwich was also a thriving community – well placed between Deptford and Woolwich shipyards – attested to by the many substantial Queen Anne and Georgian houses that still grace its streets. (*See Outer London map, pp.20–21*).

▬ ROYAL NAVAL COLLEGE **

⇌ Greenwich, Maze Hill

This masterpiece of English Renaissance architecture had a surprisingly chequered history in view of its overall grand design. Work on it was begun in 1664, under the aegis of Charles II who planned to replace the old Royal Palace. The latter was demolished except for Inigo Jones's **Queen's House,** but work on the new building was soon abandoned. It was resumed, as a naval hospital, during the reign of William and Mary. Sir Christopher Wren, then Nicholas Hawksmoor and Sir John Vanbrugh, were engaged, and the whole group of buildings – best seen from the river – was finally completed in 1726. It was used as a hospital (similar in function to Wren's Chelsea Pensioners' hospital for soldiers) until 1869. Shortly afterwards, the buildings were taken over as a naval college. (*Chapel open daily except Thu, 2.30–5pm*).

The **Queen's House** (1616–37), built for Charles I's queen Henrietta Maria, is a landmark in English architecture, for Jones introduced a pure Italian style, derived from the Venetian architect Palladio, where no such tradition had been hinted at before. All the proportions are carefully worked out (one of the halls is a perfect cube), there is studied symmetry, and decoration is strictly confined to Classical models. The main staircase (known as the **Tulip Staircase**) is circular and rises to the roof with no inner supports. The grandiose layout of the **Royal Naval Hospital** is wholly due to Wren (begun 1698 and later assisted by Hawksmoor and Vanbrugh), who used colonnades on the two long ranges, with twin domes on either side, above the Painted Hall and the Chapel, to lead the eye back to the Queen's House, which

The Queen's House, Greenwich

became the focus of his plan; he also incorporated the one part of Charles II's Palace that had been built (John Webb) in the large court opening on to the river. The **Painted Hall** (1703), where Nelson lay in state after his death at the Battle of Trafalgar, has a vast ceiling fresco (1707–17), an allegory of William and Mary handing Peace and Liberty to Europe, painted by Sir James Thornhill. It is as spacious a Baroque interior as exists in England. The interior of the **Chapel** was rebuilt after a fire in 1779 in the Neo-Classical style (J. Stuart and W. Newton) and is a perfect example of its period, with original pulpit and furnishings.

Just west of the College, in her own special dry dock, is the 'Cutty Sark' (1869), with maps, charts and other mementoes of her record-breaking days as a tea clipper on the China Run. (*Open Apr–Oct, Mon–Sat 10.30am–6pm; Sun 2.30–6pm; Nov–Mar, closes 5pm.*) Next to her, very small by comparison, is 'Gipsy Moth IV', the yacht with which Sir Francis Chichester made his solo circumnavigation of the world in 1966–7. East of the College are the **Trinity Hospital alms-houses,** with some good 16th-century Flemish stained glass in the chapel, and three riverside pubs with a nautical flavour, the **Trafalgar, Yacht** and **Cutty Sark** taverns.

THE NATIONAL MARITIME MUSEUM AND OLD ROYAL OBSERVATORY **

The National Maritime Museum is housed in the **Queen's House** and in two larger flanking wings, dating from 1809 and built to commemorate the Battle of Trafalgar. The Museum houses a great collection of globes, maps, charts and navigational instruments, model ships and barges, uniforms (including Nelson's), guns and other equipment. There are also paintings by Canaletto, Hogarth and Reynolds. (*Open Easter–Oct, Mon–Sat 10am–6pm, Sun 2–5.30pm; Nov–Easter, Mon–Fri 10am–5pm, Sat 10am–5.30pm, Sun 2–5pm.*)

The **Old Royal Observatory** at the top of the hill of Greenwich Park, dates from John Flamsteed's 1675 appointment as the first Astronomer Royal. **Flamsteed's House,** designed by Wren 'for the observator's habitation and a little for pompe' and the later **Meridian** and **South Buildings** (with a **Planetarium**), house telescopes, sun dials, clocks and other astronomical relics. (*Open Easter–Oct, Mon–Sat 10am–6pm, Sun 2–5.30pm; Nov–Easter, Mon–Fri 10am–5pm, Sat 10am–5.30pm, Sun 2–5pm; closed Bank hols.*) The famous brass meridian line divides the eastern and western hemispheres. Making a break with the nautical-navigational theme is a statue to General Wolfe, victor of the Battle of Quebec (1759), and a citizen of Greenwich.

Croom's Hill, running up the east side of **Greenwich Park,** has several notable 17th- and 18th-century houses. Below it is **St Alfege's Church,** rebuilt in 1718 by Hawksmoor. The composer Thomas Tallis and General Wolfe are buried there. Above, on the edge of Black-heath, with fine views over London, is the 18th-century **Ranger's House,** displaying Jacobean and Stuart portraits. (*Open daily 10am–5pm, 4pm Nov–Jan; closed Good Fri and 25 Dec.*) West of the Park is **Vanbrugh Castle** (1726), a fanciful dwelling which the architect and playwright built for himself.

BLACKHEATH

⇝ Blackheath, Lewisham

The Heath, above Greenwich and the Thames, stands on the historic approach to the capital from Dover and the Continent. Henry V was welcomed there after his victory at Agincourt; so was Charles II upon his Restoration. The rebel armies of Wat Tyler (1381) and Jack Cade (1450) gathered there before marching on London. In the 17th and 18th centuries, the Dover Road made it a notorious place for highwaymen. Residential development in the late 18th and 19th century gave the area its elegant character.

On the south-east side of the Heath is the **Paragon** (1790), which consists of a series of large mansions, linked by colonnades and forming a crescent — Georgian domestic architecture at its grandest. Nearby are **Colonnade House,** another splendid Georgian dwelling of exactly the same period, and **Morden College** (1695), not really a college at all, but a most handsome group of almshouses which still provide homes for the elderly. Wren had a hand in its construction, and Grinling Gibbons probably executed the carvings in the Chapel (*visits by appointment only — apply a month in advance*).

AROUND BLACKHEATH

There are other notable buildings in the vicinity. **Charlton House** (1612) is London's finest example of Jacobean architecture. (*Open Mon–Fri 9am–5pm, weekends by appointment*). **Eltham Palace** has a 15th-century Great Hall, with a fine hammerbeam roof. (*Open Mar–Oct, Thu and Sun only, 11am–7pm, Mar to 4pm*). The most prominent landmark in the whole district is **Severndroog House** on Shooter's Hill, an 18th-century Gothic folly with castellated towers, standing on the site of an earlier beacon. **Shooter's Hill** itself commands some of the best views right across London to Hampstead and Highgate, also parts of Kent and Essex. Its isolation in times past made it a favourite spot for highwaymen and footpads, and a gallows added to its fearful reputation.

PLACES TO STOP

Greenwich:

Yacht (Gateway Hosts) — pub, 7 Crane St.
Trafalgar (Host) — pub, Park Row; pub food and full restaurant menu.
Royal Standard (Chef & Brewer) — pub, 44 Vanburgh Park.
Davy's Wine Vaults, 165 Greenwich High Rd (*Mon–Fri to 10.30pm, Sat to 11pm*).
Bar du Musée — wine bar, 17 Nelson Rd (*daily to 11pm*).
Goddard's Eel and Pie House, 45 Greenwich Church St (*Tue–Sun 11am–3pm, Sat 10.30am–4.30pm*).
Jamima Joe — teashop, 279 Creek Rd (*daily 11.30am–4pm, Sat & Sun to 5pm, 5.30pm in summer*).

SHOPPING

Greenwich:

Greenwich Market (*daily 9am–5pm, Mon–Fri fruit and vegetables, Sat & Sun antiques, second-hand clothes and crafts*).
Green Parrot, 2 Turnpin Lane (*Wed–Sun 10.30am–5.30pm*); antiques and gifts.

HAMPTON COURT ***

Hampton Court Palace, several miles upstream from London, is one of the great palaces of Europe. The place name Hampton comes from the Anglo-Saxon words meaning 'farm by the river bend', and in 1236 a large manor house by the Thames was owned by the Knights Hospitaller of St John of Jerusalem. In 1514, **Cardinal Thomas Wolsey** acquired the property, demolished the manor house and had work started on the Tudor Palace as a symbol of his wealth and power. It was already one of the finest palaces in England – with nearly 500 rooms centred round a succession of courts – when Wolsey fell from favour with **Henry VIII.** Jealousy over the splendour of the building probably had something to do with it. Certainly, when Henry took possession of the Palace in 1529, he immediately made it grander still, adding new wings, a Great Hall, and other notable features. Henry himself, with five of his six wives, his daughters **Mary Tudor** and **Elizabeth I,** and the succeeding Stuart monarchs, all delighted in the Palace, each adding something to it in their turn. It was saved from probable demolition after the Civil War, when **Oliver Cromwell** decided to live there, from 1651 until his death seven years later. The last big chapter in the history of the Palace began with **William and Mary.** They appointed **Sir Christopher Wren** to restyle it for them. Wren originally planned to pull much of it down, and to build a virtually new palace around the Great Hall. In the event, he had to be content with minor demolitions; although his new East Wing, together with other work carried out by such master craftsmen as Grinling Gibbons and the French iron-worker Jean Tijou, was still a major undertaking. The Hanoverian monarchs continued to enrich the Palace, with work by Sir John Vanbrugh and William Kent. It remains, essentially, a remarkable marriage of the Tudor and English Renaissance styles, as well as the repository of many historical and art treasures. (*Open May–Sep, Mon–Sat 9.30am–6pm, Sun 11am–6pm; Mar–Apr & Oct, Mon–Sat 9.30am–5pm, Sun 2–5pm; Nov–Feb, Mon–Sat 9.30am–4pm, Sun 2–4pm.*)

MAP Outer London pp.20–21 ≹ Hampton Court

Visits to the palace start at the red-brick Tudor **Great Gatehouse** (1) which leads into the **Green Court** or **Base Court** (2), with walls

Hampton Court Palace

decorated with terracotta medallions. **Anne Boleyn's Gateway** (3) leads into the **Clock Court** (4), named after the remarkable **astronomical clock** (1540), brought here from St James's Palace in the 19th century. This records the hour, month, date, year, signs of the Zodiac and phases of the moon. It also shows the sun revolving around the earth, since the ideas of Copernicus had not yet been widely accepted at the time of its construction. Entrance to the **State Apartments** is in the south-east corner of the court. These contain an important part of the royal collection of paintings, with works by Mantegna, Titian, Giorgione, Veronese, Correggio, Brueghel, Holbein and Van Dyck. The apartments are also sumptuously decorated, with particularly fine wood carving by Gibbons, and magnificent tapestries. The **King's Staircase** (5) leads through the **King's Guard Chamber** (6) – which also gives access to **Wolsey's Rooms** (7, 8) with paintings of great historic interest – to the wing containing the **King's apartments** (9–15). The **King's Audience Room, or Privy Chamber** (11), is in the centre of Wren's new building and looks over the **Privy Garden.** Similarly, the **Queen's Drawing Room** (18), in the centre of the wing containing the **Queen's Apartments** (15A–19), offers a splendid view over the main formal gardens down the perspective of the **Long Water.** The **Public Dining Room** (20) and the **Prince of Wales's Suite** (20A) are at the end of this wing, and the **Private Apartments** (21–22A) face inwards on to Wren's magnificent **Fountain Court.** On the south side of this is the long **Cartoon Gallery** (23), perhaps the finest of Wren's rooms, designed specially to display a series of tapestry cartoons by Raphael. These are now in the Victoria and Albert Museum, while tapestries after the cartoons line the walls in their place. The **Communication Gallery** (24) displays the **'Windsor Beauties',** 11 paintings of ladies of the court of Charles II by Sir Peter Lely, and leads by way of **Wolsey's Closet** (25), the best-preserved part of the original building, to the **Queen's Staircase** (26) and her state apartments (27, 28). From this point the visit moves back into the old Tudor palace, starting with the **Haunted Gallery** (29), said to echo with the screams of Catherine Howard (Henry VIII's fifth wife) begging the king to spare her life. The **Chapel Royal** (30) was built by Wolsey, but the wooden fan-vaulted roof, with gilding and other decoration, was added by Henry VIII. It was redecorated by Wren, with a superb carved reredos by Gibbons. Beyond the **Kitchen Court** (33) the **Great Watching Chamber** (31), whose fine panelled ceiling has decorated bosses, leads by way of the **Horn Room** (32) to the **Great Hall** (34), the historic centre of the Palace, with its wooden hammerbeam roof decorated with ornate carving and gilding. Its greatest days were during Elizabeth I's reign, when she celebrated Christmas with lavish banquets and entertainments, including plays, so adding to its distinction as the oldest surviving Elizbethan theatre. The visit concludes with a tour of the **Cellars** and **Kitchen** (35, 36),which are entered from the Base Court.

The gardens and parks reflect more history. Elizabeth I cultivated tobacco, potatoes and other exotic plants brought back from the Americas by Sir Francis Drake, Sir Walter Raleigh and other great explorers of the age. The **Pond** and **Knot Gardens** date from Tudor times. The large area of the **Privy Gardens,** the **Broadwalk, Great Fountain** and **Long Water,** the **Wilderness** and the famous **Maze,** were all created during the reigns of Charles II and William and Mary. The celebrated **Great Vine** was planted by the landscape artist Lancelot 'Capability' Brown in 1768 and still bears abundant fruit (sometimes on sale in season). Three buildings in the garden which are of special interest are the Tudor Tennis Court, where the game of real tennis is still regularly played, Wren's **Banqueting House** overlooking the river, and the **Orangery,** which contains Mantegna's magnificent series of

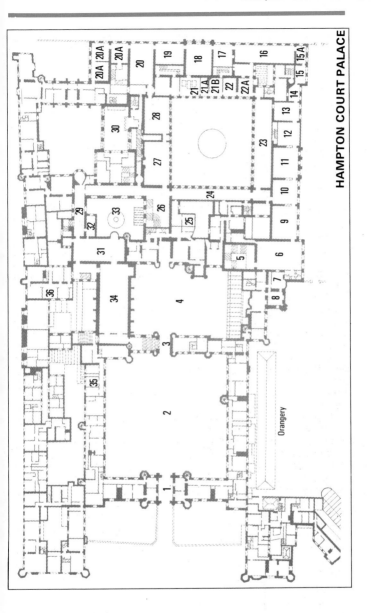

HAMPTON COURT PALACE

Orangery

cartoons for the ***Triumph of Caesar,*** which formed part of the collection of Charles I.

Across the road from the main entrance to the Palace (the **Trophy Gates**) is the extensive Green. On one side are some handsome period houses, including the old **Court House,** Wren's home from 1706 to 1723; also the **Cardinal Wolsey pub**. On the other side stands **Hampton Court House,** c.1760. In the last century it was owned by the Twining family, the tea and coffee merchants, and was the scene of many lavish social occasions. Part of it is now used as a theatre.

WINDSOR AND ETON

S ome ten miles to the west of London, in the Thames Valley, these two neighbouring towns are synonymous with one of the nation's greatest national monuments and with one of its most celebrated institutions.

≈ Windsor and Eton Central

WINDSOR CASTLE ★★★

Situated on a hill above the River Thames, the Castle can be seen at its best from the north (sometimes also from flights arriving at or departing from Heathrow airport). It has been the chief residence of English and British monarchs for nearly a thousand years. A fortification was first built in the vicinity in the 11th century by **Edward the Confessor.** The site of the present castle was chosen later in the same century by **William the Conqueror,** and building proceeded over the next 300 years. At the time of the Civil War, it was occupied by the Parliamentary side, **Cromwell's** New Model Army doing much of its training in the Great Park. Many treasures were destroyed or lost at this time, although there are important surviving works by Rubens and Van Dyck, while both Grinling Gibbons and Antonio Verrio added splendid decoration to the State Apartments in the years around 1700. Windsor Castle remained essentially a large medieval fortress until the early 19th century, when George IV began its transformation into a more comfortable and splendid royal residence. William IV, Queen Victoria, Edward VII and George V, in their turn, added both to the Castle's comfort as a home and to its grandeur as a national monument. (*Much of the Castle is closed to the public during periods of royal residence: normally the last 2 weeks of Dec, Mar, Apr and most of Jun. The precincts are open daily May–Aug 10am–7.15pm; Nov–Mar 10am–4.15pm; Apr, Sep, Oct 10am–5.15pm; Chapel Mon–Sat 10.45am–4pm, Sun 2–4pm; Apartments etc. Mon–Sat 10.30am–5pm, Sun 1.30–5pm, winter to 3pm; State apartments only open winter Suns.*)

The plan of the Castle is roughly oblong, and is divided into three main sections, from west to east: **Lower Ward, Middle Ward** and **Upper Ward.** The entrance is by **Henry VIII's Gateway,** leading into the Lower Ward. Across the courtyard stands **St George's Chapel,** the Castle's most imposing building, in Perpendicular style. Work on it was begun by Edward IV in 1477, and completed in the next century by Henry VII. The Chapel is a shrine to the Order of the Garter, Britain's

Windsor Castle from the Thames

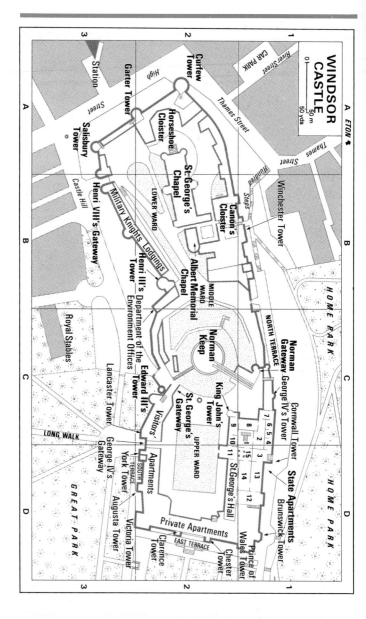

oldest and most exclusive order of chivalry and knighthood, founded in 1348 by Edward III. A special service in its honour is held there each St George's Day (23 April). The Order's title, and its famous motto, *Honi soit qui mal y pense,* probably derive from an incident involving King Edward, a lady of his court, and a missing garter, during the Hundred Years War. The magnificent interior is noted especially for its fan vaulting, the west and east windows, the exquisitely carved wooden choirstalls, and the stalls of the Knights of the Order, marked by their names and decorated with their banners and other insignia. The Chapel and the vaults beneath also house the tombs of Edward IV, Henry VI,

Henry VIII, Charles I, Edward VII, George V, George VI, and in the **Bray Chapel,** to the right of the Choir, a memorial to Louis-Napoleon, son of Napoleon III, killed in the Zulu Wars in 1879.

Adjacent to St George's Chapel is the **Albert Memorial Chapel,** built in the early 16th century by Henry VII, restored by George III, and reconsecrated by Queen Victoria to the memory of her consort, Prince Albert. The interior is sumptuously decorated with a mosaic ceiling and floor, several notable stained glass windows, pictorial inlaid-marble walls, a marble altar and communion table. A memorial to the Prince, in black and gilt marble, was designed by Sir George Gilbert Scott (who also designed the Albert Memorial in London's Kensington Gardens). In the Chapel crypt (the **Royal Tomb House**) are the tombs of George III, George IV, William IV and other royal personages.

Also forming part of the Lower Ward is the **Curfew Tower** (formerly the Belfrey Tower), the oldest surviving part of the Castle, built in the 13th century by Henry III. The exterior was refaced in the last century, but the interior, containing a large vaulted chamber, is part of the original structure. The Tower has a peal of eight bells, and a set of chimes, which play at regular intervals. It is reached by way of the **Horseshoe Cloister,** constructed in wood and brick by Edward IV and recently restored.

The **Middle Ward** is dominated by the **Round Tower** or Keep, the Castle's central and most prominent feature, raised upon its mound and once encircled by a moat. The present edifice, originally known as the Rose Tower, was built in the 14th century by Edward III, who convened within it an assembly similar to King Arthur's legendary Round Table, as well as the Order of the Garter. Its height was raised at the wish of George IV and now affords very fine views across the Thames Valley and into twelve surrounding counties. Within the Tower is a massive Russian bell, captured during the Crimean War and rung only on the death of a king or queen.

The **Norman Gate** (so called, though it also dates from the time of Edward III), leads to the **Upper Ward** and the **State Apartments.** These begin with the **Grand Staircase** (1) displaying several notable royal suits of armour. Then there are **Charles II's Dining Room** (2) with frescoes by Verrio, Flemish tapestries, wood carvings by Gibbons, royal portraits, English and Flemish furniture; **King's Drawing Room,** or the **Rubens Room** (3) with paintings mainly by Rubens, 17th- and 18th-century French furniture, Chinese ceramics; **State Bed Chamber** (4) with paintings by Canaletto, Zuccarelli and others, and French and English furniture; **King's Dressing Room** (5) with particularly fine paintings, including works by Holbein, Rubens, Dürer, Rembrandt, Memling and Van Dyck, and 17th- and 18th-century English and French furniture; **King's Closet** (6) with paintings mainly by Canaletto; **Queen's Drawing Room** (7) with royal portraits by Van Dyck; **Queen's Ballroom** (8) formerly the Van Dyck Room, now with paintings by Canaletto and Gainsborough; **Queen's Audience Chamber** (9) painted ceiling by Verrio representing an allegory of Catherine of Braganza as Britannia, Gobelin tapestries, 17th- and 18th-century Flemish and English furniture; **Queen's Presence Chamber** (10) with Gobelin tapestries, royal portraits, 17th- and 18th-century Venetian and English furniture; **Guard Chamber** (11) with arms and armour, including a shield, encrusted with gold and silver presented by the French king, François I, to Henry VIII; portraits by Van Dyck and others, a writing table belonging to Napoleon I, and Flemish tapestries; **St George's Hall**, the largest room in the Castle, with arms of all the Knights of the Garter, and portraits of the British kings from James I to George IV by Van Dyck, Gainsborough, Lawrence and others; **Grand Reception Room** (12) most richly decorated, with Gobelin and Beauvais tapestries; **Garter Throne Room** (13) with royal portraits; **Waterloo Chamber** or **Grand Dining Room** (14) decorated with heraldic devices and portraits celebrating the Congress of Vienna, 1815; **Grand Vestibule** (15) repository of royal and historic (including Napoleonic) relics. There is also the **China Museum,** displaying ceramic tableware belonging to various royal households; the **Gallery,** or **Print Room,** with drawings by Leonardo da Vinci, Raphael, Michelangelo, Holbein and many other masters; and the celebrated **Queen's Dolls House,** made to designs by Sir Edwin Lutyens for Queen Mary in 1922.

▬▬ *WINDSOR PARKS*

The Castle is bordered on its north side by the **Home Park,** with the **Royal Mausoleum,** close to **Frogmore House,** containing the tombs of Queen Victoria and Prince Albert. The Duke of Windsor (briefly Edward VIII before his abdication) was also buried in the Park in 1972. **Windsor Great Park** stretches for well over five miles south of the Castle. Its most striking feature is the **Long Walk,** a tree-lined avenue begun in 1680 by Charles II. It leads to **Snow Hill,** where a monumental **equestrian statue of George III** stands. On the Park's south-eastern corner is **Virginia Water,** a large and picturesque artificial lake, created in the 18th century. The **Valley Gardens,** lying along its north bank, are famous for their flowering trees and shrubs, (*open daily*). A **Lodge** and an **Obelisk** commemorate George II's son, William, Duke of Cumberland. Between the two lie the **Savill Gardens,** 35 acres (14ha) of woodland garden (*open daily Mar–late Dec, 10am–6pm*).

▬▬ *THE TOWN OF WINDSOR* ★

Historically the town of Windsor was divided into Old Windsor, a village about two miles from the Castle, and New Windsor, which grew up within the shadow of the Castle itself.

The **Guildhall,** or **Town Hall,** in New Windsor was designed by Sir Thomas Fitch and completed by Sir Christopher Wren in 1707. It houses another collection of royal portraits as well as displays about life in the Castle (*open Apr–Sep, Mon–Fri 1.30–4pm*). The **Household Cavalry Museum,** in Combermere Barracks, is one of the nation's finest military museums (*open Mon–Fri 10am–1pm; 2–5pm; Apr–Sep, Sat only 10am–1pm, 2–4pm*).

At Windsor and Eton Central Railway Station, Madame Tussaud's **Royalty and Railways** exhibition uses waxworks and robotic techniques to depict the military parade at Queen Victoria's Diamond Jubilee and displays a lavish reconstruction of the royal train (*open daily 9.30am–5.30pm*). Another attraction of special interest to children is the **Windsor Safari Park and Seaworld,** just to the south-west of the town, a drive-in zoo with a children's farmyard and spectacular dolphin and killer whale shows (*open daily 10am–6.30pm or dusk*).

▬▬ *ETON* ★★

A bridge over the Thames connects Windsor with neighbouring **Eton.** This is the home of **Eton College,** founded by Henry VI in 1440 and Britain's most prestigious public school. Its traditional uniform, famous **wall game**,and **playing fields** are part of the fabric of English social history. The most impressive building is the **Chapel,** a 15th-century structure in Perpendicular style, modelled closely on King's College, Cambridge, with beautiful stained glass, a splendid organ and a richly carved screen of Caen stone. This and other parts of the school, including the **Cloisters** and **Courtyard,** may be visited (*open Mon–Fri 1–5pm during school terms; 9.30am–12.30pm during vacations*).

▬ BIBLIOGRAPHY

Street maps

Geographers' A–Z of London (Geographers' A–Z Map Co, Sevenoaks)
Nicholson's London Streetfinder (Robert Nicholson, London)

Guide books

American Express Pocket Guide to London (Mitchell Beazley, London,
    1986; Prentice Hall Press, New York, 1986)
Baedeker's London (Prentice Hall Press, New York, 1986)
Banks, F.R: The New Penguin Guide to London (Penguin, Harmonds-
    worth, 1986)
Arthur Frommer's Guide to London (Prentice Hall Press, New York,
    1987)
Jenkins, S: Companion Guide to Outer London (Collins, London, 1985)
Nicholson's London Guide (Robert Nicholson, London, 1987)
Nicholson's London Pub Guide (Robert Nicholson, London, 1985)
Piper, D: Companion Guide to London (Collins, London, 1987; Prentice
    Hall Press, New York, 1987)
Reiber, B: A Serious Shopper's Guide to London (Prentice Hall Press,
    New York, 1987)

Photographic and illustrated books

Cameron, R. and Cooke, A: Above London (Bodley Head, London, 1980)
Forshaw, A. and Bergström, T: The Open Spaces of London (Allison
    & Busby, London and New York, 1986)
    The Markets of London (Penguin, Harmondsworth, 1983)
MacDonnell, K: A Photographer's Guide to London (Wildwood House,
    Aldershot, 1986)

Museums

Scimone, G.M.S. and Levey, M.F: London Museums and Collections
    (Canal Publishing, London, 1986)

Art and architecture

Jacobs, M. and Warner, M: Art in London (Jarrold, Norwich, 1980)
Pevsner, N: (revised by B. Cherry): London 1 – The Cities of London
    and Westminster (3rd ed. Penguin, Harmondsworth, 1973)
    London 2 – South (Penguin, Harmondsworth, 1983)
Piper, D: Artists' London (Weidenfeld & Nicholson, London, 1982)
Saunders, A: The Art and Architecture of London (Phaidon, Oxford,
    1984)

Historical

Barker, F. and Jackson, P: London, 2000 Years of a City and its People
    (Macmillan, London, 1983)
Hibbert, C: London: The Biography of a City (Penguin, Harmonds-
    worth, 1980)
Weinreb, B. and Hibbert, C. (eds.): The London Encyclopedia (Mac-
    millan, London, 1983)

Literary

Boswell, J: The Life of Samuel Johnson (Penguin, Harmondsworth,
    1979)
Dickens, C: Oliver Twist (Penguin, Harmondsworth, 1985)
Latham, R: The Illustrated Pepys (Bell & Hyman, London, 1982)
Pritchett, V.S: London Perceived (Hogarth, London, 1986)

INDEX

Figures in italics refer to captions